Newent   Sta   Ell Brook   R. Leadon

torsley   Long Reach

on   Taynton   Sta   Barbers Bridge   Maisemore

am   Tibberton   Alney Island

MayHill   Glasshouse   Highnam

Huntley   GLOUCESTER

Sta   Longhope   Churcham

all   Blaisdon   Sta   Minsterworth   Llanthony Abbey   Hempsted

dler   Grange Court Junction   R. Severn   Corn Ham

Abbey   Westbury upon Severn

Dean   C E S T E R

Garden Cliff   S H I R E

Ferry   River Severn   Rodley

Gloucester and Berkeley Canal

Awre

Awre Sta

dge   rpness

## A Sketch Map of FOREST OF DEAN

ays which are shown

1

D1436963

A. E. TAYLOR

# FOREST OF DEAN

F. W. BATY

ROBERT HALE LIMITED
63 Old Brompton Road London S.W.7

*First published 1952*

MADE AND PRINTED IN GREAT BRITAIN BY
WILLIAM CLOWES AND SONS, LIMITED
LONDON AND BECCLES

# CONTENTS

# CONTENTS

# ILLUSTRATIONS

ACKNOWLEDGMENTS

*The illustrations numbered 1, 3, 10, 20 and 21 are reproduced from photographs supplied by the* Gloucester *Journal; Nos 6 and 11 by Mr A. R. Barrell. The remaining 18 illustrations are reproduced from photographs supplied by the author, with the advice and help of Messrs W. R. and H. Walwin.*

# Chapter I

## ROYAL PLAYGROUND

"A certain territorie of woody ground and fruitful pastures,
priviledged for wild beasts and foules of forest, chase and warren
to rest and abide there, in the save protection of the King, for his
princely delight and pleasure."

MANWOOD, *Lawes of the Forest* (1598)

TRAVELLING westward from Gloucester, the road crosses the
Severn where that river flows in two streams around Alney
Island. And if you happen to pass this way at the season of high
tides you may see the water under the bridges running swiftly
upstream. Looking more closely you will notice, as likely as not,
that the withies on the lower parts of the banks are hung with seaweed, though this spot is some forty river-miles from the sea. You
will make a mental note (or even a diary entry) that you have seen
the celebrated Severn Bore, and then move on to the coal-mining
district.

Stop again when you see a man tipping a small truckload of
coal at a tiny loading-ramp set amongst bracken and shady oak
trees. At first you will be inclined to wonder just where he found
the coal, but the problem will soon be solved when he pushes the
truck uphill into a tunnel in the grassy bank, returning a few
minutes later with a loaded truck that needs almost no pushing on
its way from the coal-face to the open air.

You will now be ready to agree that it is no ordinary land where
everyday items such as rivers and coal mines can defy the conventions so flagrantly. With few exceptions our rivers behave just
as the poets have recorded, flowing swiftly, or majestically, or
silently, down to the sea. And the normal approach to a coal mine
is by a shaft, either vertical or steeply sloped, up and down which
men and material are hoisted in cage-like lifts. But the Severn and
the country beyond are unique in many ways, so that if the two

instances mentioned are the most spectacular they are not by any means the only ones.

History, so often stretched out stiff and dead in museum and classroom, is still very much alive here. Many places must look for history in monuments and ancient buildings, but here we have it deeply inscribed in the customs which play an important part in the daily life of many of the people. The Free Miner, as he works his Gale, is still reaping the reward of his ancestors' bravery at the siege of Berwick, more than six hundred years ago, if popular report is true. And on each 19th day of May many of our farmers should drink a toast to Blanche, daughter of Henry of Monmouth. It was by her marriage to John of Gaunt on that day, in the year 1359, that a lot of property in this area was brought into the Duchy of Lancaster, thus exempting the occupiers from payment of market tolls. They still enjoy this privilege, to the great chagrin of the market authorities. But the miner probably thinks of his early ancestors just as infrequently as the tenant of the Duchy thinks of his Benefactress. Sheep exercising their grazing rights in the shadow of a modern factory are symbolic of the history that is woven into the everyday life of the Forest of Dean.

This area consists mainly of the third, and least publicised, of the natural divisions of Gloucestershire, with a few lovely snippets taken from the adjoining counties of Hereford and Monmouth. The Cotswolds have been coaxed and hammered into print until they must suspect anyone carrying pen or pencil, while the Vale of Severn has been freely written about since the days when styre cider and the famous Double Gloucester cheese put real flavour into the words of William Marshall. But the English Mesopotamia (being the Land between the Rivers) has a character which makes it at once more fascinating and more bewildering than any other region. This is a bold claim, but I make it without hesitation, in the conviction that there are some unique qualities arising from the centuries during which this was a No-Man's-Land between England and Wales; centuries that have etched their pattern on the countryside just as the lichen imprints its design on the rock.

Several years ago a well-known American broadcaster visited the Forest of Dean in the course of a lightning tour of Britain.

There was only time for him to gather a few hasty first impressions, and these he started to record most faithfully in a notebook. As the trip proceeded by way of Tintern, St Briavels, Broadwell and Speech House his interest remained keenly alert, but his notes became steadily less coherent. Eventually he got over the difficulty by omitting any reference to what he had seen, which was probably much wiser than to attempt any opinion after a four-hour survey covering so much beauty and no small amount of squalor. In this case the fault quite possibly lay with the guide, for after living in this area for more than four years, and moving through it in the course of my work for more than ten, I approach the present task with considerable hesitation. That I shall enjoy it there is no doubt, but the same cannot be said of my fitness for the job.

One incident, more than any other, gives me encouragement to go on, and that is the first real welcome given me by a Forester. (And let it be clearly understood that throughout this book a Forester is an inhabitant of the Royal Forest of Dean.) The incident happened upon a day on which I had counted ten magpies in one field, which undoubtedly marked it as a day beyond the ordinary. So it turned out, for on that day in this Forest I was given some apples, the bloom of a flower that was new to me and a joke. The apples went, just as apples should; the flower has faded from memory, and its name I never knew; but the joke is still fresh in my mind, a typical product of the district, though generally kept for home consumption. It went this way.

Having finished my business at a small and very remote farm I enquired where I should find Mr M., who, according to my list, lived at a smaller and even more remote farm. I was given detailed instructions, including reference to several trees of various shapes, and a careful description of the dog at the cottage where Mr M. did not live. I moved on, expressing thanks as I went, when my guide called out, "Thee's 'll have to hurry, mind." I asked if Mr M. was known to be going out, to which the reply came, "Ay, they'm putting 'e under in 'arf-hour, see." I did not disturb the relatives of the deceased, but I did realise that the Forest had accepted me. They do not readily joke with strangers.

Many times I have wished that I could see into the minds of visitors to our Forest so as to understand the foundation on which their impressions are to be built. Until recent years many writers obviously regarded this country as a subject not quite worthy of their attention. People bought coal from the Dean, and it was unlikely that they would appreciate any closer acquaintance with their coal-store. Certainly there were some old customs, but they belonged to history and history belonged to the classroom. Then arose a certain amount of publicity at the time when unemployment and distress became acute; but that would not make attractive reading. In an effort to bring back a livelihood and self-respect some effort was made to reach the holiday-maker and the tourist; but who wants to listen to propaganda. In this way it is quite easy for the visitor to arrive with the impression that we are prepared to parade a few old customs in order to keep the wolf from the door. Then it is good to hear them say, as they walk in the woodlands, perhaps within a stone-throw of a coal mine, "Well, isn't this lovely!"

As the majority of people must live elsewhere, and only see our Forest in the brief weeks of holiday time, may I mention a few points in simple form:

Don't expect the woodlands to be wearing a party frock from June to September. During this time the trees are heavily leaved, so that they hide themselves and the view. The real beauty of a tree is in the shape, so that lovers of trees may find more beauty in winter than in summer. Spring and autumn are the high-spots, and it would be foolish to compare them, for that is opinion.

Don't forget that Dean Forest is primarily a workshop—though it is hard to remember this when the fairy beechwoods are carpeted with bluebells. You will find the people courteous and ready to help, but they have their work.

Don't imagine that you are better than a miner or a woodman because you have a big car and clean hands. They will not be impressed.

Don't think that all the woods in this region belong to the Crown. There are quite large areas of private woodland in which the reception will depend upon the manner of approach.

4

To avoid a misunderstanding that is very general it will be as well to start on this journey with a definition of the word forest. It does not primarily mean a large wood. There may be, in fact there generally are, trees. But these are a secondary consideration. The dictionary defines a forest as a large tract of land devoted to the chase, and as the chase was the special concern of the King, it came directly under his control, being placed outside the common law. A more picturesque definition is found in Manwood's sixteenth-century *Lawes of the Forest*: "A certain territorie of woody ground and fruitful pastures, priviledged for wild beasts and foules of forest, chase and warren to rest and abide there, in the save protection of the King, for his princely delight and pleasure." A chase is a hunting ground of less than Royal status, such as Tidenham Chase, which was the hunting ground of the Lords of Striguil.

There was, in fact, one set of laws for the country in general and a special code of very barbarous regulations for the protection of these royal playgrounds. In the same way "afforestation", which now means the planting of an area with trees, then referred to the enclosure of land for the preservation of beasts of the chase. It is necessary to make this clear, even at the risk of repetition, for the whole character of the countryside would essentially be altered by several centuries of afforestation according to the old standard. And the people who managed to survive the ordeal must bear the scars for many generations.

The Forest Laws, with all their accompanying persecution, are now just a matter of historical interest as far as they applied to game preservation, but they are still very much alive in other directions. The common man is no longer flayed alive for poaching in the King's forest; he will not even pay the price of a hand or an eye. But this is still no land flowing with milk and honey. The threat of unemployment and hardship hangs over it in the manner of the sword of Damocles, which in this case hung for so long by the single thread of coal. And the experiences of this century give little enough cause for complacence. But that is a subject to which we shall return later.

Now think of coal-mining. The mind naturally conjures up

5

a picture of dreary slag heaps and ugly winding gear, with the air darkened by the black dust that settles all around. Into the picture will also come railway sidings, carrying interminable lines of waiting trucks, gapingly empty as they queue up to play their part in spreading the dismal pall away from the central plague-spot. With this picture in mind climb to the top of the waste heap of the now disused New Fancy Colliery, which lies not far from Speech House, and so is almost in the centre of this mining area. It is a stiff scramble to the apex of this volcano-shaped mound, but every step is worth while as the view gradually widens over the tree-covered folds (or denes) that give this forest its name.

Still think of coal-mining. It is all around you, though almost hidden by trees except where the cone of another waste heap shows over the top of the green waves. And further away the glimpse of a winding wheel proves that there are shafts in this coalfield that go straight down into the earth. The valley not far from this natural grandstand is strewn with great heaps of rock, thrown aside in the search for buried treasure. But time, bracken and foxgloves have converted an eyesore into something very like a rock garden in spring and summer. Away in the distance beyond the great sandy, muddy gash of the lower Severn, from Gloucester Docks to the Bristol Channel, lies the long line of the Cotswold Hills. And if, seeing those hills, you feel a desire to exchange this rugged grey rock for the limestone that invites the chisel, remember that the country for ten miles around the spot where you stand was for some centuries the loser in the great game of Put-and-Take, while Cotswold built glorious churches out of vast profits from sheep. And a poor man may grow rhododendrons in the Forest, which he will not do on Cotswold.

Even a waste tip should not be condemned out of hand until all its possibilities have been explored. If it is not just an upstart of the last few years it will have some sort of pioneer vegetation struggling up its slopes. This may include wild thyme and mignonette; then there are worse places in which to take your ease when the early summer sun shines. If you have first climbed the New Fancy tip on a fine day in spring, before the trees have lost their multi-greens, it is well. But should your first meeting with the Forest be on a sombre winter's day, when the straying sheep look even more cold and cheerless than the tumbled heaps of rock, then your inclination to learn more of this part of the country may perish miserably for want of sun to give it life. And there is one at least who will not blame you. The balance here between natural beauty and man-made squalor is such that Nature must be in smiling mood to carry the day. And those who question this verdict will do well to walk from Ruspidge to Ruardean Hill on a raw, wet day.

Our boundary cannot be set out better than in the words of Rudder's transcription of the Perambulation of 10 Edward I (1282). But it may be well to explain that a perambulation was a boundary-fixing expedition carried out from time to time for the purpose of fixing the limits of the Forest.

"The limits of the Forest of Dean begin at Gloucester bridge and thus stretch by the main flow of the Severn going to as far as the place where the bank of the Wye falls into the Severn, and thus going up by the Wye as far as Strigoil bridge. Going up thence by the Wye as far as Monmouth bridge and going up thence by the Wye as far as the ford of Goodrich Castle and thus as far as Dunnes Cross, and thus by a certain lane called Mersty as far as Alton, and thus by the stream of Alton as far as the public way coming from Ross as far as the oak outside Weston. And so by the King's highway beyond the bridge as far as a certain tree called Bolletree. And thus by the King's highway as far as the millpond of Buriton which is Richard Talbot's. And thus by the King's highway up to a certain cross called Luce Cross. And thus by the King's highway through the middle of Gorsley as far as Gorsley Ford. And thus going down by the brook as far as Oxenhall bridge. And thus by the King's highway as far as the Prior of Newent's bridge. And by the same King's highway as far as Gloucester bridge."

The boundaries of the Forest were pulled and stretched this way and that from the earliest records until the time when they were fixed by the Commissioners in 1831 at an area of about 25,000 acres. During the centuries of struggle between the Crown and the people there were two strong moves to increase the area. The first came from the Norman kings in order to satisfy their love of hunting. This reached its peak in the above perambulation, which was the widest limit ever set. From 1282 the area shrank, as is shown by the presence of purlieus, which are lands freed from Forest laws mainly in the time of Henry II. The word "purlieu" is French, and a stranger here. It is applied in the original form to land between Lydney and Blakeney, though in this case it is usually pronounced "pearly". In other cases it has been considerably bent with the years, as at Durla Barn, near Dursley Cross, where it might pass unrecognised but for the fact that the old folk call this Purlu. This general trend continued until, in Stuart times, the value of the timber, quarries and mines proved a great temptation to a reigning House that was always in a state of great financial embarrassment.

Extensions always met with sullen and determined opposition, and this widest limit was, in fact, a claim rather than an established boundary. Apart from resistance offered by private individuals (which was chiefly made up of night raids on fences and game), there was much more influential disapproval at both ends of the Royal allotment. The Manor of Tidenham had been granted to the Abbots of Bath before the Conquest, and in those days the Abbot, supported by the Pope, was in a strong position in any argument with kings. Later this manor came into the Marchership of Striguil, so that it was never really part of the Forest. At the other extremity the Bishop of Hereford appears to have taken considerable exception to the afforestation of Chase Hill, just above Ross, and there was evidently a good deal of pressure exerted until a further perambulation in 1300 almost halved the area. It was probably at this date that a comment was written across the document of 1282, casting upon it the darkest reflections.

The reason for choosing this obsolete boundary is that it comprises a straightforward geographic district, taking in all the "Eye 'twix Severn and Wye", which for so long did not link up with England or Wales. The Royal Forest is based upon the Hundred of St Briavels, but by taking this wider area a better comparison should be obtained, thus gaining in breadth more than is lost in depth. This gives us a central core of pure forest upon which the

8

NATIONAL
FOREST PARK

FOREST OF DEAN

Manorial System, such an important factor in the pattern of much of rural England, played no part whatever, and around which a fringe of manors and parishes fall more and more into manorial shape the further they lie from the centre. For example, there is a wide gulf between the basic structures of Ruspidge and Minsterworth, as would be expected between a village that is primarily a mining settlement and one that is definitely agricultural. The former has always been inside the Forest boundary, the latter generally outside. Between these extremes are the villages which have adjusted themselves to the dual-purpose role called for by their surroundings.

It is the historic and geographic detachment of this region which provide the main excuse for this book. Much the greater part lies in Gloucestershire, but a very lovely corner in the northeast belongs to Hereford, and Monmouth provides a share that cannot be overlooked without serious loss. The county boundary has imprinted itself deeply on those books dealing with topography, so that adjoining fields may fall to be dealt with in separate volumes. In the present case the man-made boundaries are exceedingly awkward about fitting themselves to the natural division of the Wye, with the result that anyone who is interested in this particular stretch of country may find himself obliged to tackle the task of delving into the books of three counties. For example, books on the shelf marked Gloucestershire will leave us in complete ignorance about the Kymin, the hill standing guard over the town of Monmouth, though the summit lies no more than half a mile from the county boundary. Then, having digested the books on Monmouth, we shall have no clue to the ruins on Penyard Hill, above Ross. There are books on the Wye, some of them venturing quite deeply into the Forest; there are books on the Forest, but they mainly tend to restrict themselves to the Crown lands as now defined. In my opinion the fringe-lands of the Royal Forest are as important to the Forest story as is the run-back to a tennis court.

Present-day planning has touched this region with the lightest of hands, and it must be admitted that a plan to meet modern wants could only be achieved by sweeping away most of the

2* 9

*Cinderford—the Problem Town*

present layout. For centuries settlement on the Crown lands was mostly in the form of squatting. The idea was widely held for many years that anyone who could build a shack and have smoke going up the chimney in one day was entitled to the land on which the shack stood. The origin of this practice is obscure, but the result is an irregular network of lanes and tracks, as fascinating to the casual observer as it must be chaotic to those who have to bring water, electricity and other amenities. But this question is now coming to the fore as the campaign to attract new industries to the region calls for more houses and increased comfort. It is to be hoped that the old playground of kings will not be straightened and regimented by planning in the same way that a great deal of woodland has been dealt with by the Forestry Commission. In this connection, however, it should be noted that a new trend is afoot. During the last few years the solid phalanx of conifers is giving way to a planting pattern as complex as a pullover in three or four colours.

There is a fashion in the matter of scenery, just as in clothes, though the cycle is of greater length, if we may judge from the opinion of Rudge, given in his *History of Gloucestershire* (1803):

"The County of Gloucestershire may, with justice, be said to stand high in the scale of Picturesque Beauty. The Cotswolds are usually considered as an exception to this general remark; even in these, however, amongst the numerous dens and combs into which they are broken, very delightful spots may be selected."

At this point we, of west Gloucestershire, hold up our heads in pride. But fairness demands that we should read further:

". . . nor is there often sufficient traffic on its (Severn) waters to keep up a moving picture of shipping, or to give the bustle of commerce; both which circumstances contribute so essentially to render water picturesque in itself."

Here, surely, is the gospel of Industrialism, which could see no beauty in a river as a river, but was prepared to worship a system of inland navigation—until the railways held out the prospect of higher dividends. The age of Rudge did mischief enough. Let us hope that the wheel of fashion will never complete the full turn. Just at the moment, looking at the brown-green patchwork of fields and woods in springtime, there seems to be absolutely no cause for alarm. The prospect pleases in every way, with Man's villainy showing only in the aerials of the police radio transmitter. But on looking closer there are cottages which, while they fit the landscape, do not in any respect fit the requirements of mid-twentieth-century welfare. This is the biggest problem which those in authority have to tackle, and therein lies the real danger. To the layman it seems impossible to convert what is, into what must be, without losing what should be.

Please do not try to use this book as a guide, for used that way it can only lead you to distraction. Its course will be that of a grasshopper, jumping here and there as whim and circumstance suggest, taking a nibble of this and that, but never settling to any ordered route or system. It is a personal picture, painted on the site as far as possible, for whenever I turned my back on the Forest to look for information in dusty volumes I knew that I was paying in loss of colour for every fragment of exactness. For the same reason the conventions have neither been wooed nor consciously thrown aside. The terms Norm., Perp., Dec., etc., will not appear more than is quite necessary, not because they are in any way objectionable, but because they carry with them a flavour of precision that does not fit into an informal picture.

The occupier of a house will, if he is proud of that house, show his guest not only the reception rooms and the best bedroom, but also the kitchen and other less publicised but no less important apartments. All these are part of the house, and without them the inspection would give no true idea of the house as a working unit. The same will be the rule here. Though I am only the occupier of one small corner of the property I shall be delighted to play the host, if you will be my guest. And we will not deliberately turn our backs on the "usual offices" in order to look at the "very desirable features". Nature, with quite a lot of help from Man, has provided the pleasance; Man unaided is responsible for the unpleasance. But we will see both, as far as our limits of time and space will allow.

# CHAPTER II

## LOOKING FOR THE FOREST

". . . Domain that once, at early morn,
Rang to the hunters' bugle horn.
When barons proud would bound away;
When even Kings would hail the day,
And swell with pomp more glorious shows,
Than ant-hill population knows."

ROBERT BLOOMFIELD

ANY approach to the Forest of Dean, except from the north, brings to mind the names of two engineers, both supreme in their day, but separated by some thousand years. Their names are Offa and Telford, and of both it may be said that "he builded better than he knew".

Offa, prince of the Mercians in the eighth century, fought, worked and planned vigorously for his people. His province was surrounded by threatening neighbours, but it was the western boundary against the Welsh that troubled him most, and this he set out to secure. Theoretically his territory reached as far as the Wye, though his predecessors had never managed to keep a firm hold on the lands west of Severn. To make the position quite clear Offa built the great earthwork which runs intermittently from Beachley to the River Dee. The remains of this Dyke are still to be seen at many points along the ridge overlooking the Wye, and even after eleven and a half centuries of weathering it remains a deep scar at many points. In the conditions in which it was made this must have been a huge task, showing the importance that was attached to this frontier. And as an added deterrent an offer was made to remove the right hand of any armed Welshman who crossed the Dyke.

This distinction between armed and unarmed visitors indicates that the ditch was essentially a military boundary, in no way

12

resembling the "Iron Curtains" of our time. In fact, the existence of two Celtic settlements between the Dyke and the Wye (at Lancaut and Beachley) suggests that the Westland men were encouraged to retain a foothold on the Forest side of the natural boundary, for it is difficult to believe that a man of Offa's determination would have allowed these settlements to remain if he had not thought it to his advantage. It may well be that in an age when transport was a tiresome necessity rather than a lucrative industry this was an astute move on the part of the Eastlanders. By trading with their neighbours at settlements on the near side of the Wye they would avoid the work and risk of carrying the goods over a river which, if not wide, has tides and rapid floods that make it a formidable obstacle.

The struggle between east and west is still keen, but the battle has moved to the areas of civilian population, each battlefield being marked by two pairs of posts, white or striped. And the invading chariots have changed their scythe blades for ribbon favours.

The other Engineer (and the capital E is a sign of respect) did more than any other man to link this Mesopotamia with the mainland, for he built first the Mythe Bridge at Tewkesbury, where no bridge was before, then Over Bridge across the western branch of the Severn at Gloucester, which replaced an earlier structure. For his recreation Telford read and wrote poetry, and that must have entered into the flying comeliness of these spans in iron and stone. At any rate, the genius and the poetry which he put into his work are missing from the later Haw Bridge, which has neither strength nor beauty to recommend it.

The story goes that Telford took his own life when worried by the settling of the foundations of Over Bridge. This is a sad thought, for though some work was necessary when the east side settled, and there is a noticeable dip in the centre of the arch, yet the bridge was able to carry all the enormous loads that passed over it during the last war, loads of which Telford could have had no hint when he died in 1834. Yes, Telford's bridge has stood while its colleagues at Westgate Street and Maisemore are in the drawn-out agony of present-day replacement. It is interesting to note that in the fourteenth century there was a public subscription to replace a bridge at Maisemore that had come to ruinous condition. It looks as if some such action will be needed to get rid of the temporary wooden structure which now serves the purpose without in any way beautifying the scene or inspiring confidence in those who use it.

These bridges, with the help of the railway viaduct at Purton, are the only firm approaches from the east. But there are more adventurous ways of crossing the Severn. At many points it is possible to walk across at low tide without meeting any fate worse than that which befell the celebrated Dr Foster, while those who know the river well can make the crossing in waders. Unless, therefore, the character of the Severn at Newnham has altered a lot since Roman times it is likely that the soft alluvial flats on the east side were a greater obstacle than the stream itself. In more recent times Queen Margaret's army met defeat at Tewkesbury largely, we are told, because they were unable to link up with the reinforcements from the west when Gloucester barred the only bridge. Thus the Severn tides may have had an effect on the big names of history at the latter end of the fifteenth century, for Margaret's march was made at the season of spring tides; otherwise there should have been no great difficulty in crossing at one of several points.

For those who do not wish to venture on foot there are ferries of the plain utility type, or in the de luxe style as described by our poet, F. W. Harvey:

> Last fall, to sell his oldest perry,
> Old William Fry did cross the ferry,
> And there inside of an old sty
> 'A seed a leanish pig did lie:
> A rakish, active beast 'a was
> As ever rooted up the grass:
> Eager as bees on making honey
> To stuff his self. Bill did decide
> To buy un with the cider money
> And fat un up for Easter-tide.

He bought un, but no net 'ad got
To kip thic pig inside the boat.
"The'll drown wi' pig and all at ferry!"
Cried one. Said Fry, "Go, bring some perry,
And thic old drinking-horn you got,
Lying inside the piggery cot!"

'A poured a goodish swig and soon
—As lazy as a day o' June—
Piggy lay boozed, and so did bide
Snoring while him and Fry were taken
'Cross Severn: and 'a didn't waken
Until the boat was safely tied
Up to a tree on t'other side.

There must be some strong link between Charon and Bacchus, for though a number of ferries are shown on the map, they do not appear to be in use except where they run in conjunction with a riverside pub. Whether this has an archaic origin or is merely a case of symbiosis is a matter for research. But it is certain that ferries were at one time a more colourful feature of the river, otherwise there could have been no reason why Henry VIII should make an act prohibiting keepers of ferries from carrying persons, goods or cattle across the Severn between sunset and sunrise.

At the toe of the great horseshoe round Arlingham a foot-ferry runs between the New Inn and Newnham. This consists of a short or long journey in the boat, and an inversely proportionate journey in the ferryman's arms over the mud, according to the state of the tide. At one time this ferry was operated by a woman, for there is a record of the grant of two oak trees for the renewal of her boat. It has been left to another woman (Miss K. Woods) to use this as an argument that the river was narrower in those days. Others may say that the women were tougher.

During the past year or two an attempt has been made to construct a pontoon ferry at this crossing, but the first round has definitely gone to the river. After many unsuccessful attempts to find a means of anchoring the pontoons on these shifting sands the scheme has been laid aside for the time being. Some of the river-siders say they can hear the tides laugh as they shift the anchors and tear the moorings of the floats asunder, but the sound they hear is more likely to be the ghost of old Thomas Telford, sighing because he cannot step down and supervise the job.

Proposals and counter-proposals for a bridge between Beachley and Aust still ebb and flow almost as regularly as the tides. In the meantime two ferry-boats carry cars when the tides permit, and produce symptoms of the most choleric kind when, for an hour or so, the low tide says "no". To one of a sadistic turn of mind it is most diverting to watch the boiling annoyance of a motorist who arrives just when the water level has called a halt. The only alternative is to travel by way of Gloucester, a distance of more than fifty miles. In these circumstances men who are normally good citizens, kind to their wives and children and obedient to the lightest word of the Inspector of Taxes, will swell at the neck, redden in the face and emit strange gurgling oaths. I once tried to interest one of these unfortunates in sea birds, that being the pastime most readily to hand. He was certainly not amused. Yet if we have one saying in our language better known than most it is surely the one about Time and Tide.

So much for the Severn approaches; what of the Wye? The South Wales road from Gloucester has been a busy route since the days when Roman Caerwent was in its prime, so it is not surprising to find that Chepstow has enjoyed the luxury of a bridge since those days. The earlier bridge of Striguil was a little upstream from the present crossing, and therefore even more under the watchful eye of the Castle. The present bridge, with the county boundary running across the centre, is lifted high on two piers to allow for the very big rise and fall of tides. Figures as high as 60 feet have been given for the variation here, but if there is any truth in these it would only be as a contrast between low ebb and high water with flood water to help, for the normal variation of 36 feet on spring tides is unusually big for any river in Britain.

An earlier bridge on this site was built of wood, and it is said that a resident of Chepstow who had been from home for a long journey returned just when the planking was being renewed. It was dark, and while he dozed his horse crossed over by the single plank that had been left for pedestrians. On being shown what he had done the man died of fright—surely a privilege that belonged to the horse.

Of the bridges at Brockweir and Bigsweir it need only be said that they carry all but the heavier traffic over the river, and it is not until Monmouth that we find a bridge combining utility with grace and dignity. But it would be unwise to linger so near to a town with material enough to fill this book. Monmouth has allowed Newport to deal with everyday matters of commerce and administration so that she may keep faith with Henry V and the farming country that lies all around. The lower Wye did something more than carve out scenery which draws people from all parts; the rocks and rapids made the journey upstream so toilsome for barges that they gave up the struggle and left Monmouth before the mediæval pattern had been worn away. But we must stick to the rule that while hares may be followed out of the Forest they must not be allowed to run into it. Make no mistake, however, Monmouth will crop up again.

At the middle of the great loop which the river makes round Huntsham stands a narrow iron bridge that is apt to link itself, in our disrespectful minds, with a great name in our national history. But whatever the style in which it is built, the bridge forms a most useful connection between the Forest and the Hereford side. It will not carry two cars abreast, but there was no obligation on the local landowners to cater for tourist traffic. For years enough they had maintained a ferry at this point, so it was quite a move forward when the flat-bottomed boat was replaced by a firm crossing in the later part of last century, and the bridge was quite sufficient for all needs while the road at the Yat Rock remained almost impassable for wheeled traffic. And this is the best grandstand on all the lower Wye from which to see beneath the surface.

Goodrich. What a name with which to flavour history, especially when taken with the family name of Talbot. But village and castle lie across the river, so I can only point to them from the bridge, at the same time drawing your attention to the fragments of Flanesford Priory that have been built into the farm close by the river. Kerne Bridge, for all its look of permanence and sturdy middle-age, was only built in 1828, which was not until Goodrich had stepped back upon history's dusty shelves. But the bridge replaced a ferry claiming the closest association with Henry of Monmouth. We are told that Henry IV was given the news of the birth of his son by the man who ferried him over the Wye on his return from France. He was rewarded by a grant of the ferry, which grant, by all accounts, held good until the ferry was no longer needed. The earlier crossing place was above the bridge, nearer to the Castle, and this was the point at which the most extensive boundary of the Forest left the river.

The remaining boundary, some twenty miles between Wye and Severn, runs for most of its course through farmlands of a type quite unlike the rest of the area; a country of medium-sized farms on soil of the Old Red Sandstone and red marl, where machinery can be used to the full, and where a few sugar beet lying by the roadside in autumn emphasise the change from the land of the Denes, where rocks are always threateningly near to the surface.

The exact line of the various perambulations has never been traced clearly in the neighbourhood of Ross, Bromsash, Lea and Gorsley, but there are indications of bigger changes here than elsewhere. The absence of any reference to the present Gloucester–Ross road suggests that it did not exist at the time of the Norman kings, and Alton—now represented by Alton Court— may have been more important than Ross in those days. But such details are not of any consequence to us at present; we may just be grateful that the greedy intentions of our earlier monarchs now give us the freedom of looking over country which seems able to smile even when there is no sunshine. When compared with the rougher hill districts lying to the south-west farming looks easy here, which does reflect all the more credit on those who are producing food from the steep banks of the Denes.

So, having stepped over the threshold, you are entitled to ask what sort of country it is that you have entered. A first impression from the map must be of the number of familiar names lying just outside: Gloucester, Chepstow, Tintern, Monmouth, Ross. Historically you could not ask for a richer girdle, but the story is not yet half told, for by sweeping only a little wider we include Berkeley, Bristol, Raglan, Grosmont, Skenfrith, Malvern and Tewkesbury. This must be very near to the centre of mediæval England, the England that had not yet chosen London as the great metropolis. No wonder the Forest continued to figure in history long after the chase had ceased to be the main pastime of kings.

St Briavels, with the Constable holding the Castle, was for centuries the administrative centre of the Royal Forest, but it is to Newnham—quiet, middle-aged Newnham—that chief honours go. It was from here in 1158 that a document came signed by Henry II and witnessed by no less than Thomas à Becket and the Earl of Leicester. And it was here that the same king carpeted Strongbow, Earl of Pembroke, for indiscreetly allowing himself to be made King of Leinster. But the air of Newnham must have been agreeable to His Majesty, for he decided to overlook the *faux pas* on condition that it didn't happen again. And to remove any such temptation he started almost immediately for Fishguard, accompanied by the noble Earl, to conquer the whole of Ireland.

Later on, when the People took from the Nobility their privilege of initiating wars, Newnham again came into the headlines as the scene of a short-lived Royalist stand in the church and the old castle which, some say, adjoined. This would have been a well-conducted affair, with more likeness to a picnic than to our idea of warfare, had not an old retainer of Sir John Winter (of whom we shall hear more) blown a fair sprinkling of both sides out of the church by exploding a barrel of gunpowder. No one was killed by the explosion, but it quite upset the Roundhead leader, Colonel Massey, and led to the death of several of Winter's supporters, including the gunpowder enthusiast.

With her castle destroyed by Cromwell's men, the office of mayor in its last stages, and peace established in the land, Newnham came once more into the news. In 1771, so the parish records show, Mrs Sarah Hopley made clothes for the Westbury schoolmaster, and on them she sewed fifty-four Death's Head buttons. No doubt this gave the youngsters of Westbury a thrill, but no reason is given for charging this masterpiece to the parishioners of Newnham.

It might well be expected that a town with so much history would have many reminders of the past, but it seems that Newnham always has been middle-aged. At the time of the sporting Normans the castle is described as old, which must mean Saxon, though it was probably rebuilt to a great extent. The church has had no chance to grow old. The ever-encroaching river has made it necessary for the site to be moved at least twice, and one building has been destroyed by fire. The present Church of St Peter is probably the fifth to stand near to the present site, and it retains only traces of a Norman predecessor. A flourishing glass-works stood close to the river in the early part of the seventeenth century, but even the land on which it stood has now been removed by the hungry tide. In fact, it might be said of Newnham that she has something old—the sword given by King John—and something new—the daffodils that appear each spring and add so much to the Lady-Who-Never-Grows-Old.

The stretch of river between Broadoak and Purton carried quite a thriving shipbuilding industry so long as ships grew out of oak trees. But with bigger ships, and these made from metal plates and rivets, the trade left here, until now there is hardly any sign of the yards at which the work was carried on. This migration was hastened by the opening of the Sharpness Canal in 1824, for when regular traffic deserted this reach of the river the channel, always difficult, became almost impossible due to silting. But small boats carried on a trade in bark and coal well into this century, and a man living at Westbury remembers going with his brothers to Pleasant Stile to watch for boats coming up the river. When they sighted one which they recognised as bound for Broadoak they would run home with the news so that everyone could be ready. Boats had to work to the tides, and the work of taking off the incoming cargo and reloading would be rushed on without a pause until the job was finished. Hobbling, they called it, a name almost forgotten except by the few old people who still recall walking along the gangplanks carrying the freight. Men, women and children all joined in, and though the years have lent a glow of colour and romance it must have been cruelly hard work, especially for the children.

Bullo, just below Newnham, was the survivor amongst Forest ports in this neighbourhood, but the old quay is deserted now, and there is no traffic to disturb the heron as he wades on the shallow sands across the main stream. So it is left to Lydney, mile-from-the-river Lydney, to be the only point at which Forest industry has any contact with the world of ships. Lydney Harbour is a quiet backwater where rail and river meet, and where the coal trucks pour their loads down chutes into waiting barges. There is an air of tranquillity not generally associated with a port, where all is liable to be bustle and clatter. Here an engine occasionally moves trucks with a good deal of puffing self-importance, there a winch clatters self-consciously, and the whole scene works up to a gentle crescendo, reaching its peak when the tide allows the lock gates to be opened. Then, the crisis passed, the harbour settles down again to the slow rhythm of tipping coal and the plaintive cry of gulls.

But the absence of noise and bustle does not take away the interest. It is fascinating to watch the ease with which two men will move the cumbrous barges, taking all the help offered by wind or the wash of boats; never hurrying and never appearing in any doubt as they coax their charges first this way, then that, backwards, forwards and sideways. What a contrast they make with the jet-propelled aircraft screaming its way across the sky, burning up in a few hours' flight more heat-energy than could be loaded into one of these barges. But how long will a mechanised age be able to consume at the rate demanded by these giants of the air? There must be a limit to the rate of consumption and destruction called for by our present way of life. After half a century of intensive mechanisation we hear threats of the exhaustion of certain materials, just as the heavy calls of three hundred years ago so nearly exhausted our timber supply. But trees can be grown, unlike copper and lead. Is it possible that a swing of the pendulum of progress may bring us to appreciate the slow, drifting barge as a more genuinely efficient means of transport than the jet-machine, because it can continue on its leisurely way with a minimum of fuel in the form of machine or animal energy? You can do a lot of thinking while the tides rise and fall at Lydney Harbour. And you could feel very lonely.

We shall come back to Lydney, though not for the same reason that will draw us again to Newnham. At Lydney past and future will be linked, for this is sure to be the foundation on which industrial development will rest. But for the moment we are just having a quick look round.

Mention of the Forest of Dean to one of our well-known novelists called forth the remark, "That's the place with a well that cures a mangy dog if he's thrown in the water three times at sunrise." So the legend goes, but if you have a dog with this tiresome trouble, and would try the waters of St Anthony's Well, it is advisable to make a few enquiries first. Sunrise at the well must have a deadline, just as at Stonehenge; therefore the question of accommodation will crop up, unless you live within the limits of a pilgrimage on three successive days. And accommodation has been something of a problem here since Henry VIII compelled the Cistercian Brethren to give up dispensing hospitality at Flaxley Abbey.

Please do not feel discouraged, or imagine that difficulties are being put in the way deliberately, but there is one more obstacle. The well, with its stone trough large enough to hold any dog and his master, may be dry. The tradition which proclaimed the spring to be unfailing has gone the way of so many others, but with very good reason. The failing of the healing waters in dry weather is not due to any falling off in the supply of mangy dogs, but rather to the demands made by the nearby pumping station which supplies water to Cinderford.

Rudge, in 1803, tells us that the waters of St Anthony's Well have long been famed for the cure of cutaneous disorders (which shows how unrefined our writers have become in a century and a half), and says that the spring is sufficient to supply the adjoining paper mills and the iron-works at Flaxley, never decreasing in the driest season. Now the paper mills have decayed into tumbledown farm buildings, though the house still retains an architectural radiance that mud and neglect cannot entirely hide. The iron-works are long since gone, and the legend of the well is losing its hold, but forgive the small space that follows, for this is a Wishing Well and wishes must not be spoken aloud.

From St Anthony's Well there is a great temptation to wander on down the lovely Flaxley valley and through Blaisdon to Hunt-ley, especially if it is the season when the plum blossom falls like fairy snow on the fresh spring grass. Instead, let us follow the water pipe from the pumping station at Green Bottom and climb with it to Cinderford—the Problem Town—the only town coming within the present limits of the Royal Forest, and then only partly within.

Foresters will speak quite strongly amongst themselves about Cinderford, but they will unite like one man against the mildest attack from an outsider. This is mainly because they are so well aware, not only of the present shortcomings, but also of the very considerable progress that has been made, so that they are sensitive to criticism which is often lamentably uninformed. In recent years this has raised many local storms, so while angels would hesitate, the terms of reference compel me to step in.

An extract from the Medical Officer's report of 1873 will be a useful starting point:

> "In various directions, from numerous channels, and some-times out of the open house drains, at other times from ditches which issue out of gardens, or by streams that trickle stealthily out of the side entries, sewage matter finds its way into the roadways, forming in many places black and stagnant pools, which in hot weather emit a nauseous stench, and after rain fill up the roadway with an expanse of liquid mud. . . . Near some of these fragrant spots ducks, geese, pigs and children may be seen promiscuously congregated, and the observer who is acquainted with the natural history of parasites may perhaps be interested but not surprised to learn that worms form a not infrequent item in the pathology of the district."

23

Here should be enough to show that during the past seventy years the progress made by Cinderford is quite as noticeable as the loss of colour in official reports. In the following year an article in the *Western Mail* caused an outburst of indignation. It spoke of "900 houses and 4,000 inhabitants sticking to a hillside", and attributes the lack of planning to the work of the Devil when he shot the houses into position with a pea-shooter from across the valley. The people were annoyed by the obvious inaccuracy of this explanation, and it is important that the true facts should be known. It cannot be too widely known that the Devil alone could not have done this job, it needed three Devils, and it is of no consequence whether they sat on the opposite side of the valley or not, for they certainly worked in the closest disharmony. Their names? Certainly.

First comes the Devil of Common Rights, that's the wrinkled one in the middle of the group, still fancying that he possesses features that were attractive three hundred or more years ago. Then we have the Devil of Industrialism, a much younger creature, but already hideous from all the misery he has caused in his misspent youth. And the third is the Devil of Degeneracy, a subtle, persistent influence that has toiled endlessly to ensure that man's work declines steadily from the first high standard of inspiration. It is due to the work of this Devil that Stonehenge falls so far short of the magnificence that was Avebury; that the Forest church of All Saints lacks the beauty of Newland; and that the domestic architecture of the seventeenth and eighteenth centuries went to pieces in the nineteenth.

Two of these evil spirits are well known wherever human beings have been sentenced to mass imprisonment in the dreary rows of cells that were called Industrial Development, but the third, the Devil of Common Rights, is more localised and needs further consideration.

In the first place, "common rights" is intended to mean the rights belonging to certain people in common, and not any particular rights such as those of grazing or pannage. Rights and freedoms which have been won, sometimes by years of bitter struggle, are entitled to the most careful regard. They represent

24

something that was, at one time, of value to the majority and which may even have been essential to their livelihood. But conditions are always changing, and many of these rights—now stiff with age—benefit only a few, while they may be a considerable nuisance to the majority. To take a concrete example, comparatively few people in Cinderford keep a horse or pig which has the run of the adjoining common land. Probably in no case is the grazing of one of these animals essential to the welfare of the owner, yet all who frequent the town must suffer the nuisance of these animals making free use of the streets and pavements. It will be objected that these rights and customs are interesting, picturesque, a link with the past. So are stage-coaches and warming pans.

But the greatest influence these common rights have on the development of the town lies in the obstacles they place in the way of the acquisition of land. In the light of some experience I would rather have the task of obtaining land from the most flinty-hearted private owner than that of disentangling an acre of cinder-covered waste from the meshes of common rights.

On second thoughts there may be more than meets the eye in this problem of straying livestock. More than once I have seen a large pig sleeping in the gutter outside a café in the middle of Cinderford, and inside that café the most enticing bacon is served.

The names Cinderford and Coleford are unfortunate, but no one can be blamed for that. The impression they give of two upstart settlements is quite wrong, for Sinderford (as it was) is much older than the general use of coal, referring apparently to wood cinders or charcoal, a more picturesque if no cleaner origin. And Coleford has performed so many phonetic manœuvres that its origin is obscure, but it certainly does not refer to coal. There have been suggestions for renaming Cinderford, but names die as hard as customs.

The *Complete English Traveller* (1771) describes Coleford as "a small village, but situated in the most agreeable manner, near the borders of Monmouthshire. It is surrounded on every side by well cultivated fields and most delightful pastures", which is quite in order if we substitute town for village. Coleford built a Town

3                              25

Hall in 1662, on the occasion of the grant of a market charter by Charles II, and must therefore have claim to higher status than that of a small village. This Charter was probably a reward for services rendered, for in 1642 the Parliamentarians were driven out by the Royalists, in spite of having "a gun and an artilleryman to serve it". A campaign like this indicates some underground movement on the part of the Royalists.

Newland can claim a place in each chapter, so we will now only stay to glance at the main features; the thirteenth/fourteenth-century church, rich in monuments; the row of almshouses which approach more nearly, perhaps, than any other building in this area the "grown-out-of-the-earth" description so frequently applied to Cotswold buildings; the oak tree claiming superiority in years and inches over all other trees in the county; the inn oddly named The Ostrich. These items alone, without taking account of the beauty of the country, will keep bringing us back to the parochial centre of the Forest, for Newland was the parish in which the real Forest stood until quite recent times.

One other feature commends Newland. It has the great good sense to stand by a road that plays only a very small part in modern life, which gives more opportunity for ambling. But this was not always so, as will be seen by reference to the map and to the earlier importance of Redbrook as an industrial centre. The Red-brooks, Upper and Lower, were at one time looked upon as the chief centre of copper-smelting in these islands, and in those days Newland must have been a good deal busier. Otherwise the alms-houses and other charities, as well as several houses, would have been out of all proportion to the size of the village. The High-meadow mansion stood on the hill just above, and by all accounts that would have been no mean addition, though the population would have been influenced more by those who once lived in the hovels that still stand in the last stages of ruin further down the valley. Now there is no sign of the industrial past of Upper Red-brook beyond derelict mill-pools and the empty shell of an old factory, and with the present tinplate works out of sight and almost out of hearing Newland gives an impression of age taking a well-earned rest.

26

While Newland was for long the parochial centre of the Forest she is the junior member of the three villages watching over our western boundary. For St Briavels to the south and Staunton to the north have churches with signs of some two hundred more years to their credit. They offer interesting comparison, these three, and a revealing light on the development of mediæval England. St Briavels, clinging grimly to the edge of the high escarpment, is a severe and uncompromising place, built around the centrepiece of the Castle, with the church playing a part that is clearly second to military defence. There is no easy refinement here, and none of those touches of luxury which the twelfth and thirteenth centuries loved to indulge whenever the chance arose. Staunton and Newland, on the other hand, nestle in the shadow of their churches in a setting that suggests the quiet round of country life rather than the marching of armed men and the clash of steel.

The conditions giving rise to such distinctions may have gone these four hundred years, but the past is still deeply imprinted. St Briavels is exposed to every wind that blows, scorning the shelter of any hollow, but rough winds alone cannot blast creative art or we should not find the Cotswold buildings of Elkstone or Stow on the Wold. In fact, if we look to archaic times we find that soaring hilltops were the scene of inspired work by the Little People with Big Ideas. It was later progress that dedicated the high places to war.

With this sternness of aspect it is quite reasonable to find a very strong link with the past. Around St Briavels customs live so persistently that past and present walk hand in hand. The New Year gift still met with here leaves no doubt as to its extreme antiquity, for it consists of an apple mounted on three legs and trimmed with a nut and a sprig of yew. Three items, symbolising sweetness, fertility and immortality, on three legs will remind us of the Trelleck Stones across the valley, and of the Christian Trinity. Who would care to give a date or place where such a gift had its origin, and who could say with certainty that those who make their last journey by way of the Resting Stones to the Church of St Mary never take with them a coin in the hand?

Brockweir has character, but not the character of Dean Forest.

The quay where four parishes met has now gone, but still when the tide flows under the bridge there is a feeling of disappointment that it has brought no boats with it, for the echoes of trade still ring faintly amongst the old houses, fourteen of which were at one time licensed for the sale of drink. And in the evening shadows it would not be hard to see the monks of Tintern going the round of their farmland and gathering the tithes.

I have already explained that our journeys will be without system, so there need be no apology for moving on to enjoy the view from May Hill. This near-circular mound (for the slope is remarkably gentle) stands apart from the main block of high land, giving probably the widest and most detached view that can be found anywhere at the same time. Also, on account of the shape and the crowning clump of trees, it is the most familiar landmark for many miles around. At 969 feet it is the highest point in our territory, though winning only by a very short head from Ruardean Hill.

On opposite sides of May Hill are two towns that are opposite in many other respects—Newent and Mitcheldean. They are alike in having an active, thriving past, but there the likeness ends. Coal-mining was being carried on near Newent at the beginning of last century, and it is interesting to speculate on the effect this would have had on the little market town if the coal bed had justified even a few more years of activity. Newent would probably have developed a cancer of nineteenth-century industrial growth that would have changed the character completely. As it is there has been remarkably little change since the days when traffic between Gloucester and Monmouth used this route and made Newent a posting stage. The market has gone, and nothing has taken its place, but this has compensations. The landlord of the George has time to grow the most lovely geraniums in the yard where ostlers used to hiss as they groomed their horses, and in the main street it is still quite usual to see a horse and cart stopped for a leisurely conversation while the whole population of Newent looks on. But please do not imagine that the people of this mellow red brick town allow the grass to grow under their feet. Why, you can place an order with the chimney-sweeper at any time.

28

By telephone? Not exactly; but by the very simple process of writing your requirements on the paper and with the pencil hanging from the well-polished knob of his door. On the other hand a certain conservative tendency is shown by a decrepit bit of strap hanging from the bridle of the baker's pony. Long ago, it seems, this animal showed an inclination to nibble passers-by as he stood in the street, and though it is some years since the relic could have served any useful purpose, the odd piece of strap remains.

Yes, Newent still has an air of leisure, that priceless gift which is dying so fast, and which should have inscribed on its last resting place, "Killed by the twentieth-century scramble to save labour."

Mitcheldean—or Dene Magna, to distinguish it from Dene Parva—is literally and metaphorically a town of another colour. In place of warm red brick is some of the dingiest stone that the Forest has to offer. Here is the grime of an industrial past heightened by the shadow of disappointment. For Mitcheldean has backed a succession of losers until it really seems that Fate has been unkind. Coal-mining, the manufacture of nails and pins, cement-making, stone-quarrying, with grandfather clocks as a minor industry—all these have flourished here, and all have faded, the verdict in each case being that their end was due to "natural causes".

All these ventures have arisen from a supply of local material which, after it had encouraged a start, proved insufficient or unsuitable for the industry that depended on it. The clock business may have been an exception, for there is some doubt whether anything more than the cases were made here. The immediate reason for closing down was the expiration of lease on the site which was wanted for a town hall. But the grandfather clock trade was on its last legs anyhow. Now a fresh enterprise has been brought to Mitcheldean: the manufacture of projection equipment for sound films, which provides work for a number of people without being in any way dependent on local material. The future of this industrial injection depends rather upon the prevailing mode in entertainment, surely a change from the concrete to the abstract, for Mitcheldean was exporting fifty tons of cement daily in the early years of this century.

Perhaps this new industry is bringing with it new hope. At any rate the painting of houses and shop fronts during the past year or two goes quite a long way towards brightening dull stone and uninspired architecture, so it may be hoped that the clouds are lifting. But it takes more than buildings to make a town. The stones or bricks of which a place is built reflect the age that put them there, but it is on the growing spirit of the people that any judgment should be based, and in this respect Mitcheldean has something which many more elegant towns should envy—a great capacity for enjoyment. I never hope to meet more appreciative audiences than those I have had the pleasure of meeting here.

Apparently Dene Magna always has appreciated entertainment, even if the fare offered today does seem somewhat insipid by comparison with other times, as the following extracts from the local paper show:

*Gloucester Journal*, 6th May, 1732:

"They wrote from Mitcheldeane that on Friday the 28th of April last, between the hours of seven and eight in the evening (as is supposed) one Thomas Twibervile of that town, Carpenter, was in a most barbarous and inhuman manner murdered in his own shop, by having his brains dashed out, and afterwards his skull chopped and beat all to pieces with a broad axe. The deceased being a widower and having no child, lived alone, and was not found until Saturday evening, when the axe was lying with him all Gore blood. The person who is justly suspected to have commited this villanous and bloody Fact is one Ely Hatton. . . . He is now confined in our Castle, and 'tis hoped at the next Assizes he will meet with as just a punishment as so desperate and bloody minded a wretch deserves, in order to deter others from committing the like offence."

4th September, 1732:

"About 7 o'clock this morning Ely Hatton, attended by the proper officers and a prodigious concourse of People, was carried to Mitchel Deane in order to be executed near that place for the barbarous murder of Thomas Twibervile late of the same town, Carpenter."

9th September, 1732:

"On Monday last Ely Hatton was executed and afterwards hung in chains on Meane Hill near Mitcheldean. . . . He owned that he had been a great Sabbath Breaker, saying that it was usual for young people thereabouts to work all the week and on the Sunday to go and steal deer. There were 10,000 spectators present."

Hatton's body was at length taken away by night owing, it is said, to the strange fancy that the flies it fed and bred tainted the meat in the market at Mitcheldean. All of which shows how the people enjoyed the simple pleasures of yesterday, for there must have been a considerable pilgrimage from all the district round to provide so many spectators when we find that the combined population of Mitcheldean, Littledean and Ruardean at that time only amounted to about 1,550.

And there, quite unintentionally, the three Deans have grouped themselves into an association which does not exist, for Ruardean is in no way related to the Denes Magna and Parva. It is a corruption of Ruworthyn, a far more appropriate name, for it means rough farmland. The southern side of this bleak region is now being discreetly clothed in woodland, but there still remains "ruworthyn" to show that Nature and man have been ungenerous in their treatment. This loose, untidy type of growth cannot entirely blame itself on industrial pressure, for it does not carry the fingerprints of that particular Devil. It suggests, rather, settlement by people who were from time to time driven out of the royal preserve and who would, quite naturally, drift to the poorer land that had failed to attract those with any choice in the matter. Rudge tells us that the Commonwealth Protector expelled nearly 400 cabins of beggarly people from the Forest, and though we may be sure that he found Biblical authority for his action, we can be equally sure that the suffering caused by it was great. For however beggarly their cabins may have been they represented the only homes these people possessed, and we can imagine how

31

desperately they must have searched for any odd corners of land on which they could squat, building what rough shelter they could in the most inaccessible positions.

No doubt Ruardean Hill felt this invasion, for it was outside the Royal Forest at that time, and the marks are still to be seen. The victims of early industrial growth were mostly condemned to live in rows of boxes as squalid and regimented as the lives they lived in the factory-hells that provided them with some sort of living, while the people who settled in the rough farmlands at least decided, each for himself, what shape the humble dwelling should take and which way it should face. The result of all this promiscuous movement and settling must bring moments of black despair to those whose job it is to plan for us the new era in public services. For the blueprint that would bring such a scattered conglomeration into any system of wires and pipes would be a masterpiece indeed, and the estimated expenditure would put the whole idea right out of the question.

All this digression was caused by a name, but with names carrying so much history on their backs they must not be passed over lightly. In this case there is special significance, for if Ruardean is allowed to form a trinity with the other Deans we must look for some other explanation of the name of the Forest, and the various alternatives that have been put forward are not convincing.

Littledean is on an uphill road in more than the geographic sense, for while the church, with its traces of Saxon work, still remains active, the prison is no longer used as such. This "house of correction" was built as a result of an Act of 1784, and we are told that it was found to be productive of most salutary effects. It would be pleasant to believe that the one has made the other unnecessary, and this may be true to some extent, for the closing of the prison is due largely to a changed view of crime, rather than to any falling off in business for the magistrates' courts. In other words, the civilising by discipline and government spoken of by Bigland is not in fashion now.

Other changes that have come to Littledean will be open to more doubt, though they are much the same as have befallen all such small towns and villages. In 1608 there were here, in addition to miners, weavers, tinkers, shoemakers, pynners, naylors, 1 glover, 1 bonelace maker, and 1 radlecaryer. It is unlikely that any of these tradesmen have survived, while the radlecaryer is almost forgotten in name, and this specialised work of handling part of a loom in hand-weaving is finished.

In one particular the two Deans were well placed in those days, for the only registered tooth-drawer in the district lived at Abenhall. But the advantages of living near to him may have seemed less rosy when the client was confronted by the weapons of the tooth-drawer's trade. It is the privilege of every generation to regard its successors as mollycoddled weaklings, so that we take their lamentations with a large helping of salt, but if we look at any collection of old-time surgical instruments, remembering that they were used in the raw without any anæsthetic, we have to admit that the old folks certainly had something.

Though the weavers and their radlecaryers have gone there is still one example of their work left in the neighbourhood. In the seventeenth century there died at Littledean a boy of five years who, it is said, came to such untimely end by swallowing cherry stones. His little suit, beautifully made in hand-woven cloth, is carefully preserved with a photo of the tombstone, which may still be seen in the churchyard, though somewhat weatherbeaten.

This pathetic relic links itself in the mind with one at Weston-under-Penyard. In this case a little girl was killed by the poison of a pet snake, and a memorial in the form of a lovely wrought-iron gate carries a skilfully worked figure of the child's arm, round which the reptile is twined. It is unusual to be able to see these personal touches without leaving the highway, but this gate is beside the main road, and the superb house to which it belongs must be a source of joy to all who pass with eyes for more than the road ahead. When sixteenth-century timber and brick live in harmony with smooth lawns and spreading cedar trees there is only one thing needed to complete the picture—a gate of iron lacework.

Let it never be said that I recommended the car as a means of seeing this stretch of country, but a great deal can be seen without effort. Westbury is another village that makes little attempt to hide some pleasant features. Nearly all there is for the casual visitor stands near the road.

If you think Westbury-on-Severn has a worried air do not put it down to any local concern over the gap between church and spire. There is also a time-gap between them, for the handsome shingle-clad spire was first in the field by quite a fair margin. Nor does Westbury allow herself undue concern over the task of living up to the magnificent water gardens and the gazebo at the Court. The iron rails do something more than guard the yew hedges and the geometrically precise canals. They form windows where a restless twentieth century can look without effort or interruption straight into the peaceful dignity of the age that saw Dutch William to the throne. The river's threat to wash away the mill does not greatly disturb the old folks who gather in the Red Lion. They are hardened to the demands of the big tides sweeping around this great bend of the Severn, so that when the mill house —whose stone has long since ceased turning—was sold for something like one hundred pounds, they shook their heads and assured each other that the building would soon be a heap of rubble on the muddy shore. But the powers-that-be decided otherwise, and big works have since been carried out to reinforce the bank at this point.

No, Westbury's big worry is over the name by which they should call the main feature of the village. For the first decade or two of this century it was simply the Workhouse, but by a series of nomenclatural gymnastics it has received the designation Westbury Hall, a name which may bestow dignity on the clientele (who dares to call them inmates?), but which takes a bit of beating for ambiguity.

Rodley is not far from Westbury, but the two have absolutely nothing in common. You can wander through miles of narrow lanes without being able to say with certainty that you have seen this scattered hamlet. Rodley-on-the-river it might be called, for there are few houses where it would be out of place, at some time, to call upon the river to stay away from the door. In spring, if the weather and the tides are in genial mood, the orchards and meadows emerge from the flood. Apple-blossom time brings all the sudden beauty of a transformation scene, and the Peggy-whitethroat sings sweetly. Then Rodley becomes furiously busy with the making and carrying of hay, for it cannot be stacked in the lower fields. Autumn will find apples in heaps and apples in bags, all waiting for the cider mill. And in recent years quite a quantity of fruit is grown of a quality that will find its way to the market. But what happens here in winter? Only the frogmen know.

Awre stands on a loop of the Severn and on a twisted loop of by-way from the main road. And here Time winds a leisurely loop amongst the old orchards and the overgrown hedges. The chief sign of the times is the more milky look of the cows, with here and there something modern in farmbuildings. But the salmon, the cider and the celandines have not changed these four hundred years; not since the Great Sorrow came to Awre. This was a blow that fell all the harder on these land-and-water people because it was delivered by their good old friend the Severn. The lower channel of this river has always been unsettled, with sand and mud moving at the whim of tide and stream in a manner as unpredictable as it is inexplicable. And in earlier days this movement was on a much bigger scale, because no large-scale efforts were made to control the stream. So fickle was the main channel that a considerable area of alluvial land would shift at irregular intervals from the Awre side over to the Slimbridge bank, and back again, so that the people were never sure when this "new ground" would be theirs, or for how long. This was a matter of some concern, as it was very fertile soil that could quickly provide excellent pasturage. But the movement was essentially an Act of God, and therefore to be accepted philosophically, until the Berkeley Estate decided to interfere with the divine ordering by securing this shifting freehold to the Slimbridge side. Philosophy gave way to litigation, but it was only after a long and swaying struggle that Slimbridge won the day. That was in the seventeenth century, which is not so long ago in Awre. Why, time moves so slowly that they managed to make two rectors last from 1780 until 1878.

But they are not sleepy down this way. Men who own salmon fisheries can seldom afford to shut both eyes at once. Even the owl in the hollow yew tree by the church will fly away before you can come within twenty yards of him. It was here that the metrical setting of the Psalms was worked out by two local men, Sternhold and Hopkins, and the huge dug-out wooden chest which now stands under the tower must have been old then.

But with spring the gnarled apple trees will blossom again; silver-fresh salmon will run the hazard of lave net and putcheon; and the celandine flowers will gleam again like golden stars in the hedgerows.

The Severn and salmon-fishing naturally lead us to Tidenham, where the parish boundary runs to the middle of Severn and Wye. Tidenham has become widely known for the part played in *English Village Community*, that great work of Seebohm's published in 1915. It may equally be said that the book owes no small part of its success to the information available in the records of the Manor of Tidenham. In this connection it is of interest to note that the Bishop of Bath once let the manor to the Archbishop of Canterbury at a rental that included six porpoises. Apparently these creatures were more plentiful in those days, for though they are not unknown today, no one would care to bargain for the supply of six a year.

The records of this manor are an example of typical development in Saxon and Norman times, but the village now shows very little sign of the conventional pattern of village growth. It is spread on the hillside without form or plan, but with the most arresting views of the Wye-Severn reunion.

Come to Tidenham for scenery or for salt breezes, but if you come for salmon—served with salad—you may find yourself across the bridge in Chepstow before your search is ended. There is accommodation here for visitors, but in line with the general trend very little effort is made to induce the traveller to linger. Here, as in other parts of the country, the church has been used as a dosshouse by people who should have some higher sense of propriety. While there can be no defence of such behaviour it must be admitted that, for an area so attractive and so widely known for its beauty, the tourist accommodation is quite inadequate. And I make no apology for returning to this theme.

It is not easy to start writing about Longhope. There are no prominent features and no events in the past which have made any deep scratch in history. Nestling in an orchard-strewn valley it is easily overlooked, and when plum trees blossom it hides so snugly amongst the white foam that from neighbouring hills there is a glimpse of church tower and sawmill chimney, but little else. Longhope has not the wrinkles of hardship and poverty that are all too frequently met with in these parts; instead it has a look of quiet prosperity. This is probably due to the fact that no inducements drew the people to seek a living below the surface, where fate has so often been unkind. Instead they have lived by fruit and timber, which can last indefinitely if only we do not insist on taking all in the great game of put-and-take.

Yes, in spring the valley is filled with fruit blossom, and if the season is kind summer and autumn find the air heavy with the smell of plums and apples, until the people say they hate the smell of fruit. But the hatred is not too deep to be forgotten during the bare winter months when the chief reminders are cider and a goodly assortment of canned and bottled fruits. Then, as spring dawns again, an eager watch is kept for early blossom and late frost, for fruit-growing is essentially a gamblers' job. Work all you will and study all you can, if the season is against you it will all be in vain. The frost of a single night may alter the outlook for the whole season. With fruit-farming, as with betting, it is unwise to plan how the money will be spent until it is safely in the hand, and there is the added drawback of a lot of work during the close season. The fruit that is left to grow itself will often be left to sell itself—or rot on the ground. Only those varieties that are well selected and carefully tended can hope to hold their own in market competition.

So, if you happen to travel through this valley when the blossom is more beautiful than a dream of fairyland, do not make arrangements there and then to throw in your lot amongst the Arcadians of Plumland. Come back when the spraying and the greasebanding are in full swing. Then, ten to one, you will find an orchard where the time-honoured treatment of whitewashing is still carried on. And when you see these whitened stripes against the red earth or the green of early grass you will be tempted. But beware of greasebanding, which is the practice of placing a sticky garter round the trunk of the tree to stop pedestrian insects from climbing to the height of their ambition. Not long ago, in this very place, a greaseband hit back; this way.

A cow, rubbing her neck against a tree, came into touch with one of these insect traps. Later on the owner of the cow leant over her neck while tethering her in the stall, and found his ample beard firmly attached to the far side of the sticky neck. He has been heard to admit that the experience brought tears to his eyes for the first time in years.

In Longhope churchyard was a stone in memory of Thomas Bright, who is mentioned by Atkyns as being remarkable for his strength. Thomas died in 1708, at the reputed age of a hundred and twenty-four. He was succeeded by a lad still young at eighty-four, who walked the whole length of the church roof in his stockinged feet when he was eighty. But it may be as well to point out that the feat was performed in the course of building repairs, and not as part of a local octogenarians' obstacle race. Also, if you have heard that badger steak is served at one of the inns, do not look upon this as a regular event. It only happened on one special occasion.

It was not easy to start writing about Longhope, but it is even harder to stop. When approaching places that figure largely in guide-books, and places where great issues have been decided, we go on with an air of keen expectation, which is too often disappointed. It was not the outstanding names that shaped our villages, but the daily lives of all the people. Longhope boasts no ancient battlefield, nor does it claim to have attended at the birth of any of our princes or premiers. It is just one of the villages that help to make rural England, and therein lies its charm.

Everywhere in this peninsula there are viewpoints, some showing wide prospects within our territory, others looking outwards. From amongst these it is difficult to mention even a fair selection, but just as the proud owner will take you from window to window of his house, overlooking only those commanding a view of the coal shed or the neighbour's rubbish heap, so I will take you to some of our natural balconies. And my task will be made easier by the fact that our coal shed is no cause for shame, and here we have no neighbours with rubbish heaps.

Fine views across the Severn to the long Cotswold escarpment are offered from points as widely scattered as Popes Hill, Newnham churchyard, Pleasant Stile (on the road from Newnham to Littledean), Plum Point (above Mitcheldean) and Tidenham Chase. At a time when high tides are coming up the estuary my vote would go to the close-up view from Newnham, for that will give an opportunity to watch the build-up of the wave as it travels round the great horseshoe bend. There will also be no lack of sound effects, for the incoming tide makes a fine roar as it rushes over the sands, and the clock in the tower above will mark every third hour with a tune. The view from Pleasant Stile lacks these finer touches, though the height gives a much wider prospect. This spot is well known because it lies on the road, offering a wide panorama that is too often taken in with all the efficiency of an express train sucking up water. And the same applies to Plum Point. Those who really appreciate widespread scenery will walk over Popes Hill and along the high ridge above Mitcheldean, taking a leisurely fill as they go.

From Tidenham Chase you can look down on the Severn Sea where it widens to more than two miles, though only at the time of high tide will water fill the estuary from bank to bank. At low water there will be a mile and a half of sand and mud. On the stretch of heath known as Poors' Allotment, near to the cluster of windswept Scots pines, are some rocks with a story—another paragraph in our legendary history. It was here (so we are told) that the Devil and Jack Kent tried their strength in a stone-throwing contest. The Devil, having first throw, heaved the Broad Stone to the site where it now stands beside the railway at Stroat. Well thrown, Sir! A mile and a half if it's a yard. Then Jack, with some local fame as a strong man, bared his chest to the salt sea breeze and dropped his stone right across the river, winning by some three miles. Nonsense, of course, and yet history if we could but read it.

A new angle on the Wye seems to present itself every time I

39

travel that way, so it would be ridiculous to say that you simply must climb up to this ridge, or that you should not fail to keep a north-easterly look-out as you descend that pitch. Those who have enough time and energy may decide to follow the line of Offa's Dyke, which may be compared to the string which carries the pearls, but for the tourist who must glance and ride away there are such spots as Winter's Leap, overlooking the Lancaut peninsula, and the rocky balcony a mile further north on the same road. Then, if you are prepared to walk a mile, there is the rock platform of the Devil's Pulpit standing on an angle of the Dyke and looking down into the ruins of Tintern. But the trees seem anxious to protect the old monastery from the Evil Eye of the unholy preacher, for a rood screen of leaf and branch is threatening to hide the view.

At St Briavels the hills step back from the river, giving variety to the scene by widening the floor of the valley where a loop of the river once wound its way. But that was so long ago that only the rocks know the story.

It is difficult to say which is the more fortunate, Monmouth or the Kymin. Any town is lucky to have a hill close at hand (and I am thinking of Cheltenham and, further away, Reigate), and it is more than ever a blessing for a town lying low in a valley. At the same time a hill loses nothing by looking down on a town such as Monmouth. To add to the general satisfaction the top of the hill is National Trust property. The Naval Temple, erected to commemorate our great admirals, may seem incongruous, but it is a reminder that those who sailed our wooden walls took a deep interest in the sources from which the timber came. Nelson, whose name leads all the others on the Temple, only visited Monmouth twice, but he made a report on the timber of the Forest of Dean in 1803. The Temple was not built as the outcome of his splendid victories, for we are told that he visited it while at Monmouth.

The Buck Stone stands about two miles to the east, and it looks almost as if the counties had agreed to share these two viewpoints, as the boundary of Monmouth and Gloucester lies midway between them. We shall come back to the Buck Stone, just as men have been doing these thousands of years, but in the meantime the way lies across the river to the Dowards (Great and Little). These lie outside our area, but they give grand opportunities for looking at the Highmeadow Woods. Seen from this angle the contortions of the Wye will be just as bewildering, even with a glimpse of Monmouth in the distance. Between these twin hills is King Arthur's Cave, home of Early Stone Age men. The relics found on the floor of this cave can be seen in Gloucester Museum.

Symonds Yat Rock; Mecca of all who set out to see the Wye Valley; name that launches a thousand coach tours. And do not think less of the Yat because you may have to share it with others, for by comparison with many popular beauty spots this one is still unspoilt. But if you must have the Rock to yourself make a tryst with the sunrise, before the mists have left the river or the campers have folded their tents. I cannot tell the names of all the counties that may be seen from this limestone platform, though I have heard the recital many times, nor can I say anything about Symonds, or why his name is made to rhyme with pieman. The only constructive suggestion on that question comes from Alfred Watkins' book *The Old Straight Track*, in which it is put forward as the Seaman's Yat. That the word yat meant a track or way just as much as it meant a gate is beyond doubt, and according to this authority the Yat Rock was a point on a track leading past the Queen Stone, on Huntsham ham, and making towards Bristol. Chief support for this derivation comes from the absence of any legend linking the name with any individual. Land around here was owned by a man of this name at one time, but it seems as if the name was here first, and the man probably called himself SYmonds.

But this chapter is getting out of hand. It began as a hurried glimpse of the "Eye 'twix Severn and Wye", not as a guide or gazetteer. It is in danger of failing on all counts. I have kept two special favourites to the end; then we can move on.

If you lived at Lawn Farm, Penyard Park, you would have only woodland for neighbour and only the ghosts of Penyard Castle for company. At first the name may sound unsuitable, for there seems little chance that there was ever sufficient shaven turf here to attract notice. The dictionary, however, tells us that the word lawn was applied to cleared land between woods, so no place could be more aptly named than Lawn Farm. Looking carefully at the map I can find no place with which to compare this isolated farm, not more than a mile from Ross as the crow flies, but nearly three by road. As I write it is spread out in front of me, a patchwork of green and brown fields entirely hemmed in by woods. And I wish the castle had not been carried away stone by stone to be used in the church and other buildings at Weston-under-Penyard.

Wigpool Common has everything—provided you do not look for shops, or roads. This high plateau is full of interest for the botanist, the geologist, the sociologist and the tramp. Whether your inclination is to search for the tiny plants of the rock crevice and the quab-hole, or whether the eye and the fancy rove to the Malverns, the Black Mountains or the Cotswolds, you will find satisfaction. And on the outer fringes of the Common is history in the form of cabins that can have advanced but little since the days of Cromwell.

Most of the places mentioned here will crop up again, with a whole lot of others. Many more will not even find standing room. The fault is not theirs, for every village and hamlet is in the centre of the world—for those who live there.

# Chapter III

## LOOKING FOR HISTORY

"It is a degradation to man to be reduced to the life of the present; and never will he cast forth his hopes, and his views, and his efforts towards the future with due effect and energy unless at the same time he seizes and holds fondly clasped to his heart the recollections of the past."

GLADSTONE

THE Romans dug for iron in the Forest of Dean. This opening gambit has become almost a convention when writing of the Forest, and the established truth of the statement only makes it the more misleading. The earliest writings tell us of the Romans, which focuses attention on the arbitrary line between history and pre-history, based on the presence or absence of written records. But there are those who consider that the giant earthworks, the megaliths and the long barrows can be interpreted as clearly as an inscription on stone or scroll. Some may gather an even clearer picture from the works than from the words of the ancient past. However that may be, the great works of the Little People should not be overlooked.

There may be few of the early monuments in our area, but they are sufficient to show that the land was known to the small, dark-haired Iberians, though they do not seem to have been as numerous here as they were at no great distance to east and west. Their delay in getting here would be in line with later invasions. There are barrows, and the line of standing stones from Huntsham to Stroat has all the appearance of being the signposts of these folk.

The absence of well-constructed barrows is a source of disappointment, but it must be remembered that most of the higher land has been dug over so persistently in the search for metals that many traces are certain to have been rubbed out. Men who were always so handy with pick and shovel would not neglect a mound

43

in which there might be something of value. The Ordnance Survey map tells us that there are Dwarfs' Holes in the Forest, and the site of the Roman settlement at Lydney used to be called Dwarfs Hill. This information can only be gathered from local legend, for there has been nothing to see during recent times that could give rise to the names, nor is there any written record of dwarfs from whom the name might be derived.

Let us stray as far as Merrow Down, near Guildford, and meet Puck of Pooks Hill. Here was no invention of Kipling's fertile brain, but the personification of that great people who, having crowned so many of our downland heights with their creative genius, were driven westward by the all-pervading Celt. Even today the survivors of a conquered nation who cannot escape are driven "underground". How much easier was it for these people who were small of stature by comparison with those who over-ran them to take the same course literally. That they were expert miners we know, and accustomed to live in dugout huts partly below the surface. By scattering and digging deeper they survived to a place in folklore and in the ancestry of those who still preserve the mining cult.

If this sounds like wild yarning it would be well, before dismissing it as such, to look more closely into the activity of the Little People—as closely as the mists of time will allow—and then to make comparison with the inhabitants of today. Where are your Celts, your Saxons and your Romans? Surviving only as lateral intakes of a bloodstream that has Megalithic man as the source. Today, I am told, there is one band (brass, silver, or what you will) for each square mile of the Royal Forest. Even if this figure is not accurate to a decimal point it is a very strong challenge to any Anglo-Saxon community.

A mound that is said to be a round barrow stands on May Hill outside the fading circle of a circular camp. The circle is considered to be of the Iron Age, and the mound is small and flattened. It was opened this year, but I do not know who did the work, or what was found. Another likely site is on Tidenham Chase, where a round barrow is being excavated, while the name draws us to a big mound at Churcham. At one time the very

44

fact of its situation in the vale would have made this unworthy of serious attention, but that time is passed and the mound is, not un-usually, the subject of disagreement amongst archæologists. Most significant is the name, Sainthill, and in this respect it is worth recalling a case cited by Professor Boyd-Dawkins. He mentions a barrow near Mold called Bryn yr Ellyllon (the Hill of the Goblin) of which local tradition declared that it was haunted by a ghost in golden armour. When the tomb was opened—for the first time—it was found to contain the skeleton of a warrior with a corselet of bronze overlaid with gold. Memory had preserved the knowledge for more than fourteen hundred years. This is straying rather far, geographically, but it does show the impor-tance that may attach to a name. In our case it may be argued that hillocks of this type are often met with in this river-bed formation, to which I should reply that two very similar mounds, at Arling-ham and Boddington, are both called Barrow Hill.

But it is when Sainthill is approached as a possible mark on a "sighted track" that we get results which some may consider convincing. A line running slightly north of east (a likely sunrise alignment) runs through these points: Ruardean Church, Notts-wood Hill, Gloucester Cathedral, Churchdown Camp, Badge-worth Church, Leckhampton Church, Salperton, Folly Farm, Camp Farm, long barrow, Bourton-on-the-Water, Wyck Beacon and Bould. An impressive list of names to find on one line of less than forty miles. And, for what it is worth, two of the churches are orientated on this line. But all this touches on a field that cannot be explored now.

The caves of the Wye Valley limestone tell us that even earlier men inhabited this land, but beyond the fact that they left their bones and a few implements on the gravel of a river bed some two hundred feet above the present river level, we know really nothing of them. And what we know from other sources strongly suggests a complete break between them and the later inhabitants.

So we come back to the Romans digging for iron in the Forest, but not before they had been put to a very considerable amount of inconvenience, and heavy losses, at the hands of the Silures who then lived in this region and over Wye. Roman writers give the impression that the natives with whom they had to contend were barbarians; so they were, in the sense that they were bearded in contrast to the clean-shaven invaders, but they were not savages. Our word civilian derives from the Latin *civis*, meaning town dwelling, and does not necessarily mean cultured. True to their Celtic temperament, they were more inclined towards the arts than to a life of carefully ordered regimentation, and for that reason they would have presented a sharp contrast. But their resistance under the leadership of Caradoc is one of the great chapters of history. We cannot claim Caradoc (whom the Romans named Caractacus) as a Silure, for there is a rumour that he had been driven from further east in the face of the invasion, but he brought to these people their greatest need—a general. In his behaviour, first as victor, then as victim of the Romans, he showed himself to be a man of the highest qualities.

One writer says of the Forest: "Deepest of all, perhaps, is the mark left by the Roman invaders, whose sojourn lasted nearly four hundred years and many of whose roads and relics remain." Admittedly there are most interesting traces of the Roman occupation, but in spite of these I would be so bold as to say that the marks so left are insignificant by comparison with the mark that was made on the Roman Empire by the Forest. It was from here that Eurgain, daughter of Caradoc, was taken prisoner to Rome, where, under her new name of Claudia, she grew up and married Rufus Pudens, of whom St Paul writes in his Second Epistle to Timothy. It was Claudia who persuaded her husband to Christianity, and who brought up four sons so that one, Timotheus, devoted his whole life to spreading the Christian faith. And it was her younger brother, Linus, who became the first elected Bishop of Rome and died a martyr's death.

From the military viewpoint the stubborn resistance put up at this outer limit of colonisation must have added considerably to the load that eventually proved too great for the Roman Empire. For nine years Caradoc fought the invasion in a series of encounters that throw into high relief the opposing qualities of Briton and Roman. On the one hand a force that the world had found irresistible, on the other an ill-equipped band gathered from local chiefs who were themselves thoroughly disorganised by internal strife. The invaders had the problem of very extended supply lines which had to cross the Severn, amongst other obstacles, while the defenders were in their own difficult country. The highly mobile battle area moved gradually west and north, with Caradoc tormenting the massive Roman army amongst the hills of Hereford, Brecon, Radnor, and to the fateful meeting in Shropshire. A victory for the invaders, followed by treachery among their opponents, brought the leader into captivity. But even then his task was not done, for his fame caused him to be taken to Rome, where there is no doubt that his bearing raised the prestige of his people, and probably secured for them better terms than they would otherwise have received.

These appear to me important marks to be weighed in the scales against the Roman remains that we find in the Forest, for the present roads do not, in many cases, run on the track of those made by the foreign road-building specialist, and it is difficult to trace the passion for system and orderliness here as it is shown so clearly in Gloucester and Cirencester, though we know that Roman Lydney was quite an important settlement.

In Roman times the centre of Lydney, at least as regards the temple, was in the park near to Viscount Bledisloe's residence. Here, in addition to a lavish layout of guest rooms and baths, stood the temple of the god Nodens. But Nodens was no stranger in this region, being merely the Romanised form of the old Celtic god Nudd. In this way the newcomer alters the more detailed pattern of life in the land which he overruns, without causing any serious dislocation. And ultimately the old stock, carrying the fresh scion, will bear fruit which, while it may spring immediately from the new growth, is nourished by the old root.

In a field called Chesters, not far from the river at Woolaston, was a Roman villa. This has never been completely excavated, but it was of fair size and probably had some connection with a neighbouring landing place. There has been some speculation as to the most likely site for a river crossing, some placing it here, but I am inclined to go as far as Purton. Engineers of the railway epoch chose Purton as the site for a bridge because they found firm rock on which to build. This would also provide a safer foundation to a ford, and there are signs of British and Roman roads making towards this point. The British roads would have been nothing more than rough tracks, in many cases cut deep by traffic and running water, so that for much of the year they probably proved an obstacle rather than an aid to travel. In this way, of course, they would have been of considerable assistance to the inhabitants in time of invasion, for an army with equipment like that of the Romans could not make permanent progress faster than they could construct roads equal to their needs.

Having secured the route to Caerwent, by way of Lydney and Chepstow, there began a penetration into the Forest in search of iron, and we may judge the importance of this industry by the extensive working of the various scowl holes, and by the network of roads that linked up the sources of iron and wood. As both these materials were liable to run short at any particular spot it would have been necessary for the centre of activity to be moved in order to avoid excessive transport. The equipment of those days made it a more economic proposition to move the factory to the raw material rather than vice versa. This explains the many deposits of cinders that are to be found widely scattered throughout the iron-producing area, and also the short stretches of Roman road that do not fit into the popular idea of a highway as planned by these efficient organisers. Having cleared an area of woodland to provide charcoal for smelting, what is more likely than that the scene of activity would shift outwards in the same way that the fungus causing "fairy rings" in the grass grows out from the central start? Not the happiest of similes, perhaps, but descriptive because these rings leave a clear centre, whereas the outward seeping development of our towns has not yet allowed the grass to return to the middle.

The main roadway for this iron industry was the carefully paved track leading from the iron-smelting centre of Ariconium to Lydney, now known as the Dean Road, and traceable by road or pathway through most of its sixteen-mile length. This is undoubtedly our greatest reminder of the occupation, and in guide-book wording "will repay a visit". In fact, it would be safe to go further than that and say, to all who are more than faintly interested in the subject, it will amply repay the effort of walking along that stretch of some three miles lying on either side of Blackpool Bridge, running through Cockshoot Wood to Old-croft in the south and through Blakeney Walk to Upper Soudley in the north. Over this stretch paving stones may be found quite frequently, though in many places they have been completely disarranged by the timber wagons of later times, and in others they lie under a covering of turf and soil a foot or more deep.

It is at Blackpool Bridge, close to the Parkend–Blakeney road, that a stretch of this ancient highway has been uncovered so that it may be seen just as it was sixteen hundred years ago. A padlock of the Forestry Commission bars the way to vehicles, which is as it should be, for there is nothing about this road that would har-monise with modern traffic, and in the woodland quiet, sweetened by bird songs and the babbling of water, it is easier to see this track as the work of the gods (or the fairies, if you wish) making for themselves a way down to bathe in the stream, than as one of the roads leading to Rome. Even the railway close at hand plays up to this feeling of unreality, for it is no longer used, and the silver birches grow over it. These two structures, parted by so many years and so much history, raise an interesting point. Will delving archæologists of the future read the story aright? Not if they work to the popular theory of progressive evolution, for by that process the evenly laid and precisely fitting stones of the road would place it in a period much later than the dumped waste stone of the railway embankment.

Beside this road, not far north of the bridge, is the irregular mass of Forest rock known as the Drummer Boy Stone. It has two shallow depressions, one of which is lined with iron, and each having a draining groove—though these may have been made by weathering, as they run with the grain of the rock. The history of this stone is not known, but the hollows will inevitably suggest sacrificial blood, while the alternative use as a cresset to hold oil or fat will not, at first sight, make much appeal in a rather incon-spicuous valley situation.

Here I will come into the open and say that, in my opinion, the

Romans only adapted and reconstructed the road. Without questioning for a moment that they made the paved track that we now see, I would say that the work was carried out on two much earlier tracks. To see my reason for taking this view it is really only necessary to draw a line through the crossroads at Bromsash and Lydney on the "one-inch" map. Now compare the line of the Dean Road with the straight line. Given that the Romans found the country without any tracks worthy of the name, whatever induced them to take the route they did? It wanders off south of the straight line without finding easier gradients or firmer ground. Rather it seems to choose a way that will include steep banks and fords, while the straight line avoids most of them.

Now divide the Dean Road into two sections joining at Littledean and it will be found to follow very closely in the lines of two rather significant straight tracks. The first of these, working from the north, passes over the crossroads at Bromsash, through Mitcheldean Church and St Anthony's Well to Littledean Camp. The second links up Nottswood Hill (already shown as on a likely east–west track), Flaxley Abbey, Littledean Camp, Soudley Camp, Blackpool Bridge, Nodens Temple at Lydney and ending at St Tecla's Chapel. Black (or Blake) appears to be a pre-Roman name very frequently associated with trackways, and we have it on record that Patrick, Bishop of the Hebrides, gave instructions for a church to be built on the site of upright stones, or menhirs. So the Drummer Boy Stone may have served as a cresset, for they were not always on a height. The name, even after so many centuries, is probably the clue—if only we could interpret it.

But the Romans, like the Drummer Boy, had to go. And though it was only their authority and their legions that were withdrawn it is astonishing how rapidly their influence faded, particularly in this remote outpost, for our knowledge of their occupation is greater today than at any time since, say, two hundred years after the official withdrawal. Efforts were made to continue the great organisation that had been built up, but it speaks clearly of the decaying state of the Empire that even with a considerable amount of co-operation from the Britons (many of whom could look to the Mediterranean for some part of their ancestry) those who remained could not prevent the landslide. Britain rapidly returned to a state lower than that which existed before the arrival of the Roman Standard. From the material viewpoint almost nothing of the Roman influence survived for any length of time. Roads became dilapidated, with no efforts being made to keep them in repair; building of the more permanent kind came to an end; government ceased to be a unifying force; even the little refinements of everyday life had taken no deep hold on the people. Add to this the basic reaction which appears to be the inescapable aftermath of progress, and it becomes clear that the Forest of the seventh and eighth centuries possessed little or nothing that could be called culture.

Professor Haverfield, expert on Roman Britain, goes so far as to say, "The Roman has passed from Britain as though he had never been. He has left no name on hill or river; he has not even bequeathed a few drops of Roman blood. Racially, topographically, culturally, ancient Rome has nothing to do with modern Britain." And while I should hesitate to accept such sweeping words for the whole country, they do apply in great measure to the Forest. In attempting to explain the rapid decay after the departure of Roman government, too little attention is often given to the fact that the Romans were civilians, in the Latin sense. They lived in towns by choice. The Britons and Saxons were fundamentally different, preferring to settle in small isolated groups based on the family unit.

The situation can be more easily pictured by recalling that brick-making and the use of the potter's wheel were almost forgotten. And the potter's wheel is probably the most primitive piece of equipment that can claim to be a machine. This departure from the Roman way of life suggests very strongly that even after four hundred years the native population found the foreign yoke irksome, and lost no time in shunning all reminders of it. In some parts of England there are indications of an attempt to preserve at least some of the imported ideas, and the use of the foreign currency. In this area the signs point the other way, with two outstanding illustrations. At Bishops Wood, near Kerne Bridge, a great number of Roman coins were dug up in 1895. These were in three jars, two of which were already broken, while the workmen who found them broke the third. 17,550 coins were collected and classified, and many more were picked up by children. It has been suggested that such a hoard was intended for the pay of a legion that was hurriedly recalled, but whatever the purpose it seems as if the inhabitants were not greatly interested in the money or they would have found it. Aston Ingham also gave up two chests of coins last century.

At Ariconium, again, there were signs of the iron-works being abruptly and completely deserted. When the site was cleared of brambles in 1875 there were no signs of any occupation of the site during the intervening fourteen centuries. Blackened wheat and Roman ornaments still lay on the floors. And today, looking over the scene of so much early activity, the only reminder is in the earth which still ploughs up dark from the ashes of iron-smelting, and the fragments of furnace waste still littering the fields. There is no more peacefully rural scene than the well-farmed fields around Bromsash, and the excavations were only started because the people kept picking up what they called fairy coins.

While the nettles grew over Lydney, Woolaston and Ariconium the ferns took root in the iron mines, and the people of the Denes again devoted themselves to an invader from overseas. The Saxons had planted themselves firmly in southern and eastern Britain by the second half of the sixth century, but apparently they had not crossed the Severn. This was a doubtful blessing, however, for it left the country under the rule of Vontiporius, king of South Wales, though ruler is not a good title for one who is described as "spotted like the leopard with crimes and evil living". Even when allowance is made for the words coming from Gildas, a West-country contemporary with strong prejudices, it can hardly hold out hope of much uplifting influence.

During this period there are several references to campaigns against the Welsh, but this generally means the "Western Welsh", who were gradually persuaded that their future home lay in Cornwall. There is no certain mention of Saxon penetration across the Severn until the end of the sixth century. Then was established the sub-kingdom of the Hecanas, covering Hereford

and Shropshire, as well as our peninsula, and ruled over by Mere-
wald as vassal to the king of Mercia. Christianity was a growing
force, with the Forest coming within the See of Hereford. But the
clouds were still heavy, with more than half a century to go before
Offa appeared, carrying the first real ray of English daylight to
this region. He put an end to the "no-man's-land" status of this
hilly tract of woodland when he set his boundary dyke along the
rampart of the Wye. Foresters became Englishmen, however
contradictory the name may be, for they were not Angles, and
only formed a part of the human patchwork taking name from
these people. All who lived beyond the Wye were Welsh. This
happened after the middle of the eighth century.

With warfare no longer ebbing and flowing between Severn
and Wye, the country began the development that was to make it
the favourite playground of our kings. The Romans had no great
love of hunting and there is nothing to indicate that they reserved
any of the Game of the Forest for their Very Important Persons.
The Saxons and Danes, on the other hand, had all the Teuton's
love of the chase, and it was during the Danish rule that the Denes
drew covetous glances from High Places. Alfred, first King of All
England, had little time for sport even if he had the inclination,
for we know that his off-duty hours were largely devoted to
books. His daughter Æthelflæd, after her husband's death, ruled
Mercia with a firm hand for eight years until she was buried with
him at Gloucester. It was Canute who played the first prominent
part in framing the Laws of the Forest, and he is credited with the
establishment of the Court of Verderers, which survives to the
present day in the Speech House. A. O. Cooke (*Forest of Dean*,
1912) puts forward the case for a much earlier origin, based on the
following facts.

The Court meets at midday on every fortieth day; until recent
times the oath was taken by touching the Testament with a holly
stick instead of taking it in the hand. Forty days is an unusual and
quite arbitrary period, but it is arrived at by dividing the Druid
year of 360 days by the sacred Druid number 9. The Druid day
started at noon, and the holly, which grows now so abundantly
round the Speech House, had great significance for them. That is

the story, though it contains one inaccuracy. The ceremony of the holly stick is said to belong to the Court of Mine Laws, not the Verderers' Court. But this need not affect the case seriously, as the two may well have a common origin. This is an attractive explanation, and not unreasonable when we study the growth of many customs and institutions. Without voting either way I repeat that the Court does go back to the days of Danish Knut.

Thus the coming of William of Normandy, with his weakness for deer, brought no revolutionary changes, though it un-doubtedly led to a severe tightening up of the regulations intended for the preservation of the royal sport. But it is worth noting that during the earlier years of the Norman regime there is more than one reference to the forest laws of Edward the Confessor, and there seems no doubt that the newcomers used the "good old days" as a piece of bluff for putting across measures of their own devising. Something like this has been done in recent times in more than one country, and it must have been much easier to get away with such a deceit when laws and regulations may have been recorded only in one manuscript. Only the details change, while the basic ideas go on.

Up to the time of the Norman Conquest the trees had been something of an encumbrance rather than an asset, except when they were wanted by the Britons for defensive cover, or by the Romans to feed their forges. Cæsar tells us that "a town among the Britons is nothing more than a thick wood, fortified with ditch and rampart, to serve as a place of retreat against incursions of their enemies". We must admire the impersonal attitude he takes, and accept the description as particularly applicable here, though Cæsar never came so far west. But under the Norman lords trees were needed as cover for game, and renewed demands for building and iron-working had to be met. So the area included in the Forest was increased by William of Normandy and his successors, the royal wishes being enforced with a vigour that was sometimes brutal in the extreme. It is at the present time that we are reaping the benefits of this harshness, for while many great forests—including Wyre and Arden—have disappeared entirely, and others like Epping have only just escaped the same fate, the Forest of Dean now has a greater area of woodland than any of the Royal Forests except the New Forest.

The growth or shrinkage of the Forest area may be taken as a very fair guide to the confidence with which the Norman kings wore their crowns. The King, with an eye to sport and financial returns, was always looking for an opportunity to increase his property; the people lost no chance to lodge a protest or effect an encroachment. Under the two Williams the area was considerably increased, for they were men who had no doubts. Henry I and Stephen both showed caution in the face of early opposition, but in each reign the attitude changed in later years and the area was extended.

It was between these two reigns that the Forest passed into private ownership, in name at least. Maud (otherwise Matilda), daughter of Henry, struggled with Stephen for the throne. In this she was helped by Milo, Earl of Hereford, who was given the whole area complete with timber and game as his reward. When Stephen gained the upper hand he could scarcely be expected to approve an arrangement made by his opponent, so the Royal Hunting Grounds in Gloucestershire returned to the Crown.

On Christmas Eve, 1143, Milo was killed by an arrow glancing off a tree in the Flaxley valley. That is the story, though some may compare this incident with the fate that befell William Rufus and feel some misgiving that an accident may have been arranged. The present century has no monopoly of such stories, and the frequency with which arrows glanced off trees is only rivalled by the number of ladies who made excursions in the manner and costume of Lady Godiva. Such a ride is said to have secured certain rights to the people of St Briavels. For these and other reasons life must have been far from dull in those days.

But this close association of Milo with the Forest, though brief, had a lasting effect. It was as a memorial to Milo that his son Roger built Flaxley Abbey in the middle of the twelfth century. This was a Cistercian House, and it probably exercised a great local influence, both spiritual and temporal. Living in the centre of a large tract of church-less country would have given great scope for religious activity, while they were the agricultural pioneers of the Middle Ages. In this capacity their granges at Boseley, Littledean and Dymock probably stood as strongholds against the constant threat of afforestation.

The more humane attitude of Henry II may have been inspired by the view across the Severn to Frampton, birthplace of Jane Clifford—better known as Fair Rosamund. Henry had a liking for Newnham and an appreciative eye for the Forest. Though less harsh, his methods were no less successful, for he managed to extend the boundaries.

Richard the Lionheart was too fully occupied with Crusades to pay much attention to beasts of chase, but in his pursuit of bigger game he looked to the Denes for help in equipping the expeditions. It is on record that Gloucester made a contribution of 50,000 horseshoes and iron to the value of £100, the greater part of which will have come from over-Severn.

King John hunted here regularly, thus giving the opportunity for more than one house to claim distinction as "the place where King John stayed". This honour was mainly shared by Flaxley Abbey and St Briavels Castle, though others probably provided something in the nature of a stirrup-cup. Too often do we demand written evidence in such matters, forgetting that someone addicted to good living once remarked, "Where I eats I sleeps". John certainly paid more attention to sport than to the more toilsome of his duties, but the boundaries of the royal preserve were uncertain during his reign, while those who came after may have found his blackened name a useful screen for their own shortcomings.

These frequent visits of our kings to a spot which is now somewhat remote are more easily understood when we remember that up to the fourteenth century Gloucester was one of the chief cities of Britain, with the King making a practice of wearing his crown here at a Christmas Court. A fair idea of the activity in these parts during Norman times may be gathered from the building programme: Chepstow, St Briavels, Goodrich, Wilton, all heavily fortified castles on our boundary; Raglan, Monmouth, Skenfrith, Grosmont and White Castle not far away. In church building we have the grand examples at Tintern, Flaxley and Gloucester, sup-

ported by a great number of smaller works. This is a task that would tax the resources of the present day for sheer bulk, quite neglecting the skilled craftsmanship involved.

Through all these changing conditions on the Throne and on the Forest boundary one trend was developing steadily—the importance of the Forest as a centre of the iron industry. With good supplies of high-quality ore and of timber for making charcoal, this region became the chief source of supply. Records of the thirteenth and fourteenth centuries show that large orders were executed for military and civil purposes. As many as sixty forges were in operation, all paying rent to the Crown, as well as a considerable amount of black-market trade. Even the monks of Flaxley could not resist the temptation to exceed their grant of timber, so that Henry III was obliged to restrict them to a given area of woodland in place of the privileges they had been overstepping. This transaction is recorded in the name Abbotswood, close to Cinderford.

The reign of Edward I, covering the turn of the thirteenth to fourteenth centuries, was not marked by any outstanding events in the Dean Forest, but it is of particular interest as the time at which the rights and customs of the Foresters were definitely established. These were set out in the Book of Dennis, in which is found the first reference to the Forest of Dean by that name, together with the qualifications of a Free Miner and the conditions under which they might dig for iron or coal. It is likely that the Book of Dennis was the immediate outcome of the part played by miners from this part in the Scottish wars, especially at the siege of Berwick. This is colourfully told in the words of Kitty Drew:

> But I am told that many ages back,
> A foreign army did our land invade,
> And blood and carnage then were all the trade;
> They pitched their tents, and then without delay,
> They waited anxious for the bloody fray;
> But our bold miners underneath did get,
> And many a ton of powder there did set;

5\*

*The Unpleasance*

So up they blew the unsuspecting foe,
Their shattered limbs came rattling down below.
Our land thus cleared, our liberty thus saved,
Our noble miners dug the caitiff's grave.
The King with honour did them so regard,
Made them Free Miners as a just reward,
The Forest Charter granted to them was,
And firm and sure were made the Forest Laws.

While this may not be exact in detail, it probably comes very near to summing up the position. Some declare the rights to be the outcome of ancient usage alone; others consider that they arise from specific awards. Most likely the truth lies in a combination of the two, for we are told of certain decisions of the courts which strengthened the miners' position at a time when they had brought distinction on themselves by their skill as sappers. What is more likely than that they made use of a favourable opportunity for legalising a situation that had grown up on vague custom?

However that may be, from the beginning of the fourteenth century a man born and living in the hundred of St Briavels could claim a gale, or digging site. The award of these gales was regulated by the Gaveller, acting on behalf of the Crown, and he was responsible for collecting the royal dues and assessing any compensation. All matters in dispute were settled by the Court of Mine Law, made up of the Constable of the Forest (then the tenant of St Briavels Castle), the Gaveller and a jury of twelve or twenty-four. It was not until much later that additional requirements came to light, by which a man must be the son of a Free Miner and have worked for a year and a day in the pits before he himself qualified as a Free Miner. The Court of Mine Law continued until 1754.

The fourteenth century with its strife and pestilence saw a shrinking of the Forest boundaries until they came back approximately to the limits that existed at the time of the Domesday Book. This was a rough half-circle centred on Staunton, running from the Wye near Tintern and excluding Bledisloe, Newnham and Longhope. The royal sport had passed its zenith, and we may form an opinion of conditions in the early part of the century from the fact that a Cistercian outpost at Stowe, near St Briavels, was withdrawn owing to the extreme wildness of the country.

One incident of the time deserves mention, if only for the way in which it bridges the gulf of six hundred years. Guy de Brian, as Constable of the Castle, held the whole Forest from Edward III at an annual rental of £160. He was so dissatisfied with his bargain that in January 1341 he made representations to the King that he should be put in the way of something better, or have his rent adjusted. We note with satisfaction that in the following May a commission was set up to enquire into the matter. At this point the pace slows considerably, and it was not until 1350 that Guy received a reply to the effect that £40 a year would be allowed from past rents, with a future rental of £80. Comment is superfluous.

One colourful figure belongs here, and though he may have done no more than travel along the eastern boundary he is entitled to mention. Dick Whittington, childhood hero of pantomime, lived at Pauntley as a boy, so it may well have been by the road through Highleadon that he travelled to London with his inseparable companion. A stone tablet in Gloucester Museum shows a boy carrying a cat. This was found on the alleged site of the family's town house in Westgate Street. Richard did much in the way of rebuilding Newgate Prison, and when some of his work was pulled down, in 1880, a mummified cat was found in the wall. And only last year, at a ceremony to open the search for Dick's tomb, a black cat joined in the procession. So there does seem to be a strong link.

The Reformation fell heavily on Flaxley, as it did throughout the whole country, so that it had less effect here than in many parts. We may, however, wonder at the purpose of an Act of 26 Henry VIII (1534) which said that "Whosoever dwelling in Wales, or the Marches thereof, shall assault, beat, or hurt any person of the county of Gloucester, Salop, or Hereford, and shall be indicted and convicted thereof shall be one year imprisoned." But what caused Tudor to bite Welshman I do not know.

Shipbuilding was now a thriving industry along Severn-side, and it was concern for the raw material for this purpose that produced another statute from the same King ordering "replantation of forest trees to cure the spoils and devastations that have been made in the woods". But it was the threat of the Spanish Armada that caused something near to panic. Camden, Fuller and Evelyn all tell us of enemy plans to burn down the woodlands in order to stop the building of ships. This might be dismissed as wild rumour, but the whole idea of destroying large areas of English hardwood by fire gives the impression of coming from a country with a much drier climate.

The story goes that Raleigh and Drake both visited our shipyards in the course of their preparations against the invading Spaniards. Drake is said to have stayed at the house under the red cliff at Gatcombe, while the initials carved over the fireplace at Purton Manor, half a mile away, are said to be those of Dorothy Throckmorton—who became Raleigh's wife. Again there is no written evidence, but their lives are not so closely recorded as to rule out the possibility of visits to this scene of timber-growing and shipbuilding, which was so near to the home of Sir William Winter, Vice-Admiral of the Fleet. So I shall still picture Drake looking out from the little house in a situation that must have been a strong reminder of any one of a hundred quiet spots on the shores of his native Devon, and gazing down the channel that was then unmarred by any iron bridge. And when the Armada was at last sighted off the south-west coast no forest fires threatened the land, though there were alarms enough to equal any of the adventures of the Home Guard in 1940. Instead of a forest fire the beacon fire of May Hill passed on the news to other beacons around.

But the furnaces of industry were burning their way into our timber supplies. Until quite recently there was a painted sign outside the Glasshouse Inn, under the eastern slope of May Hill. It showed a "beehive" glass-maker's furnace, thus making quite clear that the name does not refer to a conservatory or a house in which tumblers are kept. The present Glasshouse (deeply concerned with tumblers) is only a reminder of an industry that flourished here until the use of wood for such furnaces was banned. The only written record, to my knowledge, is in the Newent Church Register, three entries in which are believed to refer to this place. They tell us of two baptisms in 1599, and an unspecified event in 1601 concerning Margaret, daughter of Anthony Voydyn, glassfounder. Abraham Tyzack—one of the baptised—is described as the "sonne of a frenchman". This, and the name Voydyn, suggests that here was an injection of foreign craftsmanship. For how long this glasshouse continued to work is not known. The site can be identified by glass fragments and a patch of cinders, but the buildings have completely disappeared. It is generally supposed that the trade was transferred to the riverside at Newnham, where the first coal-burning furnace was established in the time of Charles I. This was owned by Edward Mansel, but the land on which it stood has been washed away by the river, leaving only a pane of glass in the Victoria Hotel as an alleged reminder.

The House of Stuart regarded Dean Forest as a source of income rather than a place of recreation. No doubt the old folks of that day shook their grey heads at the thought of a monarch who had so little taste for the more manly sports, but it is equally certain that Stuart kings did a lot of anxious head-shaking over their urgent financial problems. There was now no sign of the firmness or the discretion of the Normans. James I leased the whole area to the Earl of Pembroke at an annual rental of £831 18s. 4d., for the Castle, land, mines and quarries. The timber was reserved. But public opinion—always sensitive on questions of common rights —was too strong for the noble Earl and his fences. The arrangement which had been made for a lease of forty years soon faded out.

At Gloucester Charles I strove to extend the Forest boundaries in 1634, citing the perambulation of 1282 and other documents. After much legal argument (for which wrangling might be a better word) the jury gave a verdict permitting the extension. The Court of Eyre, last of the Supreme Forest Courts to be held, then proceeded to collect £114,896 16s. 8d. in fines. These were mostly for timber-stealing, and the details raise a strong suspicion that the court was more interested in collecting money than in administering justice. William Kingston was charged £200 for having felled 200 acres of timber, while Henry Bish paid £100 for felling eight oaks and barking four others as they stood.

Tree-stealing (or poaching) had always been carried on, for as early as 1282 at St Briavels we find that "Adam the reeve induced John the clerk of Dean to create a diversion by sounding his horn while Adam sealed a certain oak". In the revised version this means that the parson got the people looking the other way while the mayor knocked-off an oak tree.

The punishment for tree-poaching often included confiscation of the wagon and team with which the tree had been hauled away, and there is a record of a man losing a team of four oxen in this way. This of itself would be a heavy penalty, so we may assume that a quantity of timber was taken in order to make the job worth while. It is interesting to note that there has recently been a suggestion that the same procedure should be adopted with the cars used by those who poach salmon.

Charles I met defeat at the hands of the Foresters as a foretaste of the verdict that was to come from the whole country. In 1640 he agreed to reduce the area from that fixed six years earlier, and in the following year an Act was passed confirming the boundaries as set out in 1300. Then, under financial pressure, he leased the whole Forest—land, mines, quarries and trees—to Sir John Winter. As far as we can judge, this was the height of folly, being a thoroughly bad deal for everyone except Sir John. The figures in this case bear no relation to the previous letting, since all the timber was now included, but the agreed terms were £106,000 for what may be called the goodwill, and a rental of £1,950 12s. 6d. I have always wanted to know how such sums were calculated to a sixpence, though I do remember an occasion when two dealers agreed on the price of a horse to a halfpenny—after spending six hours and more than one bottle of whisky in the process.

Rudge tells us that at the time of the sale there were 105,557 trees, containing 61,928 tons of timber and 153,209 cords of wood. Interestingly precise figures, again, and in view of the opposition that Sir John met with from the Foresters it is quite certain that he could not tell with such certainty just how many cords of wood he owned.

Then followed the Dark Ages for these woodlands. It is said that Winter had 500 axemen at work at one time, so that the effect must have been very like a gigantic mowing machine, until Cromwell brought it to a halt in 1649. On Winter's behalf it can be said that he supported the King with great obstinacy and no little courage in the Civil War, putting all he had into the struggle—including his home at Lydney—until he was driven out of the country. Around Huntley, Westbury, Littledean and Newnham he encouraged resistance to the Parliamentary Colonel Massey. Then, when the tide of events swept down to Lydney, he burnt Whitecross House rather than let it fall to his enemies, but not until Mary Winter had very bravely defied the Colonel in Sir John's absence. But it was another tide that brought resistance in these parts to an end, and as the incident was an early example of naval guns supporting land forces it is worth recalling.

Quite formidable numbers of Royalist foot and horse troops had encamped on Beachley Peninsula under the command of Prince Rupert, thinking to have the protection of the two rivers at their back and the ridge of Offa's Dyke as a ready-made forti-fication. Here they waited the attack of the Roundheads. But Massey's star was well placed at that time; he could do nothing wrong. Bringing gunboats into the mouth of the Wye, he waited for the tide to lift them to a level at which they could fire into the camp. Then he attacked over the Dyke. It was from here that Winter escaped, to give his name to the precipice over which he and his horse are said to have leapt. We will look at this again from below later on. Winter joined the King at Oxford, to be sent with messages to the Queen of France. On return he was captured and confined in the Tower of London for three years, his estates being given to Colonel Massey.

During the time that Sir John was debarred from activity in the Forest he was engaged in experiments which were closely associated with his native land. From an entry in Evelyn's diary for 11th July, 1656, we see Winter, the pioneer:

"Came home by Greenwich Ferry where I saw Sir John Winter's new project for charring sea coale, to burn out the sulphur and render it sweete. He did it by burning the coals in such earthen pots as the glass-men mealt their mettall, so firing them without consuming them, using a barr of yron in each crucible or pot, which barr has a hook at one end, so that the coales being mealted in a furnace with other crude sea coales under them, may be drawn out of the pots sticking to the yron, whence they are beaten off in great half-exhausted cinders, which being rekindled make a cleare pleasant chamber fire, deprived of their sulphur and arsenic malignity. What success it may have, time will discover."

Now we know that it was a long time before the idea was again brought to light and induced to bear fruit.

In following the fortunes of Sir John Winter I have skipped many events of these fast-moving times. But one incident must not be omitted, for those who travel by road from Gloucester to Newent will see the Memorial now standing in a field across the way from Barbers Bridge Station. This reminds us of the death of 500 Welshmen in March 1643. Here again the Royalists appear to have been hopelessly out-generalled. Lord Herbert had brought an army of 2,000 Welsh troops with the idea of closing the western roads to Gloucester, while his colleagues closed in from the east. Owing to lack of co-operation, however, Waller was allowed to cross the Severn at Framilode and attack Herbert's men from the rear while Massey held their attention on the Gloucester side. I should like to tell the story as it is still told in the neighbourhood: a story of red-stained soil and the Leadon flowing scarlet; of the blood-red glow on the dogwood, and the cranesbill that only grows in these parts where a Royalist fell. But such vivid pictures grow, they are not made. And they only come from those whose ancestors saw the event; those who have their roots in the blood-soaked soil. My ancestors were then east of Severn.

The Commonwealth did not bring peace or contentment to Dean Forest. Squatters found the new authority even less tolerant than the old, for we are told that Cromwell "expelled 400 cabins of beggarly people". Many of these would have felt a genuine sense of grievance, believing as they did that anyone who could build a hut on open ground in time to have the smoke going up the chimney in one day was entitled to the land on which it stood. It is not hard to find cabins today that were obviously set up under the same conditions. Opposition to all attempts to enclose beyond the prescribed 11,000 acres was bitter and persistent, breaking out in open rioting in 1659. Once again the Neolithic men and the Silures were in action against an invader.

With the return of Charles II Winter came back to his homeland and to his old business methods. The entry made by Samuel Pepys in his diary for 20th June, 1662, reveals more than may have been intended:

"Up by four or five o'clock, and to the office, and there drew up the agreement between the King and Sir John Winter about the Forest of Dean; and, having done it, he come himself, (I did not know him to be the Queen's Secretary before, but observe him to be a man of fine parts); and we read it, and both liked it well. That done, I turned to the Forest of Dean in Speede's mapps, and there he showed me how it lies; and the Lea-Bayly, with the great charge of carrying it to Lydny, and many other things worth my knowing; and I do perceive that I am very short in my business by not knowing many times the geographical part of my business."

It is nice to think that Winter, the man of fine parts, was so well pleased with the agreement. Turning over one page of the diary we find:

"Into Thames Street, and there enquired among the ships the price of tarre and oyle, and do find great content in it, and hope to save the King money by this practice."

But more than he was able to save on tarre and oyle was, apparently, lost in Dean Forest, for later in the same year John Evelyn mentions the subject in his diary:

"The Council Of the Royal Society met to amend the Statutes, and dined together; afterwards meeting at Gressham College, where was a discourse suggested by me concerning planting His Majesty's Forest of Deane with oake, now so much exhausted of the choicest ship-timber in the world."

There was cause for concern, for the number of trees remaining in 1667 is given by Rudge as 200. Even if this refers to mature trees only it gives a dismal picture, but one that we cannot doubt on the evidence of other observers. It also seems as if little or nothing came of the discourse of the Royal Society, for in 1789 William Marshall (a reliable observer) describes the Forest as a mere waste, which calls loudly for improvement. To show that he had no prejudice against the district, Marshall spoke most highly of the cider and perry industry, of which he regarded May Hill to be the centre.

Sir John was not the only plunderer of trees, for Pepys tells us of receiving accounts of the damage caused by storms in February 1662. Again in 1703 there was a storm that must have done great damage here. Defoe gives a most graphic description. The gale kept people from their beds for a week, and swept away the Eddystone Lighthouse with its builder. In the Severnside meadows the wind-driven tide is said to have drowned 15,000 sheep.

While Winter was still busy felling trees a commission was at work on the problems arising out of his work. The result of their report was "The Increase and Preservation of Timber in the Forest of Dean Act, of 1668", but the matter was still not treated as urgent, for reconstruction did not start until 1675, when the Forest was divided into six rides, each with a lodge for the Forester-in-charge. These lodges were given the names of famous men—King's (or Speech House), Danby, York, Latimer, Worcester and Herbert. Speech House, as it was then planned, was completed about 1680.

It was decreed that of the Forest area 11,000 acres should be enclosed woodland at any time, this being fixed as to amount but not locality. But it was not until about 1815 that the plan was completed. Plans for increased production of timber were still not popular with those who "enjoyed" common rights. It mattered not a scrap to these people whether the enclosures were carried out by Crown, Commonwealth or private tenant; curtailment of their customary rights, even when such was legal, always brought a reaction. Pulling down fences was a daily (or perhaps nightly) event, but in 1688 resentment reached such a level as to find relief

·in rioting, which destroyed York and Worcester Lodges and damaged Speech House.

During the later part of the eighteenth century coal-mining made rapid strides—elsewhere. Steam engines were replacing horse- and hand-driven winding gear in the bigger pits in other parts of the country, but they came very slowly here. This delay was largely due to the peculiar conditions prevailing in the Forest coalfield, though limited outlook and lack of co-operation played their part. The state of the roads proved a big handicap to any trade at this time. A notice appeared in the *Gloucester Journal* in 1740 announcing that the corn market at Newnham would be reopened after having been out of use for some years owing to the badness of the roads. It promised that they were now in good repair, and that there was all conveniency for water carriage.

The new prison built in Gloucester (1786) used a lot of timber from the Crown woodlands. The requisition was justified on the grounds that the building was being erected on the site of a royal castle, and that a large proportion of the clientele would come from the Royal Forest.

William Cobbett explored this neighbourhood in November 1821. He stayed at Bollitree Castle, and was full of praise for the farming round about, especially that of his host, William Palmer. Then the mood changes.

"Rode to the Forest of Dean, up a very steep hill. Pretty works are, I find, carried on here, as is the case in all the other public forests. Are these things always to be carried on in this way? Here is a domain of 30,000 acres of the finest timber land in the world, and with coal mines endless. Is it worth nothing? And cannot each acre yield ten trees a year? Is not the whole estate worth three or four hundred thousand pounds a year?"

Cobbett's estimate of the soil and the coal mines may not bear research, but it does seem that the Forest was not being conducted on sound economic lines. It had been planned at that time, however, though without the evergreens of today. So we may regard the "modern" Forest as dating from the beginning of the nineteenth century, with just a few old-timers round the Speech House.

The other Royal Forests appear to have been in even worse plight, for Rudge tells us (1803) that out of a total requirement of 25,000 loads of timber a year for the Navy they only supplied 2,000 loads, half of which came from Dean.

Other changes were going on apart from official plans. Following Cromwell's clear-up of the cabins we are told that in 1712 there were still no cottages in the Forest. In 1803 there were reported to be 696 cottages with 3,325 inhabitants. At the same time the yearly quota of four bucks and four does for the royal household was frequently not met owing to scarcity.

By the middle of the nineteenth century the control of the Crown property had been placed in the hands of the Department of Woods and Forests; it had in fact been nationalised, with Government officials taking over the duties of the Woodwards. As far back as 1688 the powers of the Court of Verderers had been restricted to matters relating to game, but with the removal of the deer in 1850 the office of Verderer became a distinction rather than a responsibility.

There is delightful evidence that the breed has not really changed much either way. This comes to us from Mr Machen's reminiscences of the earlier Commissioners of Woods and refers to a Mr Arbuthnot of rather more than a hundred years ago, comparing him with his predecessors:

"He was a very different sort of man; very polished and a courtier, and fancying he did a great deal. He used to put down the extent of enclosures he had viewed, and enquired with great earnestness the size of each, so that if we rode into one of 500 acres and out again directly, that stood for 500 acres in his report of the day's work."

It was to visit his old friend Arbuthnot that the great Duke of Wellington rode from Cheltenham to Whitemead before breakfast. But he had his reward, for he was taken to Tintern—still on horseback—over roads described as execrable, and allowed the privilege of holding an umbrella over Mrs Arbuthnot.

The Duke's trip is not the only link with Cheltenham, however, for the Kemble family have been claimed as living and dying at Lydbrook. There is a memorial to John Kemble in the little church of Welsh Bicknor, with the date 1712, and there is reason for believing him to be the grandfather of the illustrious Sarah Siddons, who made her first great hit at the Cheltenham Opera House. Even as I write this chapter there comes the news that "Sarah Siddons' House" has been purchased as a place of historic interest.

Another feature of the nineteenth century was the rapid development of coal-mining. As we have already said, coal had been used for glass furnaces at Newnham by the middle of the seventeenth century, but growth had been slow for two hundred years. Then iron-mining gradually moved into second place, with coal taking the lead. These two movements were related to the extent that the lift-up given to the iron-smelting and tinplate-making by the use of coal had hastened the working out of the richer pockets of ore. The story is still told in the lives of some of our older men who, starting work as iron-miners, transferred later to the collieries. Output figures speak for themselves: 300,000 tons of coal in 1851, 1,150,000 tons in 1898, followed by a steady decline in the early years of the present century as the more accessible seams became worked out.

Charcoal-burning naturally came upon very lean days. From A. O. Cooke we learn that the trade had nearly died out in 1912. He gives a detailed account of the life and working methods of these burners, but tells us that it was only being carried on by one team who came from outside the Forest. This was a tremendous change, for we have only to scrape away the leaves in many parts of these woodlands to find the earth blackened with ash from the burning heaps of wood, showing how widely the trade was carried on in former days. But while charcoal is no longer wanted in the quantities that the smelters had used, it is still needed for some purposes, and a considerable quantity is now being made from cordwood as a by-product of wood distillation.

Some comment on recent trends in other industries will be more appropriate in the chapter dealing with future development.

It was in a way unfortunate for this region when more advanced means of transport came to replace the packhorse train. While these strings of laden horses and donkeys were in general use the Forest was not unduly handicapped by its steep valleys and deplorable roads, and for those who have any difficulty in imagining a typical highway of a hundred and fifty years ago there are plenty of stony rough tracks and green lanes still in existence here to give some idea. These are mostly in much better order now, as they do not carry the same amount of traffic, but still in winter they are almost impassable. Water transport was the only alternative, and in this the Severn played an active part, even if shipping was at times interspersed with outburst of banditry "in manner of warre". The Wye was much more difficult to navigate, but it carried quite a lot of trade to Redbrook, Monmouth, Ross and Hereford. It may be due to the absence of barges carrying flour that we have not the same stirring records of banditry as are associated with the Severn.

Canals, the country's first real answer to the transport problem, did little for this neighbourhood. The early "cut" linking Ledbury with Gloucester, by way of Newent, appears to have been one of the wilder outbreaks of the canal fever that preceded the railways, and from the fact that it did not even wait to be put out of business, but offered its empty course for the accommodation of the railway, it obviously never met with much success. The track still lies through country which is almost one hundred per cent agricultural, in which the only threat of industrialism came from a slight attempt at coal-mining near Newent. But in the full flood of canal-building enthusiasm the economic possibilities were not always looked into very closely. This is evident in the short length of canal constructed from the Severn at Wainlodes towards Cheltenham. As this was primarily for the carriage of coal it was of some interest to a coal-mining district, but its life was short and without prosperity.

The importance that was attached to canals is shown by the protest that came from Newcastle-upon-Tyne against the proposal to link the Thames with the Severn. This protest drew attention to the importance of coastal shipping as a kindergarten for the Navy, but it is significant that it came from the town most concerned with the shipping of coal to London. That the canal did open up the way for competition from Dean Forest and South Wales is made clear by the exorbitant prices charged for coal in London when the severe frost of 1814 stopped canal traffic.

Coal was not the only product of this neighbourhood expected to benefit from the new era of canal transport. Writing in 1788, Marshall says:

"But the late extension of canals and other inland navigations, and most especially one which is now extending between the Severn and the Thames, together with the present facility of land carriage have already extended the market for fruit liquor; and there may be, henceforward, some encouragement for the manufacture of sale liquor; the right management of which is a mystery which few men are versed in, and which I have found somewhat difficult to fathom."

There is reason to believe that the mysteries connected with sale liquor were fairly well understood at that time in Smugglers' Row, Minsterworth.

The opening of the Sharpness–Gloucester canal in 1827 was the death-knell of the little shipyards and ports on the Forest shore of the Severn. Regular traffic on the river had helped to keep some sort of shipping channel, but with most of the trade taking the canal route the river soon became navigable only for shallow boats and at favourable tides. The quays at Broadoak, Newnham, Bullo and Gatcombe fell into disuse, and the fishermen and ferrymen became the only river users.

Railways came soon after canals—too soon for those who had invested much of their money in waterways. The main line from Gloucester to Chepstow was opened in 1851, and this was followed by the conversion of some mineral tramways into the present rail system—or into a system which has shrunk to its present form, for rail facilities have been greatly reduced since the early part of this century. Anyone who tries to follow the routes given by Cooke in his *Forest of Dean* will very soon notice the changes, for the writer made much use of the line from Lydney to Speech House Road and Coleford in 1911. No regular passenger services run on this route now, though there has recently been a resumption of some excursions. Branches that once linked Awre Junction with Blakeney and Lydbrook with Cinderford are now entirely disused. This trend is unfortunate, as the railways pass through some of the loveliest scenery, and they were a great help in country that can only be fully appreciated on foot.

One of the most striking results of the railway era in this locality is negative. It was originally proposed to take the Gloucester–Hereford line through Mitcheldean on its way between Longhope and Ross. At the beginning of last century Mitcheldean deserved the name Dean Magna, for it was the most thriving town in the Forest, with mining, quarrying, cement, brick and pin making; and it was a busy centre and market place for a wide area around. The buildings still show it to have been well provided with shops, and many people can still remember the busy, jostling scenes on Friday evenings and Saturdays. The one outstanding need was transport, but the chief landowners did not want the railway, so it took the present tunnelled route and left Mitcheldean in an industrial backwater. For some time the cement-works alone carried fifty tons of goods daily along the two miles of lane to the nearest station.

It may not be too much to say that from this decision arose one of our greatest problems, the abnormal and unplanned growth of Cinderford. Had Mitcheldean been permitted to take its place just at that unfortunate time it would probably have formed the centre and background of Forest industry, and it is centre and background that are lacking in the new town. However far-fetched this idea may sound it is not new, nor do I hold it alone.

In order to increase timber production the Crown purchased the Highmeadow estate in the early part of last century. This added more than 3,000 acres to the land under the control of the Commissioners, and now forming the National Forest Park, though it does not come within the boundaries of the Royal Forest. This property lies roughly north of the road through Staunton to Monmouth, overlapping that road at Knockalls Enclosure and in the small enclosure containing the Buck Stone. Northwards it reaches Symonds Yat Rock and the Coldwell Rocks, then takes in the Seven Sisters and King Arthur's Cave. These few names

*Lydney Harbour is a quiet backwater*

will give some idea of the wealth of interest this purchase brought to the National Park. By a most happy choice the official Camping Ground at Christchurch is sited in this loveliest Forest country, giving every opportunity to all who wish for more than a passing glance.

The story of Highmeadow is unusual. The estate was the home of the Hall family from the middle of the fourteenth century. During the Civil War it was fortified in the Royalist interest, and was the scene of some small incidents. When Henry Benedict Hall died in 1668 the property passed to his daughter, who, by her marriage, added it to the estate of Sir Thomas Gage, later created Viscount Gage. In 1779 Rudder gives this description of the mansion:

"The house is large and handsome, built in the form of the letter H, and from its elevated situation commands a bird's eye view of the village (Newland) and of the beautiful lawns and groves on the other side of the valley at a very agreeable distance. Were his lordship possessed of the whole landscape he could not wish to misplace a single object."

But later members of the family seldom lived here, and when it was purchased by the Crown fifty years later it is described as greatly dilapidated and past reparation. It was pulled down and the material disposed of, so that the site which did not require the misplacing of a single object now knows it no more. But we shall meet the Highmeadow woods in another chapter.

The iron industry of the Forest reached its zenith under the rule of Henry Crawshay, "Iron King of the Forest of Dean", who died at Oaklands Park, Newnham, in 1879. He came from South Wales with his father in 1835 and they very soon became associated with Cinderford Ironworks. Some idea of the size of their business may be judged from the figure of 400,000 tons which is said to have been the yield of high-grade hæmatite ore from one mine in the years 1860–70. They also owned Parkend Iron Company and Lightmoor Colliery. Henry Crawshay does not appear to have been typical of the nineteenth-century business magnates, for we read of great sorrow throughout the Forest at

6

*Staunton, the quiet round*

his death. He certainly gave liberally to the neighbourhood from the money that he caused to be dug from the ground. The restoration of the church at Awre was largely paid for by him, and he gave £1,000 towards the rebuilding of Newnham Church.

Gloucestershire is rightly proud of having the first agricultural college to be established in England, but much less is heard of the first forestry school. This was started in a room in the Gaveller's house at Coleford in 1904 for the purpose of giving some training to the foresters working on the Crown property. By slow degrees the scheme developed and moved to a shed now standing on the Recreation Ground at Parkend. Near at hand stood an empty factory building, stripped of all fittings and used as a rifle range. Now these ingredients have been combined to form a most thriving training place for students who intend to make forestry their career.

Wars have always made heavy demands on the Forest, from the time when the Silures rallied to the call of Caradoc, through the Middle Ages and the undermining sappers, right up to the names lately added to our village memorials. In material things, however, the demand has changed with the years. While there were wooden walls to be built, here was the first source of supply; if it was horseshoes, or nails, or small cannon, the iron mines of Dean produced a share. Then, when ships grew from steel plates and the iron industry moved away, timber was needed for pit props, building and a hundred more purposes, so that the woodlands were stripped far beyond the routine fellings.

The last war brought yet another need—concealment from enemy aircraft—and in this the Forest played a very big part. For miles the tree-shaded roads were stacked with explosives and other war materials wherever the verges were wide enough, and many new roads were made in the enclosures. No one will grudge this use, though it did bring with it severe restrictions on movement in the area. But there is reason to feel a lot less satisfied with the removal of (or failure to remove) some of these stores. Even now, five years after, a big area round the Spruce Drive is dangerous owing to the presence of mustard gas. Admittedly the containers have perished, so that the removal process is slow and difficult, but we are entitled to wonder if much of the trouble is not due to the delay in tackling the job. This is not just a matter of amenity for picnic parties. I have been told by men working on the site that a number of local people have been seriously injured by picking up wood that is contaminated. There are warning notices, to be sure, but they are unlikely to deter a child from wandering that way, for there are no fences.

It has been said that Foresters are not quick to accept ideas. Without swallowing this whole, it must be admitted that they were slow enough to co-operate on the question of common grazing. The privilege of turning stock on to the royal hunting ground was given centuries ago in recognition of services rendered, yet the association which now watches the interests of the graziers was not formed until 1919. Legally the grazing goes with the freehold of the land to which it was granted, so that the number of people turning out stock is limited to those now holding such lands. In practice there is a lot of 'inheritance' on Forest principles. In these circumstances it is most desirable that the graziers should speak with one voice, and since the formation of their association that has been the voice of Mr Evan Jones, their most diligent secretary since the start.

On behalf of the members Mr Jones has to deal with a wide variety of problems, ranging from claims made by (and also against) motorists involved in collisions with sheep, to attempts that are being made, by various means, to improve the quality of the sheep. But the hardest problem is that of preserving a united front. The cost to each member is small, and the benefits very clear to an outsider, so that it is surprising to find the membership well below full strength.

During the time that deer were preserved in the Forest, sheep, goats and geese were forbidden because they made the grazing unpalatable to the harts and hinds. Cattle were permitted, with pigs in certain cases and at the season of acorns and beech mast (this being known as pannage). With the removal of the deer the ban on sheep ceased to carry weight, and although nothing has been done to remove the restriction sheep are now the only animals which concern the Common Right Holders Association. There is no state of war between the Association and the

75

Commissioners, only a silent watchfulness, with each side sleeping pen-in-hand, waiting for the other to give the opportunity for the discharge of a missile. In the other hand officialdom carries the key of the pound in which sheep are held when found on enclosed land, and (let it only be whispered) some graziers have been known to arm themselves with hacksaws, though such armament is heavily frowned upon by their Association.

The Commissioners are entitled to keep 11,000 acres free from sheep at any one time, but it is their job to maintain reasonably stock-proof fences. Therein lies the main difficulty. When sheep are found in an enclosure there immediately arises the question of responsibility. How did they get there, and were the fences in a fair and fit state? In the meantime the sheep have probably been impounded, and the owners charged a flat rate against damage and feeding while in pound, also fourpence "lock fee", unless it can be established that the fences were not in order. It is easy to imagine that in such circumstances differences of opinion can arise.

While the number of grazing right holders increases, the area available to them is being steadily reduced. They have the run of the open land of the Forest. By subtracting the 11,000 acres of enclosure from the total area of nearly 25,000 acres we are left with 14,000 acres, from which must be taken the needs of building, railways, roads, pitheads and quarries. In the past all these have made heavy demands, and in the future building must take many more acres. All this is at the expense of the open grazing land. There is another factor taking an even bigger toll of the grazing area, and one which could not have been foreseen had the common rights been set out on paper when the area of enclosure was agreed. This is the effect of large-scale conifer plantations. When woodland has grown beyond damage by domestic animals the fences are removed, so that the area no longer forms part of the permitted enclosure. If the woodland thus freed carries well-spaced oaks it may provide quite a useful picking for sheep, but under closely planted conifers nothing will grow. And the effect of the carpet of needles will last for a long time, so that the loss of grazing is cumulative.

To fit all these changing conditions it is necessary for customs to be flexible so that they may adapt themselves to the needs of the day. Just as soon as they become fixed they are on the way to join the collection of interesting relics.

As evidence of the tenacity of our customs I have on my desk a piece of cheese with a background of eight centuries. And the cheese is fresh, for it was distributed only two hours ago at the Whitsun ceremony of the Bread and Cheese held outside St Briavels Church. Through all these ages the village has observed a custom, now half hidden in antiquity, by which the inhabitants enjoy the privilege of gathering wood on the Hudnalls, a steep wooded bank running down to the Wye. The bread and cheese was originally intended for the poor of the parish, and was given out in the church, until last century. According to an account given in *The Gentleman's Magazine* in 1816 the churchwardens went up into the galleries with baskets, "whence their contents are thrown among the congregation, who have a grand scramble for them in the body of the church. This is as great a tumult and uproar as the amusement of a village wake."

So it is not surprising that the ceremony was moved to the churchyard. Now, with the attendance grown to thousands, with special buses, a band and an ice-cream vendor included in the performance, the dole is thrown from a high wall into the crowded roadway. Poverty no longer gets a front seat; in fact, the bigger the hat the bigger the haul.

With all these various rights and privileges defined and watched over, only one group of Forest users seems to have been over-looked—the ramblers and the holiday-tramps, who want only to be allowed to wander amongst the miles of woodland walks without any uneasiness that they may be pulled up for trespass. Their needs were met in 1938, when the Forestry Commissioners created in the Denes the first English National Forest Park. This, in effect, establishes the public right to enjoy the Royal Forest, and nearly all the Crown woodlands, on both sides of the Wye, coming under the control of the Commissioners. The position and extent of the Park are clearly shown on the maps included in the National Forest Park Guide to the Forest of Dean, a Stationery

Office publication which makes a most excellent introduction to this country.

The benefits arising from the National Forest Park status are not as obvious as they might have been, on account of the tolerance that has always been shown to those who do not abuse the freedom of these woods. But a great responsibility has been placed on all who find pleasure in beautiful country by the establishment of this "trial" park. The way in which we use it (and others as they are formed) will decide the extent to which this freedom can be still further widened.

The chief outward sign of the New Order was the establishment of the Forest Camp at Christchurch, near Coleford, an experiment which cannot be too highly praised. The site is admirably chosen, both for itself and for its relationship to the whole area. The facilities provided for those who travel with tent or caravan are splendid, and the scheme only depends for success on the good sense of those who use it.

1948 was a red-letter day for visitors to the Forest, for it also saw the opening of the Youth Hostel in St Briavels Castle. I understand that it was the first attempt to convert dungeons into dormitories, and that the venture has been appreciated by a most gratifying flow of hostellers from many countries. Nothing could be more gratifying than to see a building which has taken a part in the darker chapters of history now turned to such good account. If a building takes on anything of the spirit of those who live in it —and who can say otherwise?—then the ghosts of St Briavels Castle will not lack variety.

History is still being made, but the events of recent times will, in the main, settle more comfortably into a chapter looking ahead. But before we reach that, it will be well to see the subject from other angles.

# CHAPTER IV

# LOOKING AT THE PEOPLE

"Together let us beat this ample field,
Try what the open, what the covert yield;

. . . . . . .

Laugh where we must, be candid where we can;
But vindicate the ways of God to man.
Say first of God above, of man below
What can we reason, but from what we know."

POPE

FIRELIGHT flickered on old polished oak; new tweed, piqued by November mist, rose in protest with the all-pervading smell of toasted teacake; the tinkling of spoon in cup added a musical accompaniment to the chatter of many voices. The others were all in pairs or parties, and though that is no excuse for eavesdropping it does increase the risk of overhearing what is being said at the next table. Anyway, we were in a small town at the gateway of the Forest, so I could not afford to miss an opportunity of watching the people.

They talked of hats, they talked of dresses; they talked of water-waving tresses. They even mentioned Mrs Blank, and how she loved attending races, but here I closed a tactful ear, because they spoke of other places, that never have been known to lie between the Severn and the Wye. But amongst all the idle chatter one piece of simple logic caught my ear. It came in reply to a fretful young woman who seemed to be chiefly intent upon trying to escape from herself. An impossible task, but I don't blame her for trying. "I can see no reason for hurrying," said her companion, "when there's absolutely nothing to do when we get home."

I left then, satisfied that wherever these people lived they did not represent our country of the Deans. For the Forest is typically not the home of people who have absolutely nothing to do.

79

"The inhabitants are some of them a sort of robustic wild people, that may be civilised by discipline and government." So wrote Bigland in 1786. A few years earlier (1779) Rudder was a little more encouraging. He wrote:

"The gentry of the Forest are courteous, hospitable and generous, and the poorer sort of people, by their example, are being brought to an obliging kind of behaviour which used not to distinguish their character; for the country was formerly so wild, and the roads so dark and terrible, that it rendered the inhabitants barbarous and emboldened them to commit many robberies and outrages, particularly on the banks of the Severn."

In 1912 A. O. Cooke tells us that the civilising process is complete; and "nowhere, perhaps, will the stranger meet with more general courtesy, whether from the coal-grimed miner or the Forest servants of the Crown." I can endorse this view, and at the same time pass on a warning from the same authority to those who deck themselves in white to explore the Forest. The stiles are used by miners—who are not normally decked in white.

Quite recently two visitors, exploring the Forest, asked the way, where the path seemed to lose itself in the garden of a cottage. The cottager, a Forester born and bred, insisted on acting as guide and, in spite of well over seventy years, helped lift bicycles over stiles, all the way keeping up a brisk story of a life that included iron-mining, coal-mining, wood-cutting and the bringing up of nine children who would gladden his later years with forty grand-children and a steadily mounting tally of great-grandchildren.

And all that, you will allow, opens up endless possibilities, and even more pitfalls, for one who has come to live amongst these people and hopes to continue so living. One feature offers the utmost encouragement, the deeply rooted dislike of all forms of artificiality and humbug which enters so noticeably into the make-up of the natives. If you bring to these parts assumed airs and graces you may keep them for your own satisfaction—your neighbours will not covet them.

It is impossible, however, even to sketch the subject without first reviewing the main racial features that have gone into Time's melting pot. It would be far easier to describe Irish Stew without mentioning the ingredients than to sum up people without tracing the stock from which they have grown. So, even at the risk of being tedious, we must go back to history and pre-history. After all, you were excused some of this in an earlier chapter.

The schooldays that taught many of us the division of kings into good and bad, clearly marked as black and white, also gave the impression that Invasion and Conquest was a complete and absolute process of Eradication and New Order. Second thoughts give a very different picture, and even in our own time there has been a surfeit of demonstration that a conquered people retain their hold more tenaciously. According to the old simple teaching we are Angles and Saxons, organised by the Normans; but the most casual glance throws a very big doubt on this idea.

First of all it will be well to leave the men of King Arthur's Cave in the misty obscurity that hides them, for a gulf of time and climatic change divides these Palæolithic folk from the next inhabitants, the Neolithic (New Stone Age) people. It is with these later long barrow builders that we must start our pedigree. It is true that no traces of long barrows have been found in this area, which may be explained by normal degeneration that would occur by the time any invasion crossed a barrier as formidable as the lower Severn, but there is no shortage of Neolithic relics. Round barrow boys arrived on their westward trek, but while they overran they did not exterminate, and there is every indication that the two races mingled even to the extent of merging the type of burial mound that characterised them. Again, unfortunately, we have few mounds, but in this connection the latest theory on the transport of material to Stonehenge is particularly significant. If these stones were carried overland it is surprising that we have not more indication of the route by which they crossed the Severn. But the return to the water-carriage idea helps very much to explain the shortage of barrows between Severn and Wye, for if these people could move such loads by raft or boat they could easily have kept in communication with South Wales without having to traverse the difficult Wye-Severn country. In physical qualities and in the choice of their gods these two streams of round-headed and long-headed people ran in one, blending as completely as the Red Brook and the White when they enter the Wye.

So it went on, with Goidels and Brythons sweeping westwards and superimposing the Celtic stamp on the earlier inhabitants. Romans came, colonised and, unlike the others, withdrew to the land from which they had come. But they left behind very many who had settled down to the Romano-British way of life and who, one would imagine, could have carried on the form of government that had been so firmly grafted on to the native stock. It was not to be so, however, and the country slipped back into obscurity and internal strife which showed a marked setback by comparison with the conditions that Cæsar had found here. Roman "culture" had smothered primitive Celtic art without giving anything permanent in return, so that the primitive lapsed into the barbarous.

Then came Saxon and Danish adventurers, the toughest and most venturous elements of North-West Europe, to add their quota, which, while it introduced little or nothing in the way of material progress, did have some effect on rural organisation and physical type.

The Normans worked more to the Roman plan, which is natural in view of the fact that they came from a country that was for much longer under Roman rule and had always shown itself less antagonistic to that regime.

All this seems to give us a mixture composed of Neolithic Man, Goidel, Brython, Roman, Saxon, Dane, Norman; with a flavouring of peoples come here for a variety of reasons, such as the Flemish weavers, Italian money manipulators and a score of others. This is the general, basic recipe, varying in the proportion of its ingredients according to local conditions. The next step is to attempt some assessment of how these conditions worked in the area with which we are now concerned.

From what remains to us of Roman writings it is clear that the inhabitants of the Forest, allied with their neighbours over the Wye, offered terrific resistance to the invader. To hold off the military might of Rome for a quarter of a century was a great effort on the part of the Silures, even when we take into account the help they received from the steep and heavily wooded country they had to defend. It is clear that they mainly employed what is now called "defence in depth", which meant that the Forest must have served as a stalking ground through which the Silures could advance, harass their opponents and retire across the Wye if necessary. This would almost entirely stop any settled life in the area of the Forest and would, at the same time, keep the opposing sides racially pure. Even after the Romans had cleared a way along Severn-side to establish a station at Caerleon, the denes were still a source of trouble to them, but from the Dean Road and the various iron-mining activities we know that they did eventually occupy the area fairly thoroughly. It had often been said that coal-mining did not come until a very much later date, but expert opinion of soot found on tiles at Lydney suggests that the Romans may have used the local coal. However that may be, it is certain that the legions did not stay long enough to change the character of the people to any marked degree, and that there was a warm (but not cordial) reception for the invading Saxons as they advanced up the Severn estuary.

The Saxons were not interested in the iron mines, but they did obtain a foothold in some strength on the lands beside the river, as is shown by their "primary" settlements at Woolaston, Alvington and Aylburton. From these they pushed on with forest clearing and cultivation until the -leys were established as the outposts of their domain, the clearings adjoining the woods. No doubt they were met with much the same tactics as those used against the Romans, but these invaders were flatlanders by origin and inclination, coveting only the richer land of the vale. They needed some iron for their weapons, but the finding of Roman coins in Forest iron-working argues strongly against the extensive use of these workings between the Roman occupation and last century. It is possible that iron was obtained from the waste heaps of "bloomery cinders" left by the Romans, as in recent times, but there is no direct evidence either way.

During later Saxon times there was considerable traffic directed towards subduing the southern Welsh. But again we may safely assume that such expeditions went either by the Severn-side route or by Hereford in order to avoid the very difficult country on both sides of the lower Wye. Not until Offa built his famous Dyke (780) would there have been any really successful attempt to cut the Forest off from Wales and thus bring it more definitely into the social and military framework of England. This boundary, being essentially military, did not attempt to sever all communications between the two sides, so there can be no doubt that the people on the west side of the Wye continued to exert considerable influence on their neighbours across the river. And the Severn still marked the limit for all but the more adventurous. Later extension of the frontier from the Wye to the Usk was a political move that had no racial effect.

Danish invasion appears to have affected this area almost less than any other part of England, for the very simple reason that there was little or nothing here to be looted. The flat riverside again probably came in for some attention, but the Danes, like the Saxons, would have little taste for thickly wooded hills unless they held some wealthy Church property offering easy swag, which was not the case here.

So at the time of Norman Conquest we have the flatter, more fertile lands fairly well settled by the Anglo-Saxons, with the wooded denes and the Wye Valley very little changed from the conditions into which it had lapsed when Roman authority was withdrawn. The inhabitants were unsettled—and unsettling to their neighbours—a people of mainly Celtic type, with strong Megalithic influence. And on these folk Norman rule fell heavily.

The only attraction of this area to the Normans was the sport of hunting. Duke William valued the deer very much more highly than he valued those whose homes interfered with his pleasure. Certainly the people were allowed to remain when, by an extension of the forest area, they found themselves living within the limits of the Royal Chase, but as they were not permitted to fence the deer off their land, or even to drive them away from their crops, this may have been a worthless privilege. Add to this John's weakness for the wild boar, and it is clear that life in the

Forest was a tough proposition even if there were no invading armies to be dealt with. A clear picture is given by William of Malmesbury who, though frequently going astray in his history, is probably right in this case:

"Husbandmen, with their harmless herds and flocks, are driven from their well cultivated fields, their meadows and their pastures, that wild beast may range in them without interruption."

By way of advice he adds:

"If one of these great and merciless hunters shall pass by your habitation, bring forth hastily all the refreshment you have in your house, or that you can readily buy or borrow from your neighbour; that you may not be involved in ruin, or even accused of treason."

All these influences will, of course, have been most intense at the centre, weakening towards the outer limits until there was probably little interference with the people who lived in the region of Churcham, Taynton and Newent. But here another feature comes into play.

The manorial system, with its trappings of open-field cultivations and varying degrees of serfdom, did not come noticeably into this area. Thus one of the chief factors in the development of the greater part of southern England and the Midlands is absent. But from that it must not be assumed that development was necessarily retarded. The manorial system, at its inception, was probably a considerable step forward, but like the majority of rigidly planned institutions it could not grow, and therefore became an encumbrance. If your only means of travel is the tram you cannot expect to do anything but follow the track, and life will be as trite as a tram. So it was with strip cultivation.

In a general way the effect of the manorial system was very marked in the layout of the village and the makeup of the villager. Strong traces of this can still be found east of Severn, where in one noteworthy case the process of enclosure is still not complete and the people live clustered about the village, leaving the big unfenced fields free from buildings. It is noticeable that new ideas penetrate very slowly there, and the whole atmosphere is of a yesterday that has lingered too long.

In the farmlands of the Forest area, on the other hand, enclosure was carried out early and, like measles in childhood, was less severe than is generally the case when it happens later in life. A survey of the Manor of Ruddle, near Newnham, made in 1618 shows that surprisingly little change of field fences has taken place since that date. A few small enclosures have been run together, but the difference in 340 years is negligible. Even the field names in very many cases remain the same, although allowance must be made for phonetic distortion. Take, for example, the wood lying near to The Haie, and shown on the present-day Ordnance Survey as Gill Birch. It is now a mixed wood, but there is a temptation to jump to the conclusion that it was once birchwood, until we see on the old map that the name is Gilberts. But there is no mistaking Fearne Brake, just over the hedge, for the centuries have not moved the bracken, which is here called fern, but pronounced according to the old spelling.

This map shows the division of the land between the various tenants, and here again the changes have not been great. So we can take it that the farming of this manor was well in advance of that being practised in many parts of England during the seventeenth century. The open-field system had the virtue of a certain share-and-share-alike fairness, but it made any improvement of method difficult, if not impossible. The manorial system depended very largely on co-operative effort, though it was so often an unwilling co-operation that had to be coaxed along with so much pressure from the manor courts that it did not tend to produce good neighbours. But it did bring all the occupiers of land under the thumb of the lord of the manor.

Conversely, the absence of these conditions gave rise to a sturdy independence and self-sufficiency that is quite noticeable today. But even that had a drawback, for the most ardent social equaliser must allow that contact with the Hall or the Court played no small part in the spread of what we may call culture, for want of a better word. Particularly was this brought about by the women of the village who, having worked in the mansion, subsequently carried with them to their own homes many reforms that they had learned. This influence, for what it may have been worth, was restricted owing to the scarcity of big houses in this area. And the past tense has been used to indicate that the whole subject is now somewhat taboo.

The influence of the Church in shaping the lives of the people must not be overlooked, for it cannot be over-estimated. Here again the findings are inclined to be negative. Pre-Norman conditions had been highly discouraging to the spread of any uplifting influence, and it would have been unreasonable to look to the Hunting Kings for help in building churches on their sports ground. Anyway they did not want people there, so why have churches? At the same time we cannot accept absence of mention in Domesday Book as proof that no church stood between Dymock, in the north, and Tidenham, in the south. Domesday was the Business King's Guide to His Realm, and as the Forest was looked to as a source of sport rather than profit it was very imperfectly recorded.

Westbury probably had a church at this time, for there is mention of the vicar in 1100, and there is some likelihood of a priest being stationed at Awre. Even where there was no church building religious teaching was often carried on by travelling friars and hermits or by holy recluses. The Cistercian Abbey was founded at Flaxley by 1150, and before the end of that century the following entry was made in the cartulary:

"Be it known to all sons of Holy Church that I, Richard called Abbot of Dene, and of the Convent of the same place, at the numerous prayers of many, have taken charge of the chapel of Herdelande in maintenance of the Divine Office, for the perpetual care as well of all things, both possessions and undertakings, of William, Solitary of the same place, for the support of the said William and of those whom he has with him, who would not that his intentions should be hindered through us, by which he resolved to inter himself in the same place in the severer life, to wit that of an anchorite, for the stability and peace of the realm, and for the soul of King Henry from whom he received the place, for the safety also of King Richard and of his peaceful subjects. Wherefore, and as long as William lives, for all the days of his life, let us minister to his necessities to wit in food and in clothing, so far as pertains to the religion of an intern."

Herdelande (or Ardland) was in Abbots Wood, about a mile from the spot where Cinderford Church was consecrated in 1844. There lies the weakness. Early industrial growth had its eyes fixed so firmly on immediate profit that it quite failed to look after its own long-term interests by studying the welfare of the workers. It was the first half of the nineteenth century that tackled some part of this problem with churches at Christchurch, Drybrook, Parkend and Lydbrook. At the same time a wave of Protestant fire swept through the land, bringing the Word and a great number of chapels. These have been subjected to a good deal of criticism, but they are no worse architecturally than those in many other parts of the country, and the service they rendered was invaluable.

This subject of church buildings comes up for discussion so regularly that a further word may not be out of place. Visitors often comment on the poor style and inferior workmanship of our more modern churches and chapels, and the comments always get a very hostile reception. No one will deny that nineteenth-century work fell very far short of thirteen to fourteenth-century; the Forest Church of the Holy Trinity cannot stand in the same architectural class as All Saints, Newland. But that is a trend not in the least peculiar to the Forest. We could point a finger of scorn at many factory buildings in Manchester and Birmingham by comparison with our own factories of the last few years. It is all part of the same process of development by which the wealth and creative genius of the country has shifted its centre. And as none of us can escape blame it might be as well if we refrained from passing judgment.

This may appear to stray far from the subject were it not that all things reflecting the lives of the people can claim a place in this chapter. Hot from the local press comes evidence that the spirit of improvement is still with us. It tells of a colliery trainee's first visit underground, during which he was shown the stables. On return to the surface he was asked his impressions. "Surry," he replied, "thay stables was a dal sight cleaner than the wallpaper is on our kitchen back wum." (In the Forest "wum" means home, just as surely as "yud" means head, so do tha take that wum in tha yud.)

Now we come to an influence which has not been left so long for lack of importance; quite the reverse. Common Rights. Whatever line a writer takes he will, if he says anything worth reading, meet a flood of opposition on this subject, so, for better or worse, here goes. Common Rights are the most damnable single factor in the lives of those who are entitled to "enjoy" them. I have heard arguments in all directions on this topic and I have formed this opinion in the face of much opposition, so I will give my reasons.

The system of using grazing, or any other property, in common really means dipping many hands into one pocket. Kipling said in verse what we are all liable to learn in hard prose:

> You can use his purse with no more talk
> Than he uses yours for his spendings,
> And laugh and meet in your daily walk
> As though there had been no lendings.

But Kipling makes it very clear that such an arrangement can only work with the Thousandth Man, and such men are just as rare here as everywhere else. It is impossible to share anything of value on such a vague basis without giving rise to a certain amount of suspicion and distrust. Each one, being human, is inclined to think that his neighbour is getting a bigger slice of the cake, which goes a long way towards explaining why these people are often so much more agreeable to strangers than they are amongst themselves.

Another drawback to this system is that small agricultural holdings, ill-equipped and of low quality, often make quite fantastic prices when they carry with them the opportunity of common grazing. Not uncommonly men will let go chances offering better prospects because they would entail moving, and

7                                    89

thereby losing their grazing rights. And all the while, as explained on another page, this common grazing is dwindling rapidly. A well-founded estimate puts it at about 4,000 acres at the present time, but a good deal of this is of absolutely no value.

This question cannot be compared with the Enclosure battle that smouldered more than a century ago, for that concerned normal agricultural land. Here we are dealing with the odd land and the woodland grazing; my suggestion for the removal of the drawbacks is made in another chapter. Another factor that should be kept in mind is that, whereas in the old enclosures the majority lost their common rights for the benefit of the few, here we have a small minority holding rights which can at times interfere with the amenities of all, particularly in the vicinity of housing estates. This is borne out by many of the garden gates being hung to open outwards, as a protection against straying sheep, though I notice that the standardisation of our times has done away with this refinement in most cases.

An amusing and illustrative story, now more than a hundred years old, is worth repeating. Forest children at Sunday school were being taught about the Inheritance of the Kingdom of Heaven. One youngster, on being asked how this could be achieved, replied: "You just takes it in." Which throws a revealing light on the method by which plots of land were inherited from the forest.

So we come back to Bigland's "wild and robustic people" to find them quite a lot like other men, though more restricted in their outlook on account of the unusual conditions in which they have been bred. Also, arising probably from the Celtic strain, they are not inclined to take the middle of the road; black is black and white is white, with very little pale grey.

The most popular story applied to nearly all rural areas is the one about the natives regarding all strangers as foreigners. The warning makes it clear that a lifetime is not long enough to bridge the gulf and to establish understanding. This has been said many times of the Forest, but it simply is not true. As between one village and the next isolationism was the rule until recently, particularly in the marriage sphere. Any lad who found his lass amongst any but his own immediate circle would be told very plainly that it was a pity none of his own people were good enough for him. To the real stranger, however, the reverse is the case, the people being very ready to talk and to give any help they can. This was particularly noticeable during the depression between the wars. Unemployed miners were bored beyond belief, and welcomed any opportunity to talk with the outside world. Their eagerness was embarrassing at times, for the cyclist or hiker who opened a map was liable to find himself surrounded by volunteer guides whose interest not only tore his map, but supplied a bewildering selection of routes. One lady has very clear recollections of this friendly spirit. While pushing her cycle up a steep hill on a hot day she looked, not unreasonably, at a tap that dripped clear, cold water by the wayside. Knowing that to drink from the tap was the surest way of cultivating a thirst for the rest of the day, she moved resolutely on. But it was not to be so. A miner sitting at his cottage door had watched, without knowing what was in her mind, and a child was sent out with a cup. Rather than give offence the lady drank—and regretted.

The isolation of this district in the past has been more complete than that of any other part of the country, not overlooking the claims that have been put forward for certain areas such as the northern edge of the old Wealden Forest, where natural barriers have produced eddies in the main stream of human movement. For so long was the Severn a natural and political boundary that we should expect to find a closer resemblance to the people across the Wye than to the dwellers east of Severn. This, in fact, only holds good to a very limited extent, which strengthens my conviction that we must go back to pre-Celtic times to find the real ancestry of the Foresters. The strip of land between Offa's Dyke and the Wye is a buffer between east and west, just as was originally intended, and contains certain features drawn from each side. This is just noticeable in the speech, for while the words belong to the Forest the tone carries a slight reminder of the Welsh. This is not surprising in view of the fact that until recent years many people from across the Wye have regarded the Dyke as the real limit of England.

The dialect of the Forest is undoubtedly derived from the plain English of Chaucer, with no frills of Norman French. Exceptions to this generalisation are found in a few place-names and in connection with the old handicrafts, indicating that certain places and trades were developed under Celtic influence. As an example we may take May Hill. This is often called Yartleton, and the western slope is liberally sprinkled with elaborations of the Yartleton theme. Efforts to explain this name have even gone to the length of deriving it from the yaffle, or green woodpecker, but they have shied at siting the Saxon *-ton* to which this loud-voiced creature is alleged to be linked. But if we listen to the old folks we shall hear the name as Yarkledon, or Iarkledun, which has a most convincing resemblance to the Celtic *iarkledune*, meaning a round-topped hill. Could any name be more likely from people with a natural aptitude for descriptive names?

The safest place in which to look for the relics of a nearly forgotten language is in the names associated with those crafts that have persisted. In this area of woods and rivers such crafts are likely to be connected with the use of wood and the taking of fish, both of which have occupied the inhabitants since long before the time of written records. We find that in the Welsh tongue *basg* means woven, *coet* is wood, and these readily join up to form basket. This is common to the whole country, but when we come to the more localised trade of fishing we meet the putts and putcheons, baskets for catching fish (and their first cousin the fruit pott). These are both taken from the word *bwt*, and the change of initial letter will be appreciated even by those whose knowledge of Welsh is confined to music-hall jokes.

There is plenty of evidence to show that in the past the people of the Severn-side frontier were amongst the more wild and robustic. Salmon-poaching was not quite the same temptation then, for we know that they were sufficiently plentiful for apprentices at Tewkesbury and Monmouth to stipulate that salmon should only appear on the menu twice a week. Now both the risk and the apprentices are gone, and so are the wilder riverside incidents, though up-to-the-waist-in-water fights still take place owing to the uncertainty of the midstream boundary.

King Henry VII received a petition from the traders of Tewkesbury complaining that when ships on their journey passed "by the costes of the Forest of Deane there came out multitudes of people from Bledisloe and Westbury with great riot and strength in manner of warre as enemys of a strange land". These multitudes made short work of cargoes of wheat and flour. It is noticeable that the spoilers came from Bledisloe and Westbury, while Newnham—between the two—stood aloof. Who would expect quiet Newnham to be a party to such things? But it is only fair to recall that Daffodil Town has had great moments. Why, at the coronation of George III the bell-ringers and others were treated to seventeen-shillingsworth of ale at the expense of the parish, and the next item in the accounts is for the repair of windows in the Church House. Let us hope there was no connection.

In 1800 bread rioting was serious, and a load of flour was taken by force from a barge at Newnham. A detachment of militia was sent to the scene and five ringleaders, all with names still well known in the Forest, were taken to Gloucester. Two of them were executed. From the fact that grain to the value of £1,000 was shortly afterwards distributed in the neighbourhood we can gather just how serious the situation must have been, for that was a very big item for Poor Relief in those days.

Do not imagine for one moment that the common multitude were the only ones given to lawlessness. On the subject of poaching Miss Woods (*Newnham-on-Severn*, 1912) found otherwise, for she wrote:

> "But the Crown Officers themselves seem to have been but frail mortals with respect to this particular sin; for it is complained of the Woodwards in the reign of James I, 'experience proveth that they, their tenants and servants, are as great spoilers as any others'."

Today we wring our hands over the crime figures, whereas the only real difference is a certain loss of colourful effect. It was at Bream that a punishment was devised equal to the best efforts of W. S. Gilbert's Mikado. In that village in 1505 Alexander Griffiths assaulted Master Thomas while the latter was celebrating divine service. Griffiths was absolved on condition that he attended the procession in the Parish Church of Newland on the next Low Sunday, carrying in one hand the stick with which he had committed the assault (or one similar) and in the other hand a candle, costing one penny, which, after penance, he had to offer on the High Altar.

The Rev. H. G. Nicholls, writing in 1863 about Edward Machen, who succeeded his father as Deputy Surveyor and Deputy Gaveller in 1805, makes some very trenchant comments:

"When he thus undertook the agency of this Crown Estate its condition was unsatisfactory and perplexing in every way. The inhabitants—though they had imperceptibly increased to several thousands—were still left to live and die as they pleased, having become exceedingly demoralised by habits of spoliation and encroachment. Totally unenlightened as respected morality and religion, but naturally intelligent, all their faculties seemed directed to the defence of their avowed privileges. Ignorant, and therefore unreasonable, suspicious because apprehensive, they were up in an instant and ready to contend for their rights with a kind of savage impetuosity."

There is the Common Rights Devil again. And the writer of those words must have seen and heard a good deal during his years of service to the Forest Church at Harry Hill, Drybrook.

Here let me again emphasise that all these remarks apply with full force only to the centre of the Forest, becoming less applicable in steps rather than gradually towards the outer limits. The mining community has for so long lived its own life that the borders of the mining locality are still clearly defined. Massingham, in his *Downland Man*, ascribes this to archaic times when stone and metal were highly valued as an essential part of religious rites, with the men who dug them forming a semi-priesthood set apart from their fellows. On the other hand, the explanation put forward by G. M. Trevelyan, in his *Social History*, is that mining became the first industry in which the owner did not take a share in the work side by side with his men, thus producing a sharp cleavage of class distinction. In this way a fence was set up between the working community and their alleged betters. Of these two views the first is more colourful, the second more practical, and I see no reason why they should not both play a part.

Another aspect that must not be overlooked is a certain lack of adaptability amongst men who have been brought up to a life in the pits. This is not now as pronounced as it was, and some will deny its existence entirely, but it was noticeable during the depression between the wars, when unemployment was causing great hardship here. Considerable road works were put in hand to relieve the situation, and workless miners came forward eagerly. They were accustomed to working with pick and shovel, so it might be imagined that all would be plain sailing. But no, habit was deeply ingrained and new tricks were learnt slowly. For example, in moving a deep bank of soil or rock it was then (without machinery) found most efficient to back lorries against the vertical face and allow the material to fall on to them, as far as height would permit. This saved a lot of shovel work. But the miners would persist in dropping on one knee and undercutting the face with a pick, so bringing a great fall of earth to ground level and bringing despair to the man in charge.

The present effort to induce new industries to take root here will broaden the outlook and brighten the prospects of the people, thus doing more than anything else towards breaking down whatever barriers still exist. Though in view of the qualities of endurance and vitality that have been such a feature of the past it is obvious that the breaking down of the centuries-old insularity will not be an unmixed blessing. The same door by which culture and a new way of life are being admitted will allow some of the robusticity to escape.

Anyone who is native to the outer area, which no longer forms part of the Forest, will stoutly resist any remark which seems, in his opinion, to link him with the real Forester. This is a form of local patriotism such as exists in many parts, and when applied to the fringe-lands of Severn-side above Newnham, and to all the red sandy lands of the Newent district, it is quite natural. It is unlikely that the ebb and flow of the evicted squatters reached so far in any strength, and the restricted matrimonial habits of the inner Forest would have frowned on such remote parts until recently. The people of this outer region are not of the same type in build, speech or temperament, though they do in many cases show an independence and sense of humour which links them with their more Celtic neighbours.

An illustration of this occurred not many years ago. The story, coming from sources beyond question, tells of a farmer (living to the east of May Hill) who found himself confronted by a generous and well-served meal, but with no guests. To a man of resource and great hospitality such a position was clearly intolerable, so he telephoned for the fire brigade. They arrived and gave what assistance they could, undoubtedly with the greatest reluctance. Telephone enquiries drew forth the information that there was a ——— good fire in the hearth and the men were needed to keep an eye on it. Maybe I am prejudiced, but I regard the slick "Stock Exchange" joke as an anæmic affair beside its country cousin.

Visitors will be astonished by the number and variety of fetes and carnivals that are organised here, particularly in the towns and villages bordering on the coalfield. In the main these are not of the subdued, or garden, type. Big boisterous affairs are the order of the day, and of part of the night, for fireworks are an important feature, with huge processions taking complete possession of the streets, thrusting dull care and normal routine far into the background, with the traffic. I wonder if there is any other town in this country (or in the world, for that matter) with a population around 6,000, with sufficient energy and enthusiasm to organise a procession two miles long, containing 2,000 characters? That has been done here, and the movement appears to be on the upgrade. Even small villages will carry through an ambitious programme with a vigour which, taken size for size, makes our national festivities look pale and lifeless. If you doubt this, just work out what length of procession London would need to equal the figures above.

There must be some explanation of all this, and I suggest that it is to be found in the past. Harshness and adversity were so heavy here in earlier days that they crushed the spirit of Merrie England; the spirit with strength enough to reveal itself through all the crudeness and brutality of life in Shakespeare's day. Here, in the Deans, there was little recreation except for an occasional public hanging and the like, and it has been left for this twentieth century to witness the awakening.

Something the same may be said of the popular sports, particularly football and cricket. The chance of such recreations has arrived rather late, but it is being grasped with a great deal of enthusiasm. Nearly every village, and many hamlets, now have their sports clubs, and the energy that has been put into the making and levelling of cricket pitches should go far towards keeping our summer game off the downhill slope. And if the goal-posts are inclined to take the wrong shape, that is just a matter of opinion.

Turning from people in bulk to individuals we find few really big names having their origin here, but a great wealth of lesser lights, together with a surprising number of "passage migrants". The latter have been drawn here for a variety of reasons, including war, the chase and the supply of timber for the Navy.

Standing out prominently amongst the native stock is the family of Winter, meriting first place not only for the prominent part they have played in history, but also for their long association with the Forest. A member of the family, now living within sight of the old boundary, has been so good as to show me an authentic pedigree going back to the days before the Conquest, at which time the family was living in the neighbourhood. Such a record must be almost unique, for most families seem to lose themselves in doubt and suspicion in no more than three hundred years, yet in this case nine hundred years have done no more than change the spelling to Wintour.

The first members of this remarkable family to figure prominently in the affairs of the country were two sailors, father and son, who held the ranks of admiral and vice-admiral in the colourful days of the Armada. Lydney was then their home town, which lends considerable support to the stories linking Raleigh and Drake with Purton and Gatcombe. Why should they have shown less interest in our oak trees than did Nelson in later years? Vice-Admiral Sir William's grandson, Sir John, walks through several pages of this book, and through some of the darkest pages of Forest history. He sacrificed his home, Whitecross, to the Royalist cause, but the Restoration revived the family fortunes, and it was from them that the Bathurst family bought Lydney Park, later to become the home of Viscount Bledisloe. In this way a link is formed between two outstanding Forest personalities.

Probably the greatest of names amongst the "passage migrants" is one that has, until recently, been almost overlooked. In fact, the name of David Mushet had even been forgotten on the neglected tombstone in Staunton churchyard, and any local enquiry would have met with blank disinterest. We appreciated that Coleford was the home of Bessemer steel, but we knew nothing of the life story of the Mushet family. Now, through the patient investigation of Mr T. A. Seed, the whole story has been recorded as it deserves. This Scots family, who settled in Coleford and enabled Bessemer to become the greatest name in steel manufactory, have at last received recognition. It is a great story of courage and enterprise, needing every page that Mr Seed has given it, and much too fine to be crammed into a few paragraphs.

We cannot claim Thomas Gambier Parry as a Forester born and bred, but we can hail him as a great figure who chose this land as his home, and as the birthplace of his son Sir Hubert. Thomas was only twenty-two when he left his home in Hereford and completed his studies at Cambridge, to buy Highnam Court. He must have been a man of quite uncommon ability in many directions, for he left the hall-mark of his talent on an astonishingly wide range of activities. The church now standing near the Court owes its origin to him, while the spire and the internal decoration are his own design and execution. The Pinetum, once a showplace but now sadly decayed, is the result of his enthusiasm in collecting trees from many parts of the world. His knowledge of painting, particularly of the Italian School, was immense, for the examples he bought at very modest prices now form a collection of rare merit and great value. And amongst all these activities he was held in affectionate regard by his tenants and neighbours.

So surely is Thomas Parry "The Squire" that it is as such that he is referred to in relation to his son Hubert. Probably he liked best to think of himself in that light, but when reading that the composer of the music to which *Jerusalem* is so widely sung was the son of a country squire it is well to remember that he was no sudden outcrop of genius. It was, no doubt, from the squire that he inherited the charm of manner and the capacity for work which earned for him a place of honour in the world of music. It was not his music alone that won him a prominent place amongst British composers, for his talent has been described as a steady glow, rather than a flashing beacon. But that steady glow of his rich personality played a big part in the rebirth of music in this country during the later part of last century. And now, after more than a hundred years, we may fairly claim this exceptionally gifted family as residents.

On account of our timber supply the Forest was never far from the thoughts of those who built our ships of oak. We saw many great sailors, and produced not a few ourselves. Let us make room for two : one of them known all over the world, the other brought to our notice only by a stone slab near the cliff edge in the church-yard at Newnham. Their names were Nelson and Greening, and our national hero would not demur at having his name linked with one who was obviously hewn from the same tree. When Lord Nelson visited Monmouth in 1803 he dined as the guest of a select dinner club which held its meetings on Kymin Hill. We are told that the great sailor was mightily pleased with the monument recently built to commemorate our leading admirals, though at that time he could hardly have foreseen the position his own name would eventually take. The table at which they dined is now in the Monmouth Museum, amongst the very fine Nelson Collection.

Now come to Newnham, and as you look out towards the sea read the story of one who was a young man when Nelson died. The story is authentic, for the hero of it left nothing to chance,

having the inscription cut—with the exception of the final date—
under his personal supervision:

"WILLIAM GREENING, Pensioner of the Royal Navy,
was present at the destruction of Washington, in America, on
the 25th day of August 1814, at that of Alexandria on the 27th
day of August 1814, when 22 ships were taken to Baltimore,
where 6,000 infantry and several hundred cavalry were attacked
and routed in 15 minutes, nearly 2,000 of the enemy being
slain, a complete and glorious victory. Was on board the Fairy
under Admiral Sir Charles Durham at the taking of Guadaloupe, in the West Indies. Also served in the Fairy under
Admiral Cockburn and General Ross. Served on board the
Impregnable under Lord Exmouth, being wounded and burnt
at Algiers on the 27th day of August 1816. Received Silver
War Medal and a pension of 22 pounds and 12 shillings per
annum. Landed at Baltimore in September 1814. Guadaloupe
was taken August 7th 1815. Was appointed at Bullo Pill,
March 1st 1818, resigned as Shipping agent August 31st 1872,
being 54 years and 6 months at Bullo Pill. Died October 17th
1882 aged 92 years."

Looking down from the cliff-top to the sleepy little derelict quay
of Bullo Pill, I think that the years 1814 to 1816 were amongst the
busiest of William's long life.

John Kent must have a place here, even though it is quite
impossible to sort out the fact from the fancy surrounding him.
His home was at Kentchurch, as far as it is possible to give a home
to such a legendary figure, but much of his time seems to have
been devoted to competitions with the Devil, many of them
being staged in the country beside the Wye. The episode on
Tidenham Chase has been mentioned. On another occasion he is
said to have made a bargain with pigs in Chepstow market, and
as there was then no road in the lower Wye valley we have some
reason to claim that the pigs were carried through the Forest. The
terms were that the pigs should be shared between John and his
illustrious rival, and the one whose pigs had straight tails in the
morning should pay for all. The Devil stayed up all night curling

the tails of his animals, with the result that they were tired and dejected by morning. But John used his head rather than his strong right arm, tucking his pigs up in plenty of straw, so that they came out lively and curly-tailed.

You will notice that John always won these encounters, which is in line with the conventional pattern of such legends as met with all over the country. It seems, also, that he won the last round of the contest, though I can only speak from hearsay. The Devil is reported to have sworn that he would have Kent's body, whether it was buried inside or outside Grosmont Church, so he was buried in the wall—and left undisturbed.

Last in this very brief review of Forest celebrities is one who shall be nameless, but who is well known in the village where, at the time of writing, he still lives. In the records of the local magistrates' court his name appears as an honest and fearless witness; a man who could be relied upon to speak his mind. It happened that he had been called by the prosecution in a claim for damage caused by rabbits. The defence sought to undermine his reliability, and the cross-examination went something like this:

"I understand, my man, that you are not averse to a glass of beer?"

"That's right, I'm none the worse for a glass or two."

"It is even suggested that you drink a considerable quantity."

"Ah, I do that, when I can get 'un."

"Now, can you tell the Court how much you would drink in a day?"

"In a day!"—with a note of hopeless alarm.

"Well, shall we say, in an evening?"

"Oh, of a evening. That's more like. Well, of a evening I sometimes haves me six or eight quarts. But (in a tone of joyful recollection) sometimes I haves a tidy drop."

I have never dared to ask the outcome of the case. The thought of such honesty going unrewarded would be more than I could bear.

# CHAPTER V

# LOOKING AT BUILDINGS

"Cities and Thrones and Powers,
Stand in Time's eye,
Almost as long as flowers,
Which daily die.
But, as new buds put forth
To glad new men,
Out of the spent and unconsidered Earth,
The Cities rise again."

RUDYARD KIPLING

THE attraction of the Cotswolds lies very largely in the works of men; in the churches, the manor-houses, the farm buildings and the cottages, all built according to the prevailing fashion, after the sharp outline of that fashion has been tempered by local craftsmanship. Here, in the Denes, it would be very near the truth to say that the country is lovely in spite of these things. We can claim for our buildings history in plenty, but when the search is for architectural beauty we shall have to look through a lot of very drab material in order to find a handful of really good examples. And in the search we shall have satisfied ourselves that the Church produced the architect—not vice versa.

This is the key to our lack of good buildings. The Church was, without doubt, the inspiration and the training ground for mediæval masons, so it is quite reasonable that good style and design should be largely absent from the area that was afforested during three or four centuries after the Conquest, with a higher standard prevailing wherever the Church exerted some influence on the lives of the people. And it was not only the mason's craft that was affected in this way. The influence spread right through the everyday life of the Middle Ages.

Our stone is certainly less amenable to the chisel than is the Cotswold Oolite, but that alone does not provide the explanation for a lower standard of work, for we shall find at Newland and a few other places that local stone can be coaxed into shape. Also, in a land of oakwoods we might look for great skill in wood-carving, such as was put into the seventeenth-century screen at Abbey Dore, but we should look in vain. This was the work of John Abell, who also built Ledbury Market Hall and the Old House at Hereford, showing that there was no lack of skill within one day's journey on foot. But the Royal Hunting Ground gave no encouragement in that direction.

A number of oak screens and galleries have gone, without leaving any indication of the workmanship they once contained, and only at The Lea can we now find a worthy example, for the one in Mitcheldean is not a local product, in addition to which it pays the penalty of nineteenth-century origin. At St Briavels we can stand at the foot of a stairway that once led to a rood loft and wonder who shaped the wood that is gone, and whether his exuberance of spirit caused him to carry out any of those practical jokes that are scattered so widely over the country—the wooden mouse to surprise the priest, or the cartoon of the priest to amuse the congregation. But we cannot know the answer, for the screen was done away with before the removal of the tower to its present position over the porch put the stairway out of use in the middle of last century.

Our mediæval churches are only in middle life by comparison with the standing stones and earthworks that remain from Saxon and earlier times, though here again we must confess to an absence of the finer examples of man's skill. We have little trace of burial mounds—the most permanent structures of their day—and our megaliths stand singly, as mark-points rather than temples. We have none of the inspired works such as are found in Wilt-shire, Dorset and on the east side of our own county, and which are considered by some authorities to belong to worship rather than war. Our earthworks link themselves with Mars, not Lucifer, and they are sited in defence positions overlooking the Severn and Wye. Many of them were used against the invading Romans, and later against the Saxons. In more than one case they were brought from the retired list by the Home Guard in 1940.

First amongst these camps, by reason of size and position, is the circular trench on May Hill. The old earthwork, said to belong to the Iron Age, is 100 yards in diameter and becomes very indistinct on the north side. It should not be confused with the more clearly defined outer ditch which marks the area purchased by the Parish of Longhope. Other sites facing east include Castle Hill, overlooking Taynton; Welshbury, a rectangular entrenchment above Flaxley Abbey; Littledean Camp, one of the smallest and at the same time most prominent; the camp in Lydney Park, where Roman followed Briton; and a camp at Sedbury, forming the end of Offa's Dyke, which was used right down to the seventeenth-century Civil War. This one, being sited on a narrow isthmus, faces the rivers on two sides and so becomes the first of the Wye defences. Its companions, working north, are the camp at Madgetts; a likely circular ditch and bank in which Hewelsfield Church now stands; the heaped-up circular camp at Stowe; Symonds Yat, a multi-trench fortification cut across the narrow ridge just south of the Rock; Howle Hill, overlooking Walford and Goodrich; and the camp on Chase Hill, above Ross.

As the first of these carries the name "castle", and as similar castles are frequently met with, it may be well to mention that many such castles never bore any likeness to our interpretation of the word. This Castle Hill is a mound at the eastern base of May Hill, carrying on its crest a square earthwork no bigger than the foundations of a house. Such a site could never have carried a building capable of withstanding siege, nor could it have been a palisaded enclosure in which a small group of people could shelter with their cattle. The most likely use appears to have been as a look-out point sufficient to provide some shelter from weather and slight protection from surprise attack. Littledean Camp is on much the same scale, but it is circular and with a higher bank. This is now being excavated, but nothing of special interest has yet come to light. Like so many other such sites, this has probably been used over a considerable length of time, with later occupants obscuring traces of their predecessors.

The fortifications at Symonds Yat are in a class apart from the conventional triple-earthworks that run around the brow of so

many out-thrust hilltops. Many of the latter type (Painswick Beacon, for example) appear hopeless for defence, since they have no protection at their backs. We can be satisfied that the need for such protection was fully understood by the trouble that was taken to supply it on such positions as Crickley Hill and here at Symonds Yat. If, as legend tells us, Caradoc held the camp at the Yat in the course of his resistance to the Romans, he was in a very strong position from whichever side the attack came.

At English Bicknor (and probably at Hewelsfield) we have a church within an earthwork, instances such as have been put forward in support of the argument that many earthworks were religious rather than military in origin. But this is a subject upon which a collection of archæologists can be relied on to divide into at least two camps and to defend their earthworks most fiercely against all comers. From a great depth of archæological ignorance I would point out that the climax of the battle at Newnham was fought out in the church; that, in fact, churches were frequently used as military strongholds, so there may be nothing at all incongruous in the transformation from earthwork to church.

Standing stones may not be buildings, particularly when they occur singly, but as they were set in position by men they have some claim to a place in this chapter. And they are probably the earliest traces of Man's work that we can offer. They are not numerous, but the placing of them, together with the various legends that go with them, are highly provocative. Casualties were necessarily high amongst these monoliths, for in many cases they stood at cross-roads or other meeting places, so that many will have been cleared right away or replaced by other marks. Some have been broken up for the stone they contained or because they formed an obstruction, while a few may have been incorporated in other buildings. From whichever way the existing stones are approached they tend to form themselves into a line running down the western uplands of the Forest, and there are strong indications that others now lost stood in the same line.

Starting with the Queen Stone beside the Wye at the tip of the Huntsham peninsula, the first step is nearly four miles to the well-known Long Stone standing on the north side of the road nearly

*Roman Road, Blackpool Bridge*

midway between Coleford and Staunton. The next stone has
gone, but the records of its position and destruction are quite
clear. It stood on Closeturf Farm, about a mile east-north-east of
St Briavels, in a field still remembered as Longstone Piece. Then
we jump three miles to Parson's Allotments, on Tidenham Chase,
followed by a jump of a mile and a half to the Broad Stone standing near the railway line at Stroat. There are big gaps in this line,
but there is also a big gap of time since they were placed in
position, and it is worth recalling that St Patrick (Bishop of the
Hebrides) gave instructions for a church to be built on each site
where an upright stone was found. If this order was in line with
general practice a great many standing stones will have been
built over, and there is a temptation to wonder whether something of the sort happened at Coleford and Hewelsfield, for these
churches fall into the line; a line which closely resembles a row of
signposts. Why else should they lead from the bank of the Wye
(at a likely enough spot for a ford) to Severn-side? The line of
these stones is not straight, but it does follow the easiest gradients
along the ridge, without deviating sufficiently from the straight
line to increase the distance appreciably. In fact, the lack of dead
straightness seems to me to add sound practical sense to the signpost idea. On Tidenham Chase the line may have forked, just as
the present roads fork, with one branch leading to the Broad
Stone while the other ended at St Tecla's Chapel, on the Beachley
peninsula. At Lambsquay (significant name) the cross-road is
marked by a square stone plinth in which is set a section of square
upright shaft. This is quite a lot like the "Black Stone" at Huntley,
and though it is, in its present form, modern by comparison with
the menhirs, its existence in such a place is some excuse for won-
dering if it replaced an earlier monument. Or it could be the old
stone in a new shape.

Each of these stones has some feature of special interest, but it is
the Queen Stone that has the most striking appearance. The
portion of this slab above ground measures $7\frac{1}{2}$ feet high, 6 feet
wide and 3 feet thick, giving a weight of over 5 tons, without the
part below ground. It has thirteen vertical grooves, some of them
6 inches deep and more than 2 inches wide. And the top of the

stone carried marks of fire—so the experts have said. As recently as the *Victoria County History of Hereford* (1908) it was suggested that these grooves were caused by some natural agency, but the number and the character of them make this appear to me the least likely explanation. The theory of natural formation is further challenged by a comparison of this stone with the Devil's Arrow at Boroughbridge, Yorkshire, which also carries grooves (though not the same significant number) and bears sufficient resemblance to the Queen Stone to set us looking for some common purpose, ceremonial or utility.

The Queen Stone is of local conglomerate, and some may be inclined to interpret this as a sign of utility, for many of the more important ceremonial stones were carried long distances, as in the case of Stonehenge. That may depend on the development of the people who set it up, but if they merely wanted a signpost there would be excellent reasons for choosing the lump of rock nearest to hand. As we stand beside this silent witness of so much history, questions naturally come to mind as to the changes that have taken place since it was put in position. The river is now some 150 yards away, but everything supports the idea that the channel has moved away from the stone, for the river is following the normal process of building up on the inside of the bend. So the stone may well have been placed near to the water. The ground level in relation to the exposed rock is perplexing to me. I am not aware of any information about the depth to which the stone is set in the ground, but the deeper grooves run down to the present field level—after allowance has been made for the hollow scooped out by the treading of cattle. On land which is so liable to flood, one might expect the general level to have risen considerably in so many centuries, even if the annual deposit of sediment is small. Many Roman sites have been covered with soil to a depth of 2 feet or more in perhaps half the time, and without the help of a flooding river. If this monolith has been covered at anything like the same rate the total bulk is above the ordinary, as the breadth makes up for any lack of height.

No opinion has come my way as to the purpose to which this stone may have been put, but taking the grooves in conjunction with the traces of fire I suggest that it acted as a base to carry a superstructure of wood. Sticks could lie in the grooves for firm support, their upper ends being woven into a container. This will surely bring to mind pictures of wicker cages in which humans are said to have been sacrificed to the flames, and while this use cannot be ruled out it is well to remember that fires were used for other purposes. In such a position it could have served to light the river crossing without being too conspicuous. But that is an elusive hare, already run hard enough in connection with the Drummer Boy Stone.

The Staunton Long Stone stands just inside the hedge of Marian's Enclosure, in full view of all who use the road from Coleford to Monmouth. The angle at which it leans is said to be due to an attempt to move it for use as a gatepost. This stone also carries slight traces of grooves, but if they ever resembled those of the Queen Stone they have suffered very severely from weathering or other action. Legend has it that a scratch with a pin at midnight will draw blood from this stone, so the grooves may have been scratched away during the centuries! The story is quite general, however, and is probably a folk-memory of some sacrificial rite. These legends have a way of linking themselves to what may be called a standard specification, like the one of John Kent and his antics on Tidenham Chase which is told elsewhere. They are all true to type; just standard folklore adapted to local requirements.

The Jubilee Stone on Parson's Allotment is the most upstanding and has the most imposing position of all this line. It must be 10 feet or more in height, and looks very upright on account of its slender figure. The name may be modern, though I have gathered no explanation. On the other hand, it may be an old name twisted out of shape by the ages. The site on which this Jubilee Stone stands has been most impressively set out by the Forestry Commission's planting scheme, which has left a wide clearing all round the stone, with rides in four directions. This was carefully planned, for one ride is aligned on the Broad Stone and another on the ruined chapel at Beachley. Standing by the stone it is easy to believe that some such clearings were made when the monolith was set up, for this seems to be the obvious point at which the ways divided—left for the flint districts of Wiltshire and Berkshire, right for the ancient settlements on Mendip. And if this looks rather far-fetched on paper I can only suggest a visit to the spot.

Parson's Allotment, of course, takes the name from having been the property of the incumbent of Tidenham. It was sold to the Commissioners because, in all probability, Parson was poorer than many of the Poor who still have right of pasturage on the adjoining Poors' Allotment. In this case the qualification of a poor person is a rateable value of less than £30, which does not represent real penury in this neighbourhood.

Without serious doubt these stones were set up to mark meeting places of tracks, whatever part they may have played in ritual. They are, therefore, the forerunners of the crosses so generally erected at cross-roads and meeting places. A number of these have now been moved into churchyards or other sites for their own protection, but many are still in the old spots, even if only the neglected base remains. Many of these crosses date back to the twelfth and thirteenth centuries, but I would venture the opinion that the majority were placed on the sites of earlier stones. A likely illustration is the rough plinth with its section of shaft standing near the public telephone box at Huntley, called the Black Stone until recent times, and the significance of the name has already been stressed. Dursley Cross still has a base, with socket, which marks a meeting of the ways at a point where the old road crossed the shoulder of May Hill. And when I say that the site appears to be primarily utilitarian rather than religious I hope not to be misunderstood—so near home.

To anyone with more than the most casual interest in such things the three crosses of Lydney, Aylburton and Clearwell will make particular appeal. They are all of local stone, standing well up on square steps, each with a square shrine between steps and column. The crosses that have been placed on the columns at Lydney and Clearwell may be ignored, architecturally, for they do not set out to indicate the original form. In fact, some will look more favourably at Aylburton because it has no such restoration. But it is in the carved shrines that the contrast lies. In each case there is a niche on each of the four sides, probably intended to shelter a figure that would look down a flight of steps. It is in the decoration of these niches and in the line of moulding above that the trend of design has revealed itself. The Lydney Cross, while standing more bravely on three extra steps, has a shrine of oddly unsatisfying Transition type. At Aylburton, Gothic has struggled for a place with Classical, giving an impression of the early struggle between Christian and Pagan. Clearwell shows the end of the struggle—Gothic triumphant—but unfortunately weathering has removed the finer lines.

Real castles, with moats and thick walls, were never plentiful here. To the one still partly left at St Briavels we can, with certainty, add only the two small private-enterprise affairs at English Bicknor and Penyard. Some claim one for Newnham, but the case is not proved, and no stone is left. This scarcity of castles on our side of the Wye, compared with abundance on the west, is due to the administrative skill of the Conqueror. Faced with the problem of maintaining military strength at a price within his reach, William allowed his chief supporters the run of the Welsh Marches, with leave to do very much as they liked (to the Welsh) so long as they kept a band of fighting men in trim for any emergency. In this way it was possible to keep a considerable army on call without all the usual problems of subsistence. And if it was a one-sided plan, the other side was Welsh—so what? Later on this plan recoiled upon William's successors, for life in the Marches did more than preserve the fighting capacity of the barons who underwent the treatment; it caused them to develop big ideas about the Crown. But that is history, though not exactly as set out in school text-books.

St Briavels Castle, now used as a Youth Hostel, is only the shadow of its former self. But while there is little sign left of the building said to have been put up by Milo, Earl of Hereford, before 1131, we are lucky enough to have the very imposing entrance towers and the kitchen, both of the later thirteenth century. I say we are lucky in having so much left because at the time the keep fell, in the eighteenth century, it is surprising that the whole building was not taken stone by stone to build houses in the village. To appreciate the attitude of those times we have only to read an account of a trip down the Wye in which the writer suggests that a mallet applied to the gable of Tintern would make the ruin more picturesque. The feature which attracts more attention than any other at St Briavels is the hunting horn, symbol of the Warden of the Forest and Constable of the Castle, carved in stone over a chimney. It is most fitting that the horn should stand over the building from which the Forest was administered for so many years. The main purpose of this castle must always have been to overawe the inhabitants rather than to resist invasion from the west, for there would be no large-scale invasion while Chepstow, Raglan, Monmouth, Goodrich and Wilton held out.

Little is known about Newnham's castle beyond what has been mentioned in another chapter. Even the site is only known approximately, and if the material was used again locally it has hidden itself most modestly amongst the red brick of the town. We are told that this castle was old at the time of the Norman kings, but it may have been no more than an earthwork before they took it in hand. It still stood when the Civil War reached Newnham, but from the fact that the resistance to Colonel Massey finished up in the church we may be inclined to think that the castle was no longer a real stronghold.

Penyard Castle seems to have attracted little attention from antiquarians, so that the origin is as obscure as the stones are now scattered. The site is still marked by a small stack of masonry standing on Lawn Farm, and a ruined cottage close at hand has a chimney as much in keeping as a coronet on the brow of a gypsy. It is said that the stone was taken to enlarge the church at Weston-under-Penyard (which I very much doubt), and to build the eighteenth-century pseudo-castle at Bollitree, while some may be more happily incorporated in the Rectory. Penyard Castle may well have been in the same class as English Bicknor, a baronial by-product of the troublous days of Stephen and Matilda, when there was no safety without a strong fortification—and very little within. A great number of these castles were pulled down within a quarter of a century of their building in the clean-up

organised by Henry II. Such is said to be the history of the stonework at English Bicknor, but the site has seen many changes since
the construction of a motte and bailey some two hundred years
before the Conquest. In conjunction with this a more extensive
enclosure took in the site which was later to carry the church. The
castle stood within the bailey, the foundations being uncovered
when the ground was cleared for a school garden in the later part
of last century.

Visitors travelling through Ruardean by the road leading down
to the Wye will inevitably slow down and tell each other, "Look,
a ruined castle!" Many local people regard the fragments of stone
wall as relics of some mediæval stronghold, and the position on
a high mound overlooking a break in the fortification of hills does
call aloud for a castle. But the facts are rather discouraging, for we
read that in 1307 Alexander of Bicknor received licence to crene-
late a house at Ruardean. This may have been to comfort him
for the loss of Bicknor Castle, but the need for a licence shows
that a close check was being kept on the private castle builder.
Ruardean Castle had no military intention, being merely an out-
break of nostalgia such as is liable to occur in any age, and which
appeared in more virulent form at Bollitree. In this case casual
visitors are frequently deceived by the look of weatherbeaten
permanence that has come to a block of farm buildings set up
some two hundred years ago, complete with arrow slits and
crenellations. The only item I know of in connection with
Bollitree Castle is that it sheltered William Cobbett and his son
Richard, as we can read in *Rural Rides*.

Between Bollitree and The Lea the map shows "Site of Eccleswall Castle". There is now only the mound, but judging by its
size and by the fact that the adjacent part of The Lea is called
Castle End I am inclined to think that here was more than an
earthwork. It seems, in fact, that Eccleswall does much to bridge
the gap between our own time and Roman days of Ariconium—
just across the road—for in addition to the castle mound the farm-
yard contains a mystery building. This is in the shape of a square
tower, the lower part being known as "The Chapel", while the
upper storey has wooden pigeon nest-boxes on the walls. There is

a lantern of sorts at the apex of the roof, but the narrow pointed windows are not in the dovecote convention. Suggestion— religious origin, pigeon afterthought.

And if you should travel past Clearwell Castle shed no tear over the threatening notice to prospective trespassers. Do not even stamp your foot and say that they can keep their castle, for there never was a castle here for anyone to keep.

As we turn to consider churches may I call attention to the heading of this chapter. We are, at the moment, concerned with churches from an architectural viewpoint. Our churches fall readily into three broad groups—Ancient, Mediæval, Modern. In the first class we can place only the ruined Chapel (or Oratory) of St Tecla, and the ruined Church of St James at Lancaut. Others undoubtedly stand on the sites of Saxon predecessors, and some have work that is declared to be Saxon—Littledean, Ruardean and Churcham amongst them—but it is only the two first mentioned that have escaped the restorer, to fall victims of neglect and decay. Norman masons were as little inclined to preserve the Saxon character of the churches they rebuilt as present-day contractors are disposed to retain nineteenth-century lines when they reconstruct a factory. But, fortunately, they were less inclined to level the site and start again. They would leave any parts that happened to fit in with their plans, or they would give a second lease of life to stones that had been shaped by earlier men, thus giving us an occasional glimpse of the things they saw. This process continued until it took a most unfortunate turn when the nineteenth-century restorers tried to copy the old styles, with deplorable results, or built anew in the characterless style of their own time.

The second class, which I have vaguely called Mediæval, covers that vigorous age between the Conquest and the Reformation, a period during which native craftsmanship could make almost no mistakes, even when it worked with imported ideas and under foreign supervision. The steadily rising fortunes of the Church throughout this time made possible the creation of our finest religious buildings, and when the work was undertaken it was carried through with a vigour that generally left little sign of the earlier structure that it frequently replaced. Taking the country as a whole it is said that the great majority of churches were built during this time, but this does not hold good for our particular area, for reasons that have already been considered. We have about thirteen churches with unmistakably Norman work (which may be taken to cover the period 1050 to 1200 in this locality), and another ten or eleven of a later date, but still pre-Reformation.

During the whole of this period the creative art of the mason was so vitally active that we must expect to find quite a wide range of styles. Unfortunately restoration and enlargement have left us with few examples that can be regarded as Norman in more than a few features. Some guide-books mention only the south door of Ruardean, with St George on the tympanum, but even when we allow that they are dealing with a more limited area they still do us less than justice. Churcham and Bulley (now in one parish) still have Norman chancel arches, with a south door of the same period at Bulley. Woolaston has a two-storey porch with inner and outer arches that have sagged under the load of stone and years until they are no longer in the original half-circular shape. For Norman pillared arcades we may go to English Bicknor, where low arches run on both sides of the nave; to St Briavels, with five arches on the south side; or to Staunton for a clear illustration of the growth from Norman to Early English. At Littledean the piers of the chancel arch are authoritatively pronounced Saxon. This is not surprising, as the present building is supposed to stand on the site of an earlier chapel dedicated to St Ethelbert, who was murdered while travelling this way and whose name is still retained.

At Linton (a church on a ridgeway) three centuries live happily together, for they are the centuries that followed the Norman reconstruction. And in the church is a coloured diagram, a happy idea that is much more explicit than any description.

The name alone should be enough to tempt the visitor to Weston-under-Penyard, and once within sight of the handsome fourteenth-century tower there will be no disappointment. The site is perfectly chosen, as if the church had taken a few steps up the gentle lower slope of Penyard Hill in order to give a benediction to the village nestling below. Restoration has dealt kindly here, leaving very much that is lovely, and adding nothing displeasing. Seven hundred years ago men built three lancet windows at the east end; a century later they roofed the nave and aisles with oak rafters; for the sheer joy of creation they carved bold figures of men and of animals, and hid tiny faces amongst the decoration of the capitals. Today the church has electric light, and the grass is carefully mown, giving an agreeable impression that the spirit of service has not dimmed through all the ages.

But it is at Hewelsfield, at the top of the lane from Brockweir and overlooking the Severn estuary, that we find a Norman church, as distinct from churches showing Norman work. Stepping in through the round-arched door is stepping back seven hundred years. Thick walls and massive pillars make the inside appear smaller than was anticipated, but we may rejoice that we have moved away from the age that described such a building as a "poor low structure". This thickness of wall is most noticeable in the three small windows on the north side. Two of these have been restored, but the third still has the original frame cut through a single piece of stone. And if you will walk half a mile down the road you can see an owl hole in a barn made in just the same way. The barn is of much later date, so we may imagine the local mason studying these windows during the sermon, then setting to work on Monday to copy the idea.

In the third—Modern—class are about twenty churches built entirely during last century. A number of these met the needs of new parishes, while others were placed on old sites without preserving any features from the buildings they replaced. In some cases a thread of continuity is carried on by some item of historic interest finding a home in the new church. I am thinking at the moment of Minsterworth, with Jacobean pulpit and earlier font, and of Blakeney, unhappily sited and styled, with a fifteenth-century font recovered from the railway cutting during construction work near Gatcombe.

When the conversation turns to lead fonts we of the Forest can lift up our heads and hold up our voices in any company. Of thirty-one such fonts in the whole of England and Wales we have four. (Incidentally, Gloucestershire leads all the other counties with nine.) Of our four, three were made in the same mould in Norman times, and now belong to Tidenham, Oxenhall and Lancaut. One of these may now be seen in Gloucester Cathedral, for Lancaut is too far gone into ruins to give it shelter, so it is lent to the mother-church for the satisfaction of all who wish to see it. Other fonts from the same mould are at Sandhurst, Syston and Frampton-on-Severn, and while the design is the same in each case the one at Tidenham differs from the others in having only five panels—one less than the rest. It is a pity that the decoration has been mutilated in a manner strongly suggestive of the Puritan outrages, but we are lucky to have so many examples when the majority of such fonts were melted down and fired from muzzle-loaders. The fourth of our lead fonts is at Aston Ingham, and it claims to be the last of its kind, having the date 1689 and the initials of William and Mary.

This does not by any means exhaust our font material. In Abenhall is one from the fifteenth century, the gift of the Guild of Free Miners and Free Smiths. Eight panels carry a wealth of history in stone, six being devoted to the arms of families then prominent in the district, the other two showing the six picks and two shovels of the Miners, and the horseshoes and tongs of the Smiths. This is unique, and the door is always open, yet in many visits to this quiet backwater I have always found it deserted. In complete contrast is the font at The Lea, close beside the main road from Gloucester to Ross. After seven centuries this piece of Italian work is a foreigner, striking in design and beautiful in execution, but still a stranger to the Forest. In contrast also is the locked door. I do not question the action of the Rector in this, but sometimes it seems that we get a poor dividend from all our investments in education.

At Newent, amongst much restoration which includes a wide span roof of Forest oak, there is a Renaissance font. And at Ruardean, long before there is any mention of the Norman south door, you will hear that a ball game used to be played against the wall of the church and that the font carries the date 1657—a time when such things were banned by the Roundheads.

The two fonts in Staunton may be taken as marking, roughly, the growing years. The one now in use is of the fifteenth century, when the addition of the tower brought the church very much to the present form, while the second one has been hailed as a Roman altar or a Saxon font. In view of the position occupied by this village on an old highway, and adjoining the remarkable Double View, it is easy to imagine that Romans and Saxons both left their mark here—probably on more than one piece of stone.

The Rectors of Staunton must bear no physical likeness to Friar Tuck, or they will be barred from their own pulpit. This may explain why a similar pulpit was, at some time, thrown out of the church at English Bicknor, for a man above average size would have the greatest difficulty in negotiating the stone stairway which provides something in the nature of a balcony on its way up to the rood screen and the belfry. Again, unfortunately, the screen has been removed but the central tower remains, though the angle at which it leans is a likely clue to the removal of similar towers at St Briavels and English Bicknor. To appreciate how our Early English style evolved from the Norman it is only necessary to stand against the west wall of All Saints, face the east and read the story from left to right, a story covering three centuries, if we include the font.

But, as often happens when we read a story, we are left with some unimportant phrase caught firmly by the imagination, so it is for me at Staunton. I have seen this village so many times, from the Buck Stone to the council houses now being built, that many views of it come readily to the eye of memory, but it is not the print of the Druid, the Early English mason or the modern villa-maker that is uppermost in mind. Across the road from the church is a house that has seen a number of changes, without achieving any outstanding merit, but it has a small round window frame of stone carved with all the delicacy of a gold circlet. It looks out from a wood store or lumber shed and has no glass, but the joy of craftsmanship is richly stored in this neglected fragment.

Newland Church is often spoken of as the Cathedral of the Forest. This is a colourful inaccuracy, as much due to the character of the building as to the fact that it served for so long as the Parish

Church for the whole of the Royal Forest. Later the area was reduced to that now covered by Coleford, Bream, Clearwell and Lea Bailey. It seems strange to think that until last century Coleford had only a chapel-of-ease under Newland, but at least that helped to support the parent church. Now, reduced to a parish of about 800 inhabitants, this fine church is faced with a hard struggle to keep the structure standing. It was while walking through this churchyard—where upright tombstones are the exception—that I first realised the vastness of the change that has taken place since the days when such churches were built. With a population that is unlikely to have exceeded five or six millions all the magnificent Norman churches and castles were built, to be added to in size and number until the end of the fourteenth century. At the same time these people were growing their own food and clothing. Now it almost seems as if Henry VIII and Cromwell were acting for the best when they destroyed so much of our finest masonry, for on present showing we could never have kept all these buildings in repair. And if such remarks are unwelcome, allowance must be made for the effect which decaying buildings can have.

The most striking outward feature of All Saints, Newland, is the five-pinnacled tower—four matching at the four corners and a bolder one over the stairway. Closer inspection will show the memorials to be of quite unusual interest for the information they give. In the Greyndour Brass we can see the costume and equipment of a mediæval Free Miner, including the candlestick which he carries in his mouth. During recent repairs the recumbent figure of Jenkyn Wyrrell has been moved back into the church for protection from weathering and other mutilation. Jenkyn was a Forester-of-Fee, and his effigy is dated 1459. There is also the figure of a forester of the time of James I, carrying a bow and arrow. But for rustic moralising you may look to the sculptured heads on the drip-arches. Here, in three straight lessons, are set out three vices and their corresponding virtues:

The Flaunting Queen  :  The Modest Maid
The Fop  :  The Steady One
The Unruly Member  :  The Bridled Mouth

There has been more than stone and brass here, however, for the vicar who followed Robert of Wakering (the Founder) rose to be Bishop of Bath and Wells and Archbishop of York. And he was followed by John o' London, a Benedictine monk who enlivened his ministry with periods of excommunication.

I have tried, clumsily it is true, to classify our buildings, but any such attempt must fail utterly at Newland, for the village has managed to bind a wide range of architecture into an inseparable whole, from the fourteenth-century cross to the wistaria climbing over the house near to The Ostrich. The layout of the centrepiece, with the early seventeenth-century almshouses, the old school, and houses of quiet charm grouped around the church is planning at a level that is found nowhere else in the Forest, reminding us that Newland was never of the Forest—though for many years in the Forest. It was the Church that brought greatness to Newland, but Industry lent a helping hand in later years. William Jones, who built and endowed the almshouses, was prominent among haberdashers, and copper-smelting brought a good deal of money to the neighbourhood. In a field not far from the church the giant oak has stood, a witness to all these events, but with a handicap of centuries the tree is fading quietly away while the works of men become mellowed with lichens.

It is the imprint of the fourteenth century that leads the mind from Newland to Mitcheldean, for there are no other features that link them except an impression of great spaciousness. The Church of St Michael has a nave, one south aisle and two north aisles, giving a width only six inches less than the length. This squareness is probably unique. A very unusual feature here is the ossuary, or bone-hole, used at one time for the storage of bones dug up in the churchyard. This is in the form of a small crypt, under part of the north aisle, reached by a continuation of the rood-loft stairs. This rood loft must have been a fine structure if we may judge by the carved wooden bosses in the roof, and by the timber panels on the wall above the central span of the three-piece section that it formed over nave and two aisles (for there is no chancel arch). The upper sections of these painted panels were exposed to the weather for four hundred years, covered only by whitewash, but the pictures can still be seen.

Pure Celtic masonry is sufficiently rare that we might reasonably expect to find the ruins of the Church of St James, Lancaut, guarded by iron railings and an unsleeping serpent. Instead there is only a weatherbeaten notice telling all and sundry that the ruins are not safe. Not safe! The danger from falling stones is of no account when compared with the danger that future generations will find nothing more than a heap of stones. And when the west gable-end falls (as it must if something is not done very soon) the Forest will have lost a pair of unique windows. But let me put on a mask of cold indifference while I give some coherent picture of this isolated ruin.

The situation is interesting, under a steep wooded bank and close to the Wye. The absence of any clear track up the slope, together with the presence of a precarious ladder leading down to the river mud, suggests that the easiest approach has always been by water. This is in line with all accounts of the roads in this part until the latter half of last century. The present dedication of the church to St James is suitable to the position, but it is the name of the parish that has caused much speculation. Various translations from the Welsh have been tried, with results such as "Church in the Wood", "Church on the Bank" and "Gateway through the Dyke". A later and more likely rendering comes from the Rev. F. W. Potto-Hicks, who attributes it to an earlier dedication to St Cerriog.

The ruin as we see it today consists of two parts, not even united by any bonding of the stonework. Looking at the western portion first, because it was built in that order, we have a Celtic oratory no bigger than the sitting-room of an average villa. It is in the west end of this we find two windows of unusual design defying storm and decay at the top of the roofless gable. These are clearly not a matching pair, particularly in width. They are separated by a flat stone and arched by two flat stones leaning together over each opening. (I do recommend a comparison of these with the doorway at Stowe, mentioned on another page.) The east wall has been cut away and provided with an arch, giving

120

access to the early Norman annexe. This is slightly larger, the extra width being due to a corresponding reduction of thickness in the walls. At the east end is a well-preserved piscina with cinquefoil head, an aumbry and four recesses whose purpose has not been established. And if we except the few tombstones of the seventeenth and eighteenth centuries, nothing has been added here since the piscina.

Now come to St Tecla's Chapel, that cartload of masonry on the southernmost point of the Beachley peninsula—the most arresting and thought-provoking work of Man in all this land between Severn and Wye. This will undoubtedly cause eyebrows to be raised, so let me state a case for putting this remote heap of rubble in the place of honour. The history is as much obscured by time as is the name; there is no record telling when it was built, or who chose the lonely site; and in the 1947th year of Enlightenment it is referred to by two writers as "the remains of Celtic St Rioc's oratory", and "St Twrog's Chapel". The problem of these two names can be dealt with by saying them both quickly a number of times. They become indistinguishable, as probably were the saints themselves. But there emerges a third name, and with it a change of sex, for Atkyns speaks of St Tecla, describing her as the first woman to be martyred in the cause of Christianity. From this has arisen the popular name—Treacle Island.

But the name and exact history are of no account by comparison with the story indelibly written in these few stones; a story taking as its plot Humanity in the widest interpretation, extending from the first appearance of dry land out of the watery waste, to the reign of science as symbolised by the unsightly modern navigation light with its iron legs firmly planted within the angles of the remaining walls. St Rioc (or what other name you wish) was no remote person to whom a chapel was subsequently dedicated. That does not fit the commonsense picture at all. No, here was a man who dedicated his whole life to the service of those who stood in need of help as they drifted at the mercy of wind and tide; a man (or woman) who must have renounced even the very limited comforts of the communal life of the time in order to provide this outpost-lighthouse.

*Charcoal-burning*

The need is obvious, and that the spot is well chosen is shown by the siting of the present shipping light. But it is a little disturbing, as we look back down the slope by which we have laboriously climbed to our present state of civilisation, to see such men who clearly belong on a higher level than our own. It is like searching with a candle for someone living under neon lights. How came the Celts—the Barbarians of Cæsar—to produce St Rioc and his kind in an age that we associate with the superstitions and sacrificial cruelties of Druidism? But they did, and we can only wonder. If you doubt these words, then walk alone out over the seaweed-covered rocks at low tide and, climbing to the ragged tablecloth of grass, thrift and stonecrop, wait while a high tide laps almost to the sill of the empty doorway. Then you will learn what sort of company you are—to yourself; how many of your thoughts rise up from the depths of your own mind and how many merely pass within reach as they travel through the air from this newspaper, that broadcast, or the remark that So-and-so made recently. And while you wait for the water to flow and ebb, watching the bees cross from the mainland to search for honey amongst the sea-aster and the ivy that struggles to live in a corner of the stonework, you will have time to count the stones forming the lintel of the doorway. Finding that there are, taking both sides, twenty-eight flattish stones set edgeways on either side of two bigger blocks, you will have time to evolve various theories bearing on the number of days in the month. And these theories will have the great advantage that no one will be able to say yes or no, for your guess will be as good as theirs.

If it is a fine summer day you will come back, when the tide permits, straight for a cup of tea or a glass of beer, for the air is salt enough to build up a capital thirst. But if you have ventured when the south-west wind brings white-topped waves up the Channel, and makes you seek shelter behind the few remaining feet of wall, then you will return to toast the memory of a saint who once kept a light twinkling across these treacherous waters, and who just as surely kept a Brighter Light gleaming in an age of shadows. In its foundation and early history this chapel is only one of many, and being so much in ruin it does not impress us in the same way as the towering walls and arches of Tintern. The unique atmosphere of this spot lies in the continuity of purpose. Through all the centuries since the chapel was built, and perhaps even further back, it has been a guide point for travellers, though some will compare the cold efficiency of the present navigation light unfavourably with the human warmth that glowed with the light of nearly two thousand years ago.

In the days when a lonely watch was kept on this pile of rocks there was probably more need of a signpost to show where travellers bound for the Wye should turn aside from the main stream, for the slightest mist is enough to hide the coastline from the occupants of a boat the size of a coracle. In Roman times the Wye will have carried a considerable amount of traffic on the lower reaches. Ferries ran from the south side of the Severn, but their landing-place on the Forest shore has been the subject of much writing, sites being claimed above and below Beachley Point. In my opinion too little account is taken of the obvious advantages of making the journey by water as far as Chepstow, a trip which entails the rounding of this corner from Severn to Wye. I can speak from experience of the assistance given by St Rioc on such a voyage.

There is yet another phase which makes the story of this ruined chapel the story of Mankind—the rise of the military epoch. Just as military civilisations have, during historic times, overrun peaceful primitives, so the War Department has overrun Treacle Island. The footpath leading from the ferry was barb-wired and hung with forbidding notices. During the war this was, no doubt, quite necessary, but it is hard to find any justification for these relics when they are no longer observed. The warning notices remain, but the barbed wire has been shorn of its terror, and those who are so inclined wander to the limit of dry land or climb across the slippery seaweed. Is it possible that we have here an omen for the future : that the time will come when mass common-sense and the spirit of Twrog, Tecla or Rioc will prevail against the rule of Mars?

And that shows what a heap of stones can do.

There is only a small step between the churches and the

domestic buildings of earlier days, for the same mason would work on abbey, manor-house or barn, giving to each the imprint of his training and creative skill. Any distinction disappears altogether in at least two cases here, for at Flaxley and Woolaston we find buildings that have stepped from one class to the other with the years. Both are Norman, though if we are to listen to legend Woolaston has seniority.

Woolaston Grange, proclaiming in the name a monastic link, is hidden away at the end of a rough lane between the Chepstow road and the Severn. As I first saw it on a shimmering summer afternoon no place could have felt more sleepy. The birds were resting from their song, the road was far enough away for the hum of traffic to blend with the grasshopper chorus, the farmer rested in the shade of his barn. But it would be a mistake to assume that these quiet low-lying meadows have always been the undisputed home of cattle, curlews and salmon fishers, for here was a busy neighbourhood during at least three periods in the past with each phase leaving a mark in stone. Just a mile to the south-west is the Broad Stone, with a wordless message from the days before written history, silent witness of the passing Megalithic Men. Less than half a mile to the north-east, and safely hidden under eighteen inches or more of soil, are the foundations and the baths of a Roman villa, partly excavated before the war and covered again as the best means of preservation.

The farmstead at the Grange is very much like many others. Past and present mingle easily and unconsciously, with an old cowhouse adapted to modern requirements, a paraffin pump waiting to refuel tractors where carters once watered their horses, a bright new combine harvester in one corner (when I saw it) and a very old building in the other. The paint on the machine was aggressively fresh, while the little bellcote on the old building sagged dejectedly. But I left the modern marvel in all its red and yellow glory, so that I might hear the story of the chapel as it is murmured from deep-splayed windows, Perpendicular arches and skilfully moulded roof timbers. And the story is full of years and of changes, of Midnight Masses and fleeces of wool, of Latin chants and sacks of potatoes. At one stage a floor was put in to increase the storage space, but it cannot hide the original purpose of the building. Now the floor is falling, as if it had no wish to spoil the lines of the east window any longer. The roof has not lately had the meagre attention generally given to a barn, so that timber work which has been praised and lectured about as far away as Australia and America is rapidly decaying. While we can be guilty of such shameful treatment it is obvious that we have far too many historic buildings. The idea of selling our treasures for removal to America has always shocked me, but the plight of this Norman chapel makes me feel that I would rather know that it was being cared for in Milwaukee than see it fall to ruin on the spot where it was dedicated.

Time has carried away the history and the name of this church-barn, but one suggestion has much to recommend it—William of Normandy, in the course of subduing this country, came to the banks of the Severn opposite Woolaston. He found the river quite a big obstacle, just as other invaders had found, but he crossed it and built this chapel as a thankoffering. Archæologists do not all accept this explanation, but at least it is in line with the story of Battle Abbey, and with a very general custom of establishing a religious house, or hospital, near to a crossing. We need go no further than Gloucester for an example, and there once stood a chapel at the end of Chepstow Bridge, on our side. The Broad Stone gives added interest, suggesting that Duke William was using an old crossing place. If this simple explanation is right, then the chapel dates from very early post-Conquest days, for William lost little time in reaching the hunting grounds of Dene.

Flaxley Abbey, though it has undergone many changes, has a history that leaves little room for speculation. From the time of its foundation by Roger as a memorial to his father Milo, Earl of Hereford, it was a Cistercian House until the Dissolution. The site was well chosen in a fertile valley, with a stream to replenish the fishpond and work the iron forge. Anyone taking monastic vows would have difficulty in finding a more agreeable spot in which to retire from the world. Of the monastery that Roger built we know only the details of the vaulted refectory and the abbot's guestroom, for these alone are left, with the guestroom considerably altered. The rest of the buildings were demolished, but from the special patronage and the many visits of royalty we may assume that it fell in no way short of the general pattern of such establishments.

The Abbey would have been a good centre from which to hunt the Royal Forest, and this probably accounted for the special favour which was shown in many forms, ranging from grants of land, including the granges of Littledean, Boseley and Dymock, down to the 5s. offered to the High Altar by Elizabeth, wife of Henry VII. This action was to be heavily countermanded by her son at a later date! But no purpose will be served by yet another outburst on the rights and wrongs of the Reformation, so it will suffice to say that Flaxley fell into the hands of Sir William Kingston after the greater part had been razed. This may have some connection with the part Sir William played in a major operation on the neck of Anne Boleyn at about the same time.

Kingston caused a house to be built incorporating what remained of the monastery, but this was quite a modest affair if we may judge from the fact that the Kingstons do not appear to have used it as a residence, and that a considerable amount of material was hauled away to rebuild the Grange at Littledean. A certain amount of work in the Elizabethan style now adjoins the refectory, with access by a door which originally led into the cloisters. Later additions in various styles caused the house to grow in size without gaining anything in architectural character. This was at the hands of new owners, for the property was sold in 1648 to the brothers James and William Boevey, wealthy Dutch merchants and the ancestors of the present owner, Sir Lance Crawley-Boevey. But more destruction lay ahead, for a wing to the north of the present house was destroyed by fire in 1777. This had its compensations, however, for the ruined portion was not rebuilt; instead a new wing was added to form the front as we see it.

So it is that visitors will meet only a late eighteenth-century house, at first, with more suggestion of serene comfort than of an historic past. The new building was by John Leck in the Adam style, so fashionable then and so satisfying today. This work covers the old part so completely that it is a surprise to move, literally in three steps, from a well-proportioned Adam stairway to a Norman vaulted dining-hall. The abbot's guestroom has charm, chestnut roof timbers of outstanding workmanship and a trap-door leading into a priest-hole. And the financial east wind that threatens most of our more attractive houses has made Flaxley Abbey available to the public during the summer months.

By looking at Littledean Grange we shall be following up the story of Flaxley, and looking at some of the ruined abbey—in ruins again. Here, but for an unusual turn of fortune, should be one of the best houses in this whole area. It was never big, but the gaunt roofless walls now standing give clear indications of design and craftsmanship vastly superior to most that we shall find. The style is shown in two lovely Tudor arches, probably cut from stone that had previously taken Norman shape, for it has not the look of coming from a local quarry. The reason for the ruined state of this house is unusual, even in a land that so often spurns the conventions. While it was in the hands of the Kingston family it was let on lease for a period of 299 years without any undertaking as to repairs. Therefore, if any lessee now lives he cannot be held responsible, nor can the owner take any action until the lease expires. So the ivy-covered walls must go on crumbling until they revert to the owner in 1961.

That is the legal position, but after exploring the ruins in defiance of falling masonry and the law of trespass I am of opinion that circumstances have merely worked out the will of the Forest. A Tudor aristocrat must have looked out of place amongst the other buildings of the day around Littledean, and the Forest would have nothing to do with such a changeling, until the roof was ready to fall through the mouldering floors. Then a man more enterprising than the rest, or more desperate, ventured in where a door had fallen from hinges eaten away with rust, and the Grange became the home of his broody hens until the roof did fall in.

Brockweir has character, but not the character of a Forest village. At the first opportunity I shall walk amongst the old houses of Brockweir, past Townsend Farm, along the path towards Tintern, and all at midnight when the last day of April makes way for the first of May. And when I find a companion walking silently by my side I shall not know at once whether he is one of the old barge-masters who used to tie up alongside the quay, or whether St Breoc has come back on his festal day. For Brockweir is said to take its name as the landing-place of the Saint, just as surely as St Briavels is derived from the same name in its other spelling—St Brieuxville.

Brockweir has a strong link with the sea, for there were four quays near to the present bridge, one for each of the parishes that touched the river at this point. This does not mean that trade ever flourished here in a big way, rather it shows that inter-parish rivalry caused each to want its own river frontage in days when the easiest route to Chepstow was by river. In this way the little settlement developed some of the features of a port, with a window-on-the-world outlook, and quite a measure of prosperity. One result was that a number of seamen retired to St Briavels Common and the Hudnalls, and as recently as the last war the young men of this neighbourhood showed a marked preference for the sea when they joined the forces. What else could be expected from houses that look across the valley to such places as Botany Bay and Barbadoes Hill?

There is no church here, yet in several of the houses there are windows and other features that whisper strange stories to anyone who cares to pry amongst them. There are traces of Gothic windows looking ill at ease in a cottage that has no other indication of masonic skill, and neatly chamfered lintels where the builder had little enough ability with trowel and hammer. And the story I seem to hear these stones whisper is one of journeys by boat to the heap of stones that had been the living quarters of Tintern Abbey.

Our forefathers lived very much more under the influence of the Church than we do, but they were not slow to make use of material that might at any time become detached from church buildings. In one case a pulpit has been built into a cottage, and at Stowe the jambs and lintel of a Saxon chapel appear to have been moved from the Cistercian outpost, and now lead down to the cellar of the farmhouse, thus telling a clearer story than any restoration could.

The idea that the Forest was, in modern language, allergic to architects is supported by an encroachment of good buildings around Weston-under-Penyard. As already mentioned, this village lies near to that part of the boundary where the line was least decisive. In fact, the Forest limit was probably never enforced in this neighbourhood, while the influence of the bishops of Hereford was always felt. It is significant that we should find here very satisfying examples of building from the sixteenth century onwards. From amongst these two stand out.

Weston Hall, beside the road to Ross, would have no cause to quiver a barge-board in any company. G. M. Trevelyan tells us that "the Elizabethan English were in love with life, not with some theoretic shadow of life", and it is their spirit which shows everywhere in this masterpiece of the builders' art. Looking at the sweeping gable lines and the generous, welcoming arches we can see an age joyfully spreading its wings after shaking off the cocoon-like casing of fortifications. The architect had not yet appeared, so the master mason was free to express himself without repressions or inhibitions, unfettered by any rules, carried on by the urge to create a home that did not resemble a castle. This six-teenth-century wave of inspiration answered the call for family dwellings that would be neither fortresses nor communal halls, and like so many outcrops of creative genius it reached a peak in early youth, before it could be cramped and stiffened by rules and conventions.

The other example here will do more than any number of words to illustrate what I am trying to explain. The Rectory is a product of the next century, and a very pleasing example of the early Classical influence in domestic architecture, where con-trolled line and carefully calculated proportion give an air of well-ordered prosperity, with none of the earlier freedom. To say that one of these houses is better than the other would be nonsense; each is a good product of the time in which it was built, and their contrast shows the changed outlook of a century. The seventeenth century had, literally, gathered itself together after the unsophisticated rapture of the earlier phase. The plan came near to a solid square, while the riot of gables gave way to precisely balanced dormers. It is all to be seen in these two houses, and without leaving the road, but the full extent of standardisation that had arisen three hundred years ago was impressed on my mind as I walked the Rectory stairs. (I use the word walked because the Spacious Days gave us stairs that needed no climbing.) Just as soon as my hand grasped the rail my subconscious self began groping in the dusty attics of thirty years ago, bringing out odd scraps and pieces: a patterned carpet as background to ferns in a jardinière; a pony whinnying in the orchard as a violin spread its plaintive notes over a sunlit lawn. At first there seemed no reason for these half-forgotten images making a return to the screen, then I realised that both pictures were linked with the present by the touch of the oak rail under my hand. In two other houses, both built in the same period and style as this rectory, I had put my hand on a rail of the same shape, though one of those houses stands nearly two hundred miles from Weston-under-Penyard.

The impressions gathered at Weston-under-Penyard (and you will please forgive the satisfaction I get from repeating this name) are endorsed at Newent. Here is a town not of the Forest, though it stands astride the old boundary, and it is a town to which the Forest pattern never really applied. A visitor meeting Newent face to face will put it down as seventeenth-century, with a few earlier buildings. On looking around, however, he will see that the "Wren influence" only came as a sort of "face-lifting", for many of the buildings are much older than they appear at first glance. In many cases the precise brick frontage has been added to a bewildering and ageless mixture of stone and half-timber. Fortunately the rejuvenating process was far from complete, so that we still have delightful examples of oak beams and white plaster. The stonework, where it comes to the surface, is evidence of a geological "break" at no great distance, for red sandstone from the immediate neighbourhood stands side by side with Silurian sandstone from quarries at Cliffords' Mesne.

So much of Newent is interesting from an architectural viewpoint that it is not easy to single out buildings for particular attention. The "black-and-whites" cannot be missed, for they stand out in any street—even when the upper storey does not project over the pavement. The Bank House, in the unmistakable Wren pattern, is an imposing feature of High Street. But the present building must have replaced an earlier one, for we are told that Mr Nash (of the Old Glos. Bank) had to take his horse through the front door because there was no back entrance. It is also said that the same man secured the door by means of a bolt let down through the floor of his bedroom. Culver House and the Old Court are both brick-built, and make interesting contrasts with Bank House. Culver House stands four-square to Culver Street for all to see, but the Old Court is well hidden at the west end of the church. Behind the church is Spicers Croft, a small field leased by Sir John Winter (then Lord of the Manor) for 10,000 years. That was in 1657. Two hundred years later the field was sold, subject to the lease but without any known claimant, so it looks as if at least 9,800 years of that lease will be wasted.

The Town Hall (or Butter Cross) in Newent is the only such building in our area standing on legs. The other two, at Mitcheldean and Coleford, started life that way but had their lower parts enclosed in later life—Coleford some eighty years ago, and Mitcheldean quite recently. No doubt they are more useful now, but let us hope that no alterations will be made to Newent's timber-framed Hall. The only adjustment that is called for is the removal of a particularly unsightly telegraph pole standing near to the apse-like addition on one end. After all, with a perfectly good Posting House just round the corner there can be no great need of these new-fangled devices.

The architectural good taste of the period running roughly from mid-sixteenth to later seventeenth centuries crops up in a number of examples scattered mainly on the eastern side of this Forest country. But they are not confined to any district, as is shown by the bold red-brick front that was given to Hartsbarn, Longhope, and the wing added to the house at Gunns Mill, near Flaxley. These are improvements that must have come with a wave of prosperity and confidence (perhaps faith is a better word) in both farming and the other industries, for some of the houses carrying this imprint are situated in the towns, while others are farmhouses. Highnam comes first to mind in this connection, for in addition to several pleasant farmhouses it has the outstanding local example of the style that I have in mind. Highnam Court is, without doubt, the architect's greatest achievement within our boundaries—a fine house standing on an historic site.

The story of Highnam Court begins, for our purpose, before the Norman Conquest, when the owner took part in the murder of seven monks from the Abbey of Gloucester. The penalty for this crime brought the property into the hands of the Abbey, where it remained, as a grange, until the Dissolution. During the later part of this time, however, it was let by the abbots, though always with the reservation that it should be available for them as a retreat during times of plague. At the Dissolution it was acquired by the man who was then the tenant, passing by inheritance through three families until it was sold in 1837. But in the meantime there had been great happenings here during the Civil War.

At the time when Gloucester was in the storm-centre between King and Parliament Highnam Court was in the hands of a Roundhead named Cooke, but it must have fallen into Royalist control, for we are told that Colonel Massey attacked the house during the battle of Highnam (or Barber's Bridge) in March 1643. The building appears to have been completely destroyed by fire. The owner died not long after, and his son, Colonel William Cooke, had some difficulty about compensation owing to his Royalist leanings. But this was overcome by a change of coat (or headgear) on his part. The new Court was built before the Restoration, and in all its more pleasing aspects retains the character of that period. From the Cooke family the property passed by marriage to a member of the well-known Guise family. In this way it became linked with the Elmore estate and the barony, until it came into the hands of Thomas Gambier-Parry by the first sale in three hundred years.

The house is of brick with stone dressings, in the style so closely associated with Inigo Jones that the plans have been attributed to him. But it is more likely to be the work of one of his pupils. It is of two main storeys, with dormer windows above the eaves-line, and built on the half-H plan. Looking at the delightful mellowed brickwork today it is hard to believe that it was once covered by stucco, yet such was the case. Inside is a staircase which, by reason of the marks of fire it carries, has been put forward as a relic of the former building. But this is now said, on good authority, to belong to the Commonwealth period. The most remarkable feature here is the collection of Italian art, which really belongs to the Squire.

I have commented on the shortage of skilled woodwork in the buildings of the Forest, so it is only fair to mention two outstanding exceptions. Stears Farm, Newnham (also known as The Staure), has oak beams and panelling of exquisite quality in a most agreeable state of preservation. So good is it that preservation has the wrong descriptive sound. There can be few houses carrying their years and history with so much vigour and so little self-consciousness, from the progressive farming outside the door to the "priest-hole" tucked away in the attic.

At Purton the story is not so happy. Before the last war this hamlet was a scene of the most depressing desolation, and the process of decay has not been entirely arrested. Even the Manor House, for all its alleged association with Sir Walter Raleigh, was in no better state. In this house is one room, at least, which should be preserved amongst the nation's treasures, whereas it has been treated with little more respect than the Norman chapel at Woolaston Grange. Even a thick layer of hideous paint cannot hide the beauty of the oak, or the inscription over the fireplace— DTM 1618. This was obviously added after the house was built, and one story is that the letters stand for Dorothy Throck-Morton, who became Raleigh's wife, after a little unpleasantness with Queen Elizabeth. Some may not think the date supports this idea, for it is some years after their marriage and is, in fact, the year in which Raleigh was executed. But that need not dim our appreciation of the beautifully decorated plaster ceiling.

Another example of the carpenter's craft, though in quite a

different class, is the spire of the old church at Westbury. This
landmark still serves for the present church, though standing
apart by some fifty feet. The square stone tower base is of the
twelfth century, but the most remarkable feature is the spire with
its massive beams and silver-grey roofing shingles, for the whole
structure is of wood. An earlier set of shingles is said to have been
made from cider casks, but the present covering was cut in the
sawmills at Huntley.

If this chapter is inclined to be jerky and disjointed the fault
does lie, in some degree, with the material. At first glance there is
so little, but closer search reveals so much that should not be left
out. Even now we shall have to leave Poulton Court with no
more than an acknowledgment that its stones have a history; at
Box Farm we must stretch our arms wide to measure the thickness of the walls; at Bream we can do no more than admire the
handsome drip-stones of the New Inn. Longhope can show us a
house once belonging to a Duke of Kent, with the deeds by which
it passed out of his family, and a heraldic design on the wall.
Added to this, it is called Knap House, which may suggest a link
with Knepp (or Knap) Castle in Sussex. Also in Longhope is a
farmhouse of medium size having only one door to the outside world—surely a big drawback when unwelcome visitors
appear. And not far away is an inscription showing that Pound
House was rebuilt by an insurance company within a year of its
destruction by fire. So perhaps there was some good in the old
days.

Mitcheldean is the scene of our greatest building loss in recent
times; a loss that is intensified by the silent swiftness with which
it happened. One day the George Hotel stood here as one of our
most interesting features, the next—or so it seemed—there was
only a mutilated shadow of its former self.

It has even been claimed that this pin mill, and probably one-
time shot factory, was the most striking architectural work in all
this land between Severn and Wye. Consisting of two square
tower-like wings, three storeys high and joined by a recessive
middle portion, it strongly suggested Flemish origin. I have no
knowledge of the date of building, but it was probably in the

seventeenth century. No doubt there were excellent reasons for the removal of the upper parts last year, but the result is most unfortunate, and there is a temptation to wonder if there really was no practicable alternative. We are already familiar with the Jacobean and the Commercial Gothic styles, but this can only be described as Brewer's Reclamation.

Having wandered at random round the area let us finish up in the centre of the Forest, at Speech House, nominally the seat of local government. The original building on (or near) this site is as difficult to date as the various customs with which it is so closely associated. There has been a building here since very early times, but the King's Lodge was built in 1676, and the date is preserved on the lintel of a doorway. Since that time there has been at least one major operation—in the middle of last century—but this has not in any way interfered with the architectural style. In fact, it is very difficult to detect which is Restoration and which is only restoration. It is of local stone, which is very resistant to weathering, and has a lofty first floor and jutting eaves-line giving an expression of alert surprise.

Very naturally there has grown up a wealth of legend and story around this lodge. Quite a lot of it is not strictly accurate, but it provides an endless source of conversation in the lounge. Charles the Second and Nell Gwyn cross the stage, which need cause no surprise, even if we doubt the rumour that His Majesty planted the holly trees here with his own fair hand. The trees claiming the touch of this royal hand would, I am told, keep a whole-time forester busy for years. The outsize beds are a fact, though we may well question some of the stories told about them.

The meetings of the Verderers Court are, theoretically, held at the appointed times. In practice these meetings are very infrequent, and have been so for at least a century past. Perhaps this is as well, for there is almost no business to place before the Court, and there are many visitors hoping to lunch in the historic courtroom. It was a most fortunate event when Speech House became an hotel. The alternative would probably have been something in the nature of a museum, or offices for Forest administration. Our history is still too much alive to be put into a museum, and offices are now horribly abundant, while we are in need of commercial hospitality. And if there should be any delay in the dining-room (which I have not noticed), it will not be long enough to allow you to reach any solution of the mystery picture on the wall. I am thinking of the Wild Life scene of lady and gent with tablecloth, not the Still Life of man and gun.

# CHAPTER VI

# LOOKING ROUND WITH A HAMMER

"And God called the dry land Earth; and the gathering
together of the waters called he Seas: and God saw that it was
good."

*Genesis i*, 10

THIS land between Severn and Wye is a geologist's paradise,
worthy of treatment by an expert. Therein lies the weakness. That
I am no geologist you will very soon discover, but I do lay claim
to a very deep interest in all that belongs to the subject of this
book. An expert might be sorely tempted to take the subject
beyond the depth of the average reader, a danger to which I shall
not be exposed. My own observations convince me that geology
is not a popular subject for general consumption. As light recreation it probably falls rather far short of the serial in the Sunday
newspapers. Taken in small doses, however, it should not be
unbearable, so please try just one more page. Then, if you give up
the struggle, I will admit defeat. But please look upon geology as
an outdoor science, not a dry-as-dust subject found in books.

Just as the times which we choose to call historic carry the story
of Man written in the form of buildings, so the countless ages of
pre-history carry in the rocks the story of Nature's gigantic works.
If we accept the standing stones as buildings, Man can claim to
have written his story in this land for some three thousand years,
which may seem a long time until we compare it with the ages
that were needed to fashion the rocks. Experts have decided that
the oldest rocks which come to the surface here, a small area of
Silurian formation, are about 375 million years old. I say "about"
that age advisedly, for even the experts are not prepared to tie
themselves within a matter of a few million years either way. In
order to keep a sense of proportion it is well to remember that
Man only figures in the last million years.

So we may regard these rocks as a book with countless pages telling the story of the earth in their own way. The book may appear difficult to read at first, but scientists are interpreting fresh pages from it every day, and it has the advantage of being completely free from bias or propaganda, which can seldom be said of other history books. Another great feature is that while old documents are liable to fade and perish the story of the rocks is becoming clearer with every new research and discovery. Certainly very much change has been caused by weathering, but this is part of a natural process of development, and cannot be compared with loss of documentary evidence.

There can be few areas showing such a great variety of rocks within such a relatively small compass, and probably none where there are so many opportunities to read the story. The whole region is so dotted with shafts, quarries, cuttings, river banks and scowles that it is as if a great history book stood open, and with the leaves turned back ready for inspection. And it is not only in the quarrying and mining districts that these opportunities occur. Even in the quiet undulating red lands of Newent and Taynton there are high banks to some of the twisting lanes, giving a glimpse of what lies below the surface. Then, on Severn-side, the cliffs of Westbury, Newnham and Sedbury keep the lines vividly clear by the ceaseless undercutting of the tides.

As rocks are, in the main, covered by the layer of soil in which plants grow they might at first be regarded as of little importance in a survey as superficial as this. But they cannot be overlooked, even when they do not assert themselves with the boldness of the cliffs overhanging the Wye. Rocks have been described as the skeleton of a country; the bones of a landscape. They are all this, and more. For the bones only govern the shape of the body, whereas the rocks decide to a great extent what vegetation shall grow and what use man shall make of the land. In this area the rock formation is of particular importance because it has so largely controlled the industrial activities of the inhabitants. Deposits of iron and copper led to the building up of quite flourishing trades, while the hope of finding gold induced men to tunnel deeply under Wigpool Common. Let us look into some of these points in more detail, for it is well to be satisfied why, before we consider how.

First of all, rocks are the raw material from which the soil is formed; the main raw material, for there are other ingredients. If the earth's surface were flat, and there were no strong winds, the soil of any locality would be in a close and simple relationship to the underlying rock. This would be very nice and easy from that particular aspect, even if it had certain disadvantages! But with conditions as they are there is a very considerable movement of material from disintegrating rock. This may happen in a spectacular form, as in a landslide or a fall of cliff; it happens more quietly, but on an enormous scale, in every flooded river; it happens when frost and wind dislodge particles from the exposed surfaces of rocks. Always there is movement, downhill except where occasionally the wind chooses to carry the grains upwards. This movement results in a great deal of mixing of the rock material, so that the surface layer, or soil, is rarely the product of just one particular type of rock. But the underlying rock usually exerts a big influence on the soil above.

A factor of great importance is the dip, or angle at which the rocks lie, for, owing to various earth movements, they seldom remain horizontal. This obviously affects the slope of the land and the uses to which it can be put, but much more vitally it affects the direction in which the water will drain and the streams run. This question may be greatly complicated, as where the porous nature of the upper layer of rock allows the water to soak through to a lower layer which may not have the same slope (a geological unconformity).

The Thames is a fair example of a river that has followed the general rule and the prevailing slope of the rocks that form the foundations of England and Wales, while the Severn and Wye have been more wayward. Broadly speaking, these rocks slope downwards towards the east, and the Thames—except for a slight check where that river had to cut through the Chiltern Hills at the Goring Gap—follows that eastward slope. But while central and eastern England was comparatively quiet, the Forest of Dean and surrounding areas experienced foldings and fracturings that would have been disturbing in the extreme to Man, had they not happened so many millions of years before he arrived on the scene. And it is these upheavals, together with various raisings and lowerings of the land in relation to the sea, that give us the giddy meanderings and the outstanding beauty of the valley of the lower Wye; scenery which cannot be found on rivers further east. The folding of the rocks here causes the main streams to run towards the south-east, the ones flowing westwards into the Wye being short and swift as they plunge down the escarpment.

The other close relationship between rocks and scenery is clearly to be seen in those buildings which have been made from local material. This was the last feature to appear, for even when we include the stone monuments of Megalithic times as the earliest works of Man in this country, we are only scratching on the surface of time. This is also likely to be the first feature to disappear. For when we see Cornish housing units being carried to Hereford, while bricks from the eastern counties travel to South Wales, it is obvious that local character in building will not be preserved. Admittedly they often provide absolutely no clue to the stone of the district. Part of Stonehenge was carried from Pembroke, showing that even to the ancients one stone was not just like another. So it has continued, with stone for the building of churches and other works of special importance sometimes being carried considerable distances throughout all the ages of the masons' craft.

The result is that only the smaller houses and the farm buildings can be accepted as indicating the rock that lies near at hand. Broadly speaking, they will have been made from local material, with a fair sprinkling of exceptions that are too obvious to be deceptive.

That, then, is my defence, and if its ramblings have exceeded those of our two boundary rivers those ramblings have at least postponed the moment when we must quit generalities and face the more important details.

Given that the general inclination of the rocks is towards the west, and knowing that the hills do not continue to rise after the first ridges of May Hill and the Wigpool-Cinderford uplands, we may reasonably expect to find various layers of rock coming to the surface. They do, though their appearance is anything but regular owing to the wrinkles that age has given to the earth's crust. It is important to keep in mind that all the hills in this area are only the shortened remains of their former selves. No one can say how high they once stood, but it is certain that the tops have been very much lowered and the edges worn away by weathering. During millions of years this weathering has, in some cases, removed hundreds (even thousands) of feet, so that beds of the same rock which are now separated by several miles were at one time joined by a continuous arched layer. Some idea of the enormous extent of this upheaval and weathering can be gathered from the fact that the rocks now forming the mountains of North Wales were at one time covered by layers of Silurian rock, and Old Red Sandstone, and others, no doubt. These layers have been completely removed, to expose the older Cambrian formation.

Then comes the geologists' main joy—the fault. And no others get so much satisfaction out of their own faults! A fault is described as "a dislocation of the rocks, where one side has moved relatively to the other", and in view of the part these faults play in Forest scenery there need be no apology for bringing in the term. Several of these faults will be met with, and in one instance at least an example can be pointed out which gives a better idea than any amount of description.

Looking back through the history book of the rocks we find that the earliest page to which we can refer is number 375, or thereabouts, remembering that we number backwards in millions of years. Here we find Silurian rocks, belonging properly below the Old Red Sandstone (because they are older) and only coming to the surface on account of the very sharp folding of the rocks. Such folding encourages faulting and weathering, with the result that the whole thickness of Old Red Sandstone has been removed, together with any layers that may have existed above it, leaving the upturned pattern of the older rocks. In this way we get a glimpse of some 50 million years, plus an almost equal number of hammer-carrying enthusiasts who have come to read the story.

The top of May Hill, after losing several thousands of feet during all these ages, now consists of Llandovery Sandstone, first coming to the view of those travelling from the east in the small quarry just above the church at Huntley. From here it may be followed right across the hill as far as the old lime kiln at Aston Ingham. But if the hill consists mainly of sandstone, which is obvious to anyone who looks at the samples lying near the top, it may be something of a surprise to find the remains of lime kilns on the western slope. In this, as in many other things, the old folks knew what they were doing. Amongst some queer superstitions and customs they had few illusions as to the needs of the land and the problems of transport. They needed lime, and they did not intend to do more carrying than was necessary; therefore they spread the kilns over the area where the limestone could be found and carried the coal to the kilns. For three miles along this hillside a narrow outcrop of limestone has been quarried to an extent that must have caused quite a scar at the time. Now the kilns have fallen into disuse and ruin, while the diggings are overgrown with hazel and honeysuckle, but the limestone is marked by occasional yew trees standing like Nature's ranging rods on the line of soil which favours their growth. This is the Woolhope Limestone.

On the lower side of the Woolhope is a strip of grey rock of the Wenlock Shale type, nowhere more than two or three hundred yards wide, followed by a narrower band of Wenlock Limestone. A further layer of shale of the Ludlow type brings us to the fault that has allowed a glimpse of the union of Old Red with Silurian. By the grace of the Gloucestershire County Council (Highways Dept.) all who travel the Gloucester–Ross road can view the meeting place of the Silurian with the Devonian (Old Red) rocks without the trouble of leaving their cars. As the road approaches the railway bridge from the east a steep bank has been cut back on the south (left) side. Here the join is clearly visible after some years of weathering, for the soil that is being formed retains the characteristic colours, grey for the shale, red for the sand.

In saying good-bye to the oldest of our rocks I should mention that at the time when they were being formed the animal kingdom had not risen beyond the level of primitive fish, as is shown by the fossil remains in the rock. These are quite a move forward from the earliest forms of life found in the Cambrian formation.

The Old Red Sandstone, which by order of formation lies immediately above the Silurian, covers a large area round Dymock and to the west of Newent, then it runs through Newents Wood and on each side of May Hill, ending on the east side at Castle Hill Wood, while to the west it forms the north–south ridge of Breakheart Hill and Shapridge. It then extends through Flaxley and widens out to form the floor of the undulating country around Blakeney, Lydney and Purton. It also runs under the coalfield, to appear again on the slopes facing Monmouth and between Staunton and Tintern. The red, rather coarse-grained stone from this formation will readily be identified in many buildings.

It is in this red sandstone that fossilised amphibians first appear, which means that at the time of its formation the first air-breathing animals developed. It is, however, the colour that is of chief interest, a mellow red which may be found in many parts, particularly Devon from which it is named. The sand has been reddened by oxide of iron derived from the breaking down of other rocks. Decaying vegetable matter produces acids which remove this colour, so it has been concluded that there was very little plant life during the period. Later formations belonging to periods of plentiful plant growth sometimes have a red colour, such as the New Red Triassic rocks, but this is explained by the experts as due to the prevalence of arid conditions at the time and place of their formation. Not being in a position to argue with experts I will move up one layer, and forward some 50 million years to the next period, the Carboniferous layer.

The structure of the Coalfield has been described as a limestone saucer containing the coal-bearing rock. But mention of a saucer carries with it a suggestion of even smoothness that is noticeably lacking, and I would rather liken it to an old limestone trough, the edges of which have been chipped at many points, while the floor is far from level. This irregular trough of limestone rests upon the Old Red Sandstone, and in its turn holds the mixture of rocks that go to form the Coal Measures. On the east side it may be traced as an outcrop from north of Yorkley Slade, through Upper Soudley to Littledean, where it crosses the main road near the foot of the steep hill; then passing to the west of Mitcheldean (where it supplied material to a cement works situated just above the Stenders), and around the slopes of Wigpool Common to the west side of Euroclydon; thence along the edge of the hills to the west of Hope Mansell, until, as we might have guessed, it passes through Kiln Green, above Bishops Wood.

To anyone first taking an interest in this subject no area could be more helpful than the spur of hill on which stands Wigpool Common. At first sight a clear cross-section, such as the Garden Cliff near Westbury, may seem the ideal first stage. Certainly Garden Cliff is more spectacular, putting all it has in the window, but it does not give the same incentive or opportunity to follow up the course of the various layers. At Wigpool there is a sharper contrast between adjacent layers (as between Old Red Sandstone, Limestone and Conglomerate), and it is easy to trace the dip of the narrow limestone layer under the Coal Measures because it is visible all round the northern end. The natural breakaway of the hill, combined with very frequent small quarryings, will allow the novice to trace this without difficulty. And at several points on the east side where the quarries fail the limestone can still be traced by the yew trees. It has been said that these yews have grown from pegs used by iron-miners as steps to help them climb in and out of the workings. This I am very much inclined to doubt, for yew is not one of the easiest trees to grow from a cutting, and these yews are found even where there is no sign of digging. Having a strong preference for lime it seems only natural that yew trees should mark this stratum.

On the west side of the common, about a mile north of the road cutting at Euroclydon, is a quarry rather bigger than the rest, in which the uptilted layer of limestone and the overlying bed of Drybrook Sandstone are very clearly visible. And here can be seen an example of the red staining of the limestone by hæmatite. Quite near is a smaller quarry, long disused, where great blocks of stone lie in a disorder that suggests a giant's playground, with fantastically rooted trees climbing about amongst the boulders.

On the west side this limestone formation is much more spectacular, giving us the Coldwell Rocks and Symonds Yat Rock. It then withdraws from the Wye until we get to Winter's Leap and the precipitous cliffs between Lancaut and Chepstow. Across the river it is continued in the Trelleck plateau, and geologists tell us that there was no deep valley here until, by a gradual changing of levels, the Wye cut the channel that has become one of our top-line beauty spots. From this it will be clear that most of the scenic beauty of the lower Wye is due to this limestone which, owing to the presence of various compounds, has a colour-range from near-white to red. Without it there would be none of the caves that have yielded so many interesting finds, for the action of water on limestone is by far the most prolific cave-maker.

Almost a bird's-eye view of this coalfield area is seen from the Longhope–Monmouth road in the neighbourhood of Worral Hill. A wide irregular valley runs southwards, with Cannop Pond in the centre and the narrow gully through Lydney at the far end. The roof and chimneys of Speech House show through the leaves nearly two miles away standing on a ridge within the trough. But it is unwise to describe too closely the spot from which a particular view may be seen, for the clearing of one area and the rapid growth of conifers on another will play havoc with any such directions in a matter of two or three years.

It is in pockets of Crease Limestone, particularly on the east side of the area, that Forest iron has been found and worked for so many centuries. The name "scowle" given to the old workings is Gaelic, so it is safe to assume that mining started before Roman times. When the Roman way of life was withdrawn iron-mining fell into disuse, to be started again at an uncertain but very much later date. The industry fell away rapidly at the beginning of this century as the deposits near the surface were becoming worked out, and although the ore is of good quality the drainage of these small workings by pumping was an obstacle that could not be overcome economically.

The scowle holes can still be examined, though in some cases caution is needed because of the depth. The only information I have on this subject comes from a man who was an iron-miner in his youth and who has since been lowered into one of the scowles to rescue a goose. He assures me that he went down the length of two wagon ropes, found the goose on a ledge and went no further, though the hole went on beyond the light of his candle. So, in scientific language, we may say that "er goos down a vairish way, mind".

In addition to the cliff overlooking the Wye, examples of this limestone formation may be seen in the quarries at Drybrook, Lydbrook, Whitecroft, Bream and Tidenham, as well as at the Gloucestershire end of Brunel's tubular railway bridge over the Wye at Chepstow. In the Lydney neighbourhood the rim of the trough was not high enough to stop the rock of the Coal Measures flowing out and overlying it, so that there is a break in the normal sequence.

The bed of Millstone Grit which lies immediately above the limestone, forming part of the Coal Measures, consists of coarse-grained grit and shale, originally laid down in the form of a delta to some vast unknown river. It produces a poor type of soil, and is responsible for the inferior quality of much of the land, notably the Drybrook Sandstone. It should be kept in mind, however, that probably no region on earth has been so persistently worked and dug over for such a long period in the search for coal, iron and other metals. So the formation of soil from the rock has seldom proceeded in a natural way and the evidence of the surface layer should be treated with extreme caution.

The Forest Coalfield covers an area of about 22,000 acres in a rough heart-shape centred on Speech House and Parkend, being traced by the pits, large and small, even more readily than the limestone is indicated by the quarries. It will be noted that the area of the Coalfield is very much the same as that of the present-day Royal Forest. This is not coincidence, but the outcome of the planning which had necessity as its basis. The Coal Measures, being naturally the poorest soil, were of less value for agriculture, and there was less pressure for their disafforestation.

The Coal Measures are shown in diagrams as sloping gently to the centre of the saucer, but some idea of the sharpness of the rock-folding may be gathered from the fact that the greatest depth of this formation reaches at least 2,700 feet in some parts. As far as is known the maximum depth is around Speech House, and as the highest land in this neighbourhood is about 550 feet above sea level, it will be seen that the floor of the limestone trough goes some 2,200 feet below sea level.

As every schoolboy proverbially knows, coal is the product of forests of long ago—something like 280 million years ago in the opinion of geologists. But this coalfield needed more than the growth and decay of a single forest, for there are four main beds of coal, all now taking the general trough shape of the underlying rock, but separated by layers of sand deposit. These Coal Measures are a complex study in themselves, but for our purpose they consist of a layer of Millstone Grit, or Drybrook Sandstone, with a thickness of more than 600 feet in some places, overlaid by Pennant Grit in which the coal seams are situated. This Pennant Sandstone varies greatly in colour and texture according to conditions at the different times when it was laid down, but it is mainly grey or blue, and very resistant to weathering. Study of this rock can be started well outside the Forest, for it was used by the Romans as the blue constituent of their pavements at Chedworth and elsewhere, as well as in the more recent building of the Old Bailey (London), Cardiff Castle, Salisbury Barracks and Eastnor Castle. And it has been recommended for use in the proposed Severn Bridge.

The four coal seams represent four periods of luxuriant growth, divided by intervals when the whole area was completely under water. We are told that 15 feet of rotting vegetation go to make 1 foot of coal, so that the Coleford High Delf seam, with its 3–5 feet of coal, is the product of a layer of rotting plant matter 60 feet thick. There is now no exact counterpart of the forests that formed our coalfields, for in the course of evolution the plants of that period have become extinct, so it is impossible to study the process except from the results that are left to us. But even with the Giant Horsetail type of tree, and in swamp conditions that controlled the action of decay, the process must have gone on over a period of years that staggers the imagination. To most of us figures that run into millions mean very little—even when they appear in budgets.

There are several features adding to the interest and the intricacy of these rock formations. First there is the rather curious overlapping of the upper layer of the Coal Measures at several points, so that while the chronological order is applicable in the main, it has certain exceptions. The most noticeable of these lies between Soudley and Lydney where the intermediate layers of limestone and Drybrook Sandstone are completely submerged, bringing the Pennant Grit into direct contact with the Old Red Sandstone. The result of this can be detected in the scenery, for at all other points around the irregular rim of the Coalfield the outcropping limestone is inclined to cause a sharp variation in the contour (as is clearly seen above Littledean and Mitcheldean), whereas in the area mentioned there is a more rounded outline between the highlands and the vale.

Another important feature is the presence of a number of faults within the coal basin. These may have a most pleasing scenic effect, but they can cause a lot of trouble underground. Imagine that a seam of coal is being worked at a depth of 300 feet. It lies at a gentle slope and given that the pumps can deal with any incoming water, all is well. Then the fault is reached; the seam ends abruptly against a wall of rock; it continues at a level that may be many feet above or below that of the existing gallery. A mining engineer will, of course, be able to read the story of the rocks and estimate the new level. In fact, he has probably foreseen just what was going to happen, but if the fault has a big "throw" (that is the distance one side has moved in relation to the other), it may be quite impossible to continue the old workings, and a new shaft may have to be sunk. The chief fault in this area, at least in so far as it affects the surface, is one which runs roughly north–south through Miry Stock and Parkend. This gives us the ponds of the Cannop valley.

All through the Coalfield there is that most easily recognised of rocks, Conglomerate (or Puddingstone), so named from the mixture of pebbles embedded in the sand. This is the material of the Buckstone, the Suck Stone and the majority of the large boulders that do so much to dictate the uses to which a lot of the land shall be put. Quite apart from any question of fertility it is not a practical proposition to farm land strewn with boulders or which has large rock masses close to the surface. Forestry is the obvious answer on such land.

The Carboniferous Period did, literally, see big things happening. It was the experimental age of the earlier plants, the mosses and ferns. In the struggle to survive they developed the huge tree-mosses that played such a big part in coal formation. At the other end of the scale they adapted themselves to conditions which would not support anything but the most humble plants, and lived in the forms we know so well on damp walls, roofs, rocks and the bark of trees. The Calamites (a variety of today's Horse-tails) flourished until they reached a height of 80 feet before they fell into the swamplands. There was also the Lepidodendron, a huge tree-moss which staked everything on size in the fight to live. But it backed a loser and paid the penalty by fading out during the next rock-forming period. Many varieties of fern were present. Flowering plants were still a long way off, the plants of this time spreading by spores and by growth from the roots, though something in the nature of a cone was developing.

In the animal kingdom there was a marked tendency to crawl out of the water on to the shore. True amphibians (starting life in water and changing to air breathing) made great progress, thus bringing in the era of those great reptiles which have captured such a prominent place in our museums and adventure stories. At the opposite end were plant lice and snails.

So we pass to the next chapter, moving forward some hundred million years and eastward in direction to the Triassic formation. This is the Rhætic red marl that overlies the Old Red Sandstone in the north-eastern part of our area, its southern limit ending in a geological climax at Garden Cliff, Westbury, and in the Beachley peninsula. Here is certainly the most graphic passage in the rock story of the peninsula. Many of us may find the greatest difficulty in distinguishing between Wenlock and Magnesian limestones, but no one can fail to recognise the sandy beach that lies many feet below the present turf, and just about the same height above today's river level. The sand has been compressed under the weight of the upper deposits so that every ripple made by the tides of 150 million years ago is as clearly visible as when the last tide withdrew and the land surface was raised. Fresh sections of this beach are continually being uncovered as the river undercuts the cliff, for the red marl with its green-grey stripes offers little resistance. Even on the calmest day there is a steady patter of small fragments as they rattle down the rough surface. But the old beach is made of sterner stuff and stands out from the cliff in the form of a shelf until with its own weight it breaks off in great slabs. In this way there is always a possibility that some fossil or footprint may come to light after being buried for so long. The casts of sandworms look as though made yesterday and frozen; the fossilised shapes of many marine creatures are found embedded in the sandy layer; footprints of bigger game, including the Dinosaur, have been found, and so may be found again. A walk along this stretch of river shore always carries with it the possibility that something may turn up, even if it is only a young rabbit that has walked too near the edge, as happened to me recently.

Amongst the fragments of this old beach the children search for "gold" and their efforts are rewarded with pieces of rock on which is a shining substance having the general appearance of the precious metal. This is coprolite, varying in colour between copper and brass, and in near crystalline form. The fact that prosaic grown-ups have declared this to be the droppings of the reptiles of the period does not in any way detract from the children's pleasure.

Closely related to the Keuper Marl is the Keuper Sandstone. They both belong to the Triassic Period, and come under the broad title of New Red Sandstone. A wedge of this Keuper Red Sandstone divides the Old Red Sandstone from the Keuper Marl at Newent, with the southern point reaching the quarry above Huntley Church. At two points the limits of the red marl are made clear in local names, and although they lie outside our north-eastern boundary they are worth mentioning if only for the light they throw on the problems of place-names. At Redmarley and at Hartpury there are farms carrying the name Murrell's End. As both of them lie on roads which have no outlet it might be thought that they both, at some time, belonged to someone named Murrell. But when we see from the geological map that both farms stand at the edge of the marl there seems good enough reason to think that marl has been corrupted to Murrell—a very small step in our dialect.

On the east side this red marl is overlaid by Lias Clay of that same bed which forms so much of the floor of the Severn vale before it slopes down under the Cotswold Oolite. This clay influences the soil of parts of Churcham, Minsterworth and Westbury, showing as the upper layer in Garden Cliff, and appearing again in some quantity at Awre. A small amount occurs in Highnam, to the discomfiture of a mechanical excavator recently engaged in digging a trench beside Pipers Grove. The alternating layers of clay and stone-bearing marl made it necessary to use two machines of different type, within a small area. But the extent of clay is not great on this side of the Severn, which is fortunate, for the supply of men who can handle a clay farm successfully is limited.

Now we skip all the formations of about 100 million years, because if they existed here they have long since disappeared, and we come to the most recent, the alluvium (or river deposits) of the present age. My own opinion is that we have a collection of rocks sufficiently large to give all the variety that can be asked for in such a small area. By going further up the scale we should certainly get some very heavy clay.

The alluvial soil that is being spread over the lower riverside fields whenever the Severn is in flood is of interest for two main reasons. The first is the fertility that is brought from upstream by this means and distributed wherever the floodwaters come to comparative rest. This is of very considerable value to farmers whose land is liable to flood, for they gain much rich soil that has been lost from land higher up. And this is not the only source of nourishment in flood water. When the great floods of 1947 subsided more than one artificial manure store was found to contain only empty bags. The contents, being soluble, had been removed by the water!

The other feature of interest in this new soil lies in the clear illustration it provides that the process of rock formation is still going on. In time to come this layer of fine-grained sedimentary soil will be just another layer of rock, and geologists of the future will be eagerly searching for our footprints in the sand and mud which now form the Severn shore. And if you are inclined to think that the rate of alluvial deposit is too slow for words, go to the New Grounds at Slimbridge and, having come to terms with the Severn Wildfowl Trust and looked at the geese, take a look at the relative levels of the land inside and outside the flood wall. You will find that during the time that the bank has held the floods back there has been about 2 feet 6 inches of soil added on the river side by sedimentation. And we know that the land did not make up its mind to stay on that side of the river until the sixteenth century. This may not seem like hustling, but it compares quite favourably with all attempts to use glaciers as a means of transport.

This building-up process is less noticeable on the west side of the river because the banks are less liable to flood, being for the most part higher. To a lesser extent it is happening at Minsterworth and Lydney. The rate of deposit is even slower in the lower Wye valley, where the river has little scope for overflowing. When it does break the banks the narrowness of the valley keeps the water moving rapidly so that it does not have the same chance to leave sediment. Also, the Wye mostly flows through country of harder rock, where it is less likely to pick up a load of fine-grained material.

Tides play a big part in this process of sedimentation, as the salt water has the effect of causing the fine particles to run together (or flocculate). In this state they behave like heavier particles, and sink. This is largely responsible for the mud deposit that is normally associated with tideways and is carried on at a rate far in excess of that which would happen without this action of salt water.

I have tried to put this sequence simply on the broadest general

152

*Newent has an air of leisure*

principle of an upward slope from east to west, which is the rule in this country. Exceptions and faults there are, too numerous to go into, but two features must be mentioned as having a distinct influence on the scenery. The first is the complex alternation of Rhætic beds and alluvium that is met with on a journey from Lydney towards Chepstow. Here the valleys that have given the road such a switchback contour have cut through the upper layer of alluvium, thus bringing the red marl to the surface.

The other feature, in the same neighbourhood, is the extension and broadening of the carboniferous rocks in the south-west. The limestone trough is extended until it overhangs the Wye at Chepstow. Above this limestone is a widening of the Drybrook Sandstone, which accounts for the poor heathy soil of Tidenham Chase, especially the enclosures known as Parson's and Poor's Allotments.

A feature mentioned in most books dealing with the relationship of scenery and geology is the prehistoric "ox-bows" which have been formed by the Wye in the reach between Monmouth and Tintern. We are all familiar with the meanderings of a stream along the soft floor of a valley, and its habit of cutting away the outside of the bends until a loop is completely cut off. The process can be watched on the great bend of the Severn at Newnham, and the same thing happened at Redbrook when the Wye valley was, geologically speaking, middle-aged. This can be seen on a good contour map, and better still on the site. At one time the river turned sharply east just above the point where the Redbrook now enters; then, by an irregular loop passing through the spot where Newland now stands, it returned by the hollow in which the Valley Brook runs. From the fact that this loop now stands, in places, 400 feet above the present river level it is clear that the narrow neck was cut through in the earlier stages of the present valley formation.

There are signs of a much smaller loop below St Briavels, but the bow here is not more than 100 feet above today's river level, and therefore correspondingly later.

These two ox-bows explain the comparative straightness of the Wye between Monmouth and Tintern. But in doing so they call attention to the unusual character of this river below Goodrich.

11*                          153

*Come to St Tecla's Chapel*

Meanders or windings of this kind are typical of a river running through a broad valley on a soft floor. Here they occur in exactly opposite conditions, the river cutting a winding channel through limestone and sandstone rock when an easier course would seem to have been offered further west. The explanation must lie in successive liftings of the rocks, so that the river was able to cut out the present deep valley by a series of easy stages.

It may well be argued that the rock pattern of this or any other area can only be followed with a geological map, a lens and much close study, none of which forms part of the equipment of the ordinary visitor. As an answer to that argument let me give two routes across the Forest, pointing out the junctions of the various formations, so that anyone looking about them as they travel this way may decide for themselves whether there is anything in it all.

The first route will be by the main road from Gloucester to Monmouth, passing through Huntley, turning left for Longhope, and through Mitcheldean. Starting from Over Bridge there is a narrow belt of alluvium reaching no further than the point where the road comes down to field level from the railway bridge. This is followed by Lower Lias Clay until just over the crest of the small hill known locally as Beauchamp Pitch, rather more than two miles, where the soil shows a change to red marl. This New Red continues through Huntley to the beginning of the hill on which Little London stands, where the May Hill (Silurian) formation starts with a bed of Llandovery Sandstone. The upper part of this hill is made up of belts of Woolhope Limestone—Wenlock Shale—Wenlock Limestone, in that order, occupying about half a mile, followed by Ludlow Shale on the downward slope to the railway bridge at Longhope. Old Red Sandstone begins at the bridge, shows itself boldly in the quarry beside the road to Mitcheldean, and meets the Carboniferous Limestone at the crest of the hill near Plum Point. The limestone layer only reaches the surface for a width of about 400 yards, forming the rim of the trough in which the Coalfield rests, and then gives way to a narrow belt of Millstone Grit (Drybrook Sand) running along the top of the ridge. The beginning of the Coal Measures is marked by small pits on each side of the road, these being at the point where the coal seam comes to the surface.

The Coal Measures extend here to about their greatest width, more than seven miles, until, within about a furlong of the Staunton Long Stone, the Millstone Grit returns to the surface in a belt not more than 450 yards wide. Beyond this is the rim of the Carboniferous Limestone reaching to the far end of Staunton village, where it gives way to the Old Red Sandstone, which reaches to the Wye.

The other route is from Gloucester to Chepstow, and as it runs roughly along the line of the outcropping formations it is less varied. Also, it does not touch the Coalfield. The start again will be alluvium and Lower Lias, the latter stretching for about a mile and a half from the Highnam road junction. Here the clay changes to red marl for more than a mile, until a small patch of alluvium occurs by the riverside. Then there is a return to Lower Lias Clay until we reach the top of Wintles Hill, where a wide prospect of Severn comes into view, and the New Red formation returns until the road has climbed well up the hill towards Bledisloe.

Here—opposite Oaklands Park—is a return to Old Red Sandstone, lasting as far as Woolaston, though at several points at Lydney and Aylburton the alluvium comes very near to the road on the river side. The Old Red then falls away to the right, leaving the road on the red marl again, with alluvium still close at hand on the left. This continues as far as Tutshill, where (neglecting small patches of Dolomitic Conglomerate) the road runs on the Carboniferous Limestone right to Chepstow Bridge.

These are the bare bones upon which this peninsula is built; the framework on which Man has been carrying out his small-scale works for some four or five thousand years, for any earlier works have been levelled by Time's bulldozer. In that time he has completely changed the patchwork pattern of field and woodland, waste-heap and village, until the men who cut the thirteen grooves in the Queen's Stone at Huntsham would probably find little of the land they knew except a few surviving menhirs and the outline of hill and vale. But throughout all these changes the rocks have continued to dictate certain terms which have profoundly affected all that we see today. It is not too much to say that the rocks played the biggest part in preserving this forest as a great tract of woodland, for our Norman rulers, with all their passion for the chase, were by no means careless of the natural capabilities of the soil. That is why we find deer-parks, chases and forests, with very few exceptions, on the less fertile soil. Local dictators though the early nobility may have been, they had more sense than to till poor land and hunt game across fertile acres. Their good judgment is now apt to recoil on those of their descendants who still retain the family seats, for coal is seldom found under naturally rich soil—and certainly not the coal that can be got by opencast mining methods.

The effect of the geological formation on the industrial history of this region can be read in the industries of the present day. The coal deposits have played chief part, both in the value of their produce and in the effect on scenery. The iron mines come a close second, for though they are no longer worked the result of them is still with us in the shape of several small foundries, and in the wire and pin manufactories which originally came to the iron supplies, and have stayed with us even though they now use material from "foreign parts" across Severn and Wye.

Deposits of copper in the Redbrook neighbourhood were sufficient to start a thriving smelting trade, which had to import raw material when local supplies ran out. This trade has now gone, but without the incentive of copper there would probably be no tinplate works here today.

Gold often occurs in the upper layers of the Old Red Sandstone, though seldom in quantities that justify any attempt at mining. During the past six centuries, at least, there have been trial diggings, and at one time Taynton was regarded as a promising site. More recently a syndicate carried out considerable work around Wigpool Common, but the samples of ore were not of high enough quality to encourage a gold rush.

Our quarries tell their own story to all who travel this way.

In all this land between the rivers the unkindest soil is found where it arises from the Drybrook Sandstone, whether in the vicinity of the village from which the rock takes its name or on

Tidenham Chase. The most casual observer will notice the resemblance between the poor, heathy waste-land lying above Drybrook—towards the Wilderness—and at Poor's Allotments on Tidenham Chase. On the many patches where even ling and whortleberry do not grow the sandy soil lies bleached and lifeless, ready to be drifted by rain and wind. Where this land is in agricultural use it is, in many instances, a source of greater joy to the student of botany than to the struggling farmer. Pastures that are not treated very liberally will quickly become a carpet woven with sedge, crowfoot, daisies (large and small), cowslip, self-heal, yarrow, early purple orchis and dozens more, leaving the grasses and clovers to play a very small part. As arable it will not return the amount of the seed that has been sown unless generously treated.

The peak of natural fertility is found on the dark alluvial soil of the riverside fields, where the accumulated fertility of centuries may be called upon to yield a succession of heavy crops without any noticeable impoverishment. But as if to draw attention to the danger of generalisations, figures have recently been published showing a farm at Drybrook to have a production which, acre for acre, probably exceeds that of any other farm in the county. This does not disprove the statement that much of the soil within the Coal Measure formation is of poor quality. It means that the basic composition of the soil is only one factor in the farming business, with capital and management as the other partners. It means that the natural soil is acting as no more than the foundation upon which the farmer has built according to his own design. The lesson of this case is that only soil with rocks coming to the surface, or land covered by waste-heaps, or the small area of bog, can really be looked upon as outside the pale of productive agriculture—provided that economic conditions permit, and that there are men of the right type to farm it—which is not geology.

Next we are met by the fact that while the richest soil is found in the alluvium of the riverside, especially between Awre and Woolaston, the best farmers are, generally speaking, on the red soil to the north-east of our area. This will only be a paradox to those who are quite unfamiliar with farming practice, and the explanation is geological in part. Good farming seems to be indigenous in the Dymock–Ross area; the well-trimmed hedges and clean headlands of Weston-under-Penyard being regarded as the prerogative of Hereford, were it not that they are just as much in evidence in the Kempley–Dymock corner of Gloucestershire. This land is not of very high natural fertility, but it responds well to generous treatment, carrying almost any system of farming, a quality that does not belong to the deep, dark soil near the Severn. This latter type of land does not encourage arable farming, not because the crops will not grow, but on account of the difficulty of working such soft, bottomless land except in dry weather and at low tides. Much of this land is so near to sea level that it cannot drain when the river is being filled by high tides.

Farmers need to be practical men, so we will not dwell on the idea that they cultivate the red soil more thoroughly for the satisfaction they get out of seeing the colour of the freshly turned earth, but I do think that the weakness of the human element is in some degree responsible for the rough farming methods that are quite frequently met with on the most fertile land. Good soil and a soft climate have yielded an easier living than can be found in other situations, and in these conditions there is a tendency to work to the old saw, "God makes the grass grow greener while farmer be at his dinner."

And that is a very rough outline of the rocks coming to the surface in the King's Hunting Ground in Gloucestershire. Putting it together has greatly deepened my own interest in the subject until I am almost tempted to study the thing closely. But it is not with geology as a science that we are concerned, but rather to discover the link between the rocks, plant growth, land use and industry, with the bearing that they have all had on history. All these go hand in hand, and the picture would not be complete otherwise.

# Chapter VII

## LOOKING FOR COAL

"Pray don't put too many coals on the fire, Mary. It makes me
shiver when I think that in three hundred years we shall have none
left."

*Punch*, 25th April, 1868

IN reply to casual enquiry you will probably learn that a Free
Miner has the right to dig coal anywhere in the Forest of Dean.
This statement is broadly true, but at the same time it may give an
impression that is very wide of the mark. Since "time out of
mind" the Free Miner has enjoyed certain privileges which have,
in the course of centuries, come to be accepted as rights. This is in
line with the much more general custom of allowing all the
residents in a parish to collect wood for firing and house repairs
from the common land of that parish. Such collection of house-
bote and fire-bote was controlled by the lord of the manor for the
benefit of the whole community, because the well-being of everyone depended on a sharing of this common property. In the Forest
of Dean the King was in the position of lord of the manor, and for
all the severity of the Forest Laws the earlier kings had some
regard for the welfare of the people—while they did not interfere
with the deer.

To understand the growth of mining in this district it is
important to have in mind the change that has taken place in the
demand for coal. After the fuel crises of recent years, with coal
output figures coming so frequently into the news, it is difficult to
appreciate that coal was regarded as a second-rate fuel until the
seventeenth century. The fireplaces of our older houses show the
trend, those of the Tudor period obviously being designed for
wood fires, while the following century admitted coal as the leading means of house-warming. During the fourteenth and fifteenth
centuries there were frequent protests against the use of coal on

grounds that it was injurious to health, and these may well have
been justified in cases where the smoke had to find its way out
through the roof. In the course of repairs to old buildings there are
many cases of soot being found on roof beams that were subsequently hidden by ceilings, showing that coal had originally
been burned on open hearths. All this is just history now, but it
throws some light on the conditions in which people secured the
privilege. The coal they were allowed to dig—near the surface—
was a rather unpopular substitute fuel that would keep them from
taking the wood which provided cover for the deer.

Let us be clear on the definition of a Free Miner. He is a male
person, born in the Forest of Dean or Hundred of St Briavels, of
the age of twenty-one, having worked for a year and a day
underground in a coal or iron mine. Under an Act of the opening
years of Queen Victoria's reign it is necessary for application to
be made to the Deputy Gaveller for registration as a Free Miner,
and certificates of birth and employment are required. In this, as
in all matters concerned with mineral workings in the Royal
Forest, the Deputy Gaveller represents the Crown as absolute
owner of the land. The term "mineral workings" is broad, but for
practical purposes in this area it may be taken as covering coal,
iron and stone. The rights of the Free Miner cover digging of
coal and iron and the quarrying of stone, whereas the rights of the
Free Quarryman are confined to the quarrying of stone.

A comparison of the boundaries of the Royal Forest and of the
Hundred of St Briavels is interesting for the light it throws on the
planning of other days. Detailed information on the history of
these boundaries is given in a booklet printed and published by
C. E. Hart, which will be of great interest to those who wish to go
into the matter more closely. For our purpose the position is that
the Royal Forest contained most of the coal and quite a lot of the
iron, and the Hundred contained most of the miners. The two
areas run together over the greater part of the coalfield, but while
the Forest boundary was shaped to avoid the main centres of
population, the Hundred extends widely enough to include the
majority of homes that were likely to be closely concerned with
mining. This looks like very sound planning, for it would be

embarrassing to have the towns and villages undermined, and the boundary that put them outside the area of mining activity would have excluded most of the people, for English Bicknor, Staunton, Newland, St Briavels and Hewelsfield are all situated within the Hundred of St Briavels, but none of them comes within the boundary of the Royal Forest. Cinderford has become an exception to the broad rule, for the upper (and older) part lies outside, and it is only the growth of last century that has carried it into the area in which Free Miners may dig.

After this brief outline of the Free Miner and his territory we come to the very complex question of procedure. A great deal of well-intentioned nonsense has been written on this subject, so that anyone wishing to learn the details may easily be lead astray. Accounts picked up at random are inclined to be most confusing, and it was not until I approached the man who handles the business that I had any feeling of being on firm ground. But this is such an important feature of the Forest of Dean that accuracy is essential, even if it means the loss of a little glamour.

From quite early times the Royal Forest has been divided into sections, or gales. The name is probably taken from the same word which in the past meant a regular payment or rent, for a rent must be paid to the Crown for every gale during the time that it is held. These gales were reorganised, mapped and recorded by the Deputy Gaveller's office in 1841, and the volume containing the information is still in the office at Coleford, and is a real master-piece of penmanship. The names of some of the pits are altogether fascinating—Work of Hang Pit, Uncertainty Colliery, Pluck-penny, Catch Can, and Gentlemen Colliers' Colliery are among them, while the one called Dick's Ready Penny surely has a story behind it. The map shows that the gales vary greatly in size. This is due to the geological formation, large gales being of more use in the middle of the coalfield where the seams run at considerable depth, as they can only be worked by companies with capital for equipment. Around the outside edges of the limestone trough, and at other points where the coal comes to the surface, gales are of a size to suit the needs of individual miners or small partner-ships. It is on these gales that the Free Miner may dig; here he may exercise his ancient rights—if he can find the opportunity. Please do not go away with the idea that any Free Miner is entitled to take up a pick and start work where he likes.

Thinking for the moment only of the near-surface coal that can be worked single-handed or by a small number of men, the first step is registration, as already mentioned. Then the Free Miner must secure a gale, either by purchase from the holder or by award from the Deputy Gaveller. Awards are not made very frequently, because a gale forms part of the personal estate of the holder (subject to payment of rent) and is therefore generally passed from one to another. For certain reasons, such as non-payment of rent, a gale may be forfeited, or it may be surrendered, in either case returning to the Crown for re-award. This provides one of the opportunities for the Free Miner who is on the look-out for a gale. At one time notice of the gale being "in the market" was only posted in the Free Miners' room at the Coleford office, but this meant that a man must call there every day to be sure of missing nothing, so arrangements were made some years ago for notice to be given in the local press. For reasons that will become clear there are generally a large number of applicants whenever a gale is offered, and the method by which a decision is reached is interesting—and probably unique.

The only point at which the Deputy Gaveller stands aside is in the selection of the successful applicant from amongst a number. Should there be only one applicant he can proceed to make the award, but when there are a number he will arrange for the men to meet at Speech House to decide the matter amongst themselves. And though the Speech House is an hotel in the hands of a well-known firm, they hold it on the condition that it shall be available for such meetings. When the miners meet they appoint from amongst themselves chairman, secretary and treasurer for the business on hand, and then proceed to dispose of the gale by a process that is really no more than an auction. The applicants make offers according to their estimate of the value of the gale, and the name of the man making the highest offer will be given to the Deputy Gaveller so that he may make the award.

The reason why the Crown representative has not taken part in the allocation is that he is not concerned with the payment that is made at the Free Miners' meeting. Whatever price is offered and accepted at this stage is a matter only concerning the applicants, for the sum is divided amongst them. The only initial payment to the Crown is a fee of 5s. on award.

From this stage onwards there will be three parties concerned with all arrangements that are made: the Free Miner, the Forestry Commission and the Deputy Gaveller. A fourth party comes on the scene in the case of land that is privately occupied. The Commissioners, as the body responsible for the Royal Forest, must be consulted on any proposed workings; the occupier will be awarded compensation by the Deputy Gaveller for land that is put out of use by the operations; the Deputy Gaveller, in addition to approving the site and fixing compensation, is responsible for collecting rent for the gale and royalty on all coal dug. Subject to these conditions the Free Miner is what the name suggests.

Small workings, where the digging is more or less horizontal, are called levels, and every effort is made to ensure that water from the level will be able to drain away without pumping. In some cases the adit (which is the name given to such a tunnel) runs slightly uphill all the way to the coal-face, in others it is necessary to dig a special outlet for the water. The height of the adit will be governed by the thickness of the seam, for only the mechanised pits can afford to move much rock in order to make the passage more convenient. The roof must be propped as the adit is dug, and this is a big item of expense, for even larch (which is the favourite timber) does not last long in the damp air of the workings. This coalfield has the big advantage of being free from explosive gases, so that naked lights can be used. The memorial in Newland Church shows a miner carrying a candle held between his teeth, but small acetylene lamps are now in general use, though candles are met with.

In the small levels and pits the coal is generally hauled out by man-power in trucks running on light railway track, each one carrying about 5 cwt. This gives an impression of inefficiency to the outsider who may watch a man splash his way out of the adit, tip his load of coal, then wade back again to the coal-face with the returned empty. What this job must have been like before there were any rubber boots does not bear thinking about, and I cannot get away from the idea that quite a lot more mechanical power could be used with advantage even in the small undertakings. Some are using stationary engines, and a few still employ ponies, but without leaving the roadway a number of workings can be seen where everything is done by hand. It would be interesting to see comparative figures, but under a system so closely related to common rights no such figures will ever be available.

Free Mining is an extension of the more widespread common rights that apply to grazing and wood-gathering, but it has been organised, as already described, so that the worst features are cut out. There is no casual dipping into the common pocket, and competition is confined to the meeting at which bids are made. The unquestioned authority of the Crown, acting through the Deputy Gaveller, has a steadying effect on a system which might otherwise become chaotic. But there is one feature that appears to be contrary to the normal practice of common rights. The coal may be got by men who have absolutely no link with the Forest. The gale can only be awarded to a man (or men) with the necessary qualifications, but during the time that he rents that gale he is free to enter into a contract with any other party for the working of the mine. In fact, in a number of cases a Free Miner only comes upon the scene for the purpose of securing the gale for a party who is not qualified to apply on his own behalf.

There are two chief points at which friction is likely to occur. The first is soon met when the site of the working is chosen, if that site happens to lie on privately occupied land, and the second arises out of damage caused by the working. Both of these lead to a good deal of local ill-feeling, but both appear to be inseparable from the system. It is only natural that a farmer will feel intense annoyance when he finds that a level is to be opened in one of his fields. High words are often set free at this stage, and much local gossip may be put on the wing, but the choice of site is not entirely in the hands of the miner, as it must be approved and valued for compensation by the Deputy Gaveller. In practice the first shock and volley of words generally fall upon that official's assistant when he first goes to peg out the land, yet such is the degree of "civilising by government" that bullet-proof waistcoats are not generally worn. While a certain amount of annoyance is quite understandable in the circumstances, it should be kept in mind that anyone holding land within the Royal Forest knows (or should know) the position. It is not a case of being hit with a stick that had been hidden behind the back.

While the farmer has no legal grievance against the miner—when he has been compensated for the land actually put out of use—the system is far from satisfactory in its effect on food production. Quite a lot of land has been put out of agricultural use by this means, and the process continues. Admittedly the land overlying the coal is seldom of high natural fertility, but we have reached the stage when land can no longer be frittered away as in the past. Approaches have been made to the subject, but there seems no likelihood of any change in the foreseeable future. In fact, any alteration of this system would be quite illogical while much bigger areas of better land are being sacrificed to opencast workings.

It is only natural that there should be many claims for compensation arising out of mining activities. At the time of making the award of a gale arrangements are made covering the land occupied by the entrance to the level and the waste-heap, but further damage will often arise as the work proceeds. When the coal has been removed and the tunnel is no longer used the props will not be renewed, so the roof will fall in sooner or later. This causes a subsidence, or wrack on the surface, and the course of old workings can be traced in many places by these wracks. At first the wrack will have sharply broken edges, showing quite clearly what has happened, but these gradually become softened by weathering until the wrack looks much more like the result of shallow surface digging. In either state it will seriously affect the value of any field in which it may occur, and there should be no difficulty in imagining the feelings of an owner who sees one wall of his house quietly slipping into the subsidence. In such circumstances miners are generally very ready to take to the law. Indeed, there is probably no community more prone to legal action. This is unfortunate, for though the court may settle the amount of compensation payable, such actions do absolutely nothing towards promoting goodwill between neighbours.

Free Miners have been given first place because they are such an essential and peculiar feature of Dean Forest, but they produce only a small proportion of the coal mined in this area. In order to make the position clear (or as clear as lies within my power) it is necessary to go back to the rough limestone trough mentioned in an earlier chapter. This is the trough, or basin, into which the coalfield is folded, not as one seam of coal between two layers of rock, but three main beds each having more than one seam. A passable illustration of this could be given by laying three thick hearthrugs in a shallow trough, or sink, and trimming off the edges where they come above the margin of the trough. The cord on which the rug is built represents the coal seams, while the woollen body of the rug stands for the intervening layers of rock. In the centre of the trough the rugs will lie comparatively flat, while the sides will be folded in varying degrees. One defect in this illustration is that it takes no account of certain "faults" occurring within the coalfield, but as none of these have a throw of more than about 55 feet they would not be big enough to show on a model the size of our trough.

The hearthrug that went first into the trough represents the Trenchard Group, with a total thickness of about $4\frac{1}{2}$ feet of coal, in a rock bed varying between 50 and 400 feet. There are technical difficulties which make the working of this uneconomic at the present time.

The next layer (middle hearthrug) is the Pennant Group, carrying three seams of coal—Coleford High Delf, Whittington and Yorkley. The Coleford High Delf, which is the lowest and has a thickness of 3–5 feet, yields the great bulk of the coal produced in the Forest. In a number of places it overlies the Trenchard in such a way as to reach the edge of the trough in contact with the limestone. In such situations it is worked by Free Miners, and levels into this seam may be seen beside the road leading from Christchurch to Symonds Yat Rock, on the right side about half a mile before reaching the Rock, and again on the left side of the road climbing the hill above the Forest Church at Harry Hill, Drybrook. The Whittington and Yorkley seams have been worked in some places, but their thickness varies considerably, and they are not regarded as a likely source of much coal in the future. All the seams mentioned so far contain "steam" coal, which is in demand for forced-draught furnaces but of no use for open fires.

The upper layer (top hearthrug) is known as the Supra-Pennant Group, and contains as many as eight seams of coal in some places. But I would not attempt to describe them even if I could, beyond saying that they yield house-coal. Owing to the thickness of the Pennant Group this upper layer is widely separated from the rim of the coalfield, as is illustrated by the level beside the road between the Dilke Memorial Hospital and Foxes Bridge. The disused Lightmoor and New Fancy Collieries worked the coal in this layer for many years, as may be seen from the size of the waste-heaps they have built up. The slow growth of vegetation at New Fancy tells of the barren nature of the shale in which this coal is found.

From what has been said it should be apparent that the main source of coal is the Coleford High Delf seam, where it lies relatively flat and at a depth of anything up to 3,000 feet. On the east side, in the neighbourhood of Staple-edge Wood, there is a vertical fold of some 700 feet, but at other points the upward slope is usually more gentle.

In 1904 an Act amalgamated the small gales in the central part of the coalfield into six groups of sufficient size for the working of the deep coal, and it is as a result of this Act that we now have the six main pits—Cannop, Arthur & Edward, Princess Royal, Norchard, Eastern United and Northern United. But all these are run on lines that are so near to the practice in other collieries throughout the country that any description lies outside the scope of this book. Much more accurate information on the mining of coal in general can be found in books devoted to the subject.

Only at two points does the Free Mining system come into contact with the bigger collieries. The first is to do with the arrangements by which some shallow workings are operated by

individuals on the gales held by the big pits, and the other concerns royalties. It is one of the conditions of the amalgamation of
gales in the central area that the Free Miners shall receive some
share of the royalties from the output. It is this share-out that
forms the main feature of the annual rally held at the Speech
House. The amount to be paid out varies quite considerably,
sometimes being as little as a halfpenny a ton, and the number of
Free Miners claiming a share is around 1,200 at the present time.
From sundry comments overheard this year I gathered that the
sum received by each man was small, little more than a token, in
fact.

One question has probably been asked more than any other
during the past two or three years. What is the effect of nationalisation on an industry which has grown up so much under the
influence of custom and ancient usage? And the answer is a trifle
complicated. The Act of 1946 authorised the State to take over all
"Colliery Concerns", which is interpreted as meaning all companies and partnerships in existence when the Act came into force.
This means that all the main collieries, and any others included in
the description, are now worked by the National Coal Board.
Individuals are not taken over, so the Free Miner working his own
gale, or any individual who has acquired a gale through a Free
Miner, can say that he is in the same position as before. But while
the individual has not been nationalised he has been hobbled—at
least in theory—for he is not allowed to sell coal without a licence
from the Board. It can still be said that no genuine application for
a licence has been refused, but the very existence of such a condition makes it incorrect to say that nationalisation has not
touched the Free Miner. In practice nearly all the small men sell
their coal through the Board, but this is not the outcome of
nationalisation, as they have mostly used the central selling
organisation for the past twenty years.

The only other aspect of the coalfield that need concern us here
is the amount of coal still available and the likely life of the pits
and levels. Experts are unwilling to make any forecast, so I can do
no more than attempt to point out some of the difficulties tha
face a would-be prophet. The trend during the last two centuries

*An ill-advised rabbit*

is shown by the following figures of production, drawn from various sources including the local press:

| 1788 | 100,000 tons |
| 1851 | 300,000 ,, |
| 1898 | 1,150,000 ,, (peak) |
| 1907 | 1,000,000 ,, |
| 1908–9–10 (av.) | 900,000 ,, |
| 1949 | 750,000 ,, |

If we accept an estimated figure of 100,000,000 tons of coal in this coalfield it would look, at first glance, as though we need not deny ourselves an extra lump on the fire now and then. On the other hand we have been told that the larger pits may not be able to continue for more than about ten years. These two statements do not appear to rest happily on the same page until we appreciate the difference between total coal and available coal. A great deal of the 100,000,000 tons lies in the Whittington and Yorkley seams, which present great technical difficulties, and the vertical folds of the Coleford High Delf, which cannot be handled by any ordinary methods. There is also the Trenchard Group, which has not proved attractive so far.

In the first quarter of 1949 the nationalised collieries in Dean Forest showed a loss of £42,909, and this was at a time when the Board claimed a profit on their workings over the whole country. Each one of us is entitled to his own opinion of these figures in general, but there is no reason to doubt that our pits are below the average standard of the country when judged as economic production units. This does not reflect any discredit on the miners, as efficiency now depends to a great extent upon equipment, and it would be unreasonable to spend vast sums of money on pits that can only have a very limited life.

There are other technical questions that cause experts to be shy of forecasting. Under the National Coal Board a lot has been done in an attempt to assess the position, with the result that the figure already mentioned for total coal left in the Forest may be adjusted quite a lot—in either direction. Within the broad outline that has been given many irregularities are being found, and while these are

*Garden Cliff, Westbury-on-Severn*

not big when considered on the basis of a country-wide survey, they can upset mining calculations quite severely. For example, relatively small folds are being found where it had previously been thought that the seams ran horizontally, and in places a seam has been found to scatter as through some terrific impact in earlier earth movements. Such irregularities have done a lot to make the scenery beautiful, so we can only hope that mining surveyors have an eye for beauty.

Most of these problems do not concern the shallow workings, so that, all things considered, it seems likely that the present century may see the close-down of the deep workings, while the Free Miner continues to exercise the rights he has claimed for so many centuries.

CHAPTER VIII

## LOOKING FOR BIRDS, BEASTS AND FLOWERS

"The world is so full of a number of things,
I'm sure we should all be as happy as Kings."

R. L. STEVENSON

AT the cross-roads in the centre of a small town in the Forest an old man idly swished a bracken stem to drive off the flies. There is no need to identify the small town, much less the man; it is just a trifling incident, but at the same time it has a certain significance for it is an admission that even a long life does not carry with it immunity from the summer plague of flies. It is also symbolic, for the bracken with which Age was defending himself is almost synonymous with flies. Wherever it grows in quantity a particularly lean and hungry type of fly abounds. Over the wastelands and the sheep-turf these buzzing tormentors hold sway, but only for two or three months of summer, and they will not leave the open country for the house or the conifer plantation. Not that you will find much consolation in this knowledge when one of the pestering horde decides that life holds no joy for him unless he infests one particular square inch of your sweating forehead. Drive him away as often as you will; he returns with maddening accuracy to the same landing strip. But the reign of the fly is brief, so that they must not be allowed to occupy too much of the stage, and a rival is easy to find if you will follow these simple instructions.

Park the car, or bicycle, where it will cause no annoyance to passing traffic or the Commissioners of Forests; unhitch the picnic hamper and carry it into the shade of a pinewood; cast around for a spot where pine needles are waiting to take the place of spring cushions and a tree-trunk offers to support the back (but watch out for the gum that is liable to ooze therefrom); lean contentedly back and gaze at light fleecy clouds sauntering across a blue gap in the tree-tops. After about three minutes you will have reason to be thankful if the party consists only of those nearest and dearest to you; otherwise it is advisable to scatter as widely and rapidly as possible in search of seclusion in which to free oneself from a widespread infestation of ants. A well-trained army, this, according to modern standards, for they do not advance in a solid phalanx which could be dealt with at a single blow, but range far and wide in a well-organised attempt to cause maximum dislocation with a minimum of ant-power.

Perhaps it is unfair to start with these two creatures, especially when they are not included in the chapter title. But the heading is merely rhetorical, being intended to include everything that lives and there is so much on the credit side to go into this chapter that it seemed as well to deal straight away with the aspect that is sometimes put forward as a grievance; then it can be set aside without incurring a charge of making the picture brighter than the scene.

There are few, if indeed there are any, districts in the British Isles where such a variety of conditions are compressed into such a small area, and so it is reasonable to expect a correspondingly wide selection of wild life. Sites are offered from sea shore to near-mountain, on soils that vary from clay to millstone grit, by way of marl and limestone cliffs. And all in a climate favouring a wide range of plant life. Rainfall varies from an average of over 40 inches in the neighbourhood of Coleford and St Briavels to below 30 inches on the east side. Temperatures are essentially moderate, though there are days when such a word seems inapplicable to Ruardean Hill, May Hill and other such exposed situations.

Against the wide scope allowed by Nature we must take into account the influence exerted by Man. Forestry (in the modern sense), farming and mining have done much to alter the natural pattern. Even in the Highmeadow Ecological Reserve the picture will be prejudiced by the control of the animal population, for it would be quite unreasonable to allow such a pest as the grey squirrel to live here undisturbed, using the Reserve as a centre from which to infest surrounding woods, and squirrel-proof fencing is not a practical proposition, even if it is a possibility. One aspect, important in some areas, does not seriously affect us; that is the harmful effect of smoke and industrial fumes. This has a very adverse effect on vegetation, particularly conifers, in some parts of the country, but it is gratifying to know that the industry of the Denes does not noticeably interfere with farming or forestry in this way.

It is disappointing to find no red deer in a forest that was preserved for so long as their home, but there would certainly be no place here for them today. The last of the old brigade were destroyed just a hundred years ago, because, it was alleged, they presented too much temptation to the poacher. Against this may be set a widespread belief that mankind can, with few exceptions, be divided into poachers and non-poachers. If this is so, no appreciable good will have been done by removing one source of temptation, for the real dyed-in-the-wool poacher will always find something to poach. And on strictly moral grounds the taking of a rabbit, illegally, must be a crime just as hideous as taking deer. By coupling mathematics with morals we get an equation something like this:

$$1 \text{ crime} + 1 \text{ rabbit} = 1\tfrac{1}{2} \text{ lb. food} = 1 \text{ family for } 1 \text{ day}$$
$$1 \text{ crime} + 1 \text{ deer} = 100 \text{ lb. food} = 66 \text{ families for } 1 \text{ day}$$

therefore less crime will be needed to supply a given number of families for a given period when taken in terms of deer as compared with rabbits. For the prime motive of the poacher is normally the call of hunger, and in response to that call men have risked torture and death.

There may have been other reasons, however, for a later attempt was made to reintroduce the species, but it was given up when the harts were found guilty of attacking those who were unlucky enough to come within their reach at the wrong moment. These animals would certainly be an intolerable nuisance to modern forestry, for the damage they do to young trees is very considerable. In hard weather particularly they will eat young shoots and bark, and at the rutting season nothing is safe from their slashing horns.

For the protection of game, in the past, the most brutal

punishments were devised, including that of nailing the skin of the accused to a door. I use the term "accused" deliberately, because there was little need to prove guilt, and even less opportunity to establish innocence.

Vile as this undoubtedly was, it was further aggravated by the practice of making the punishment fit the criminal. Thus a villein (or serf) might lose his life for killing one of the King's deer, while a man of higher rank would only be deprived of 5s. This sounds incredible today, even when we adjust the fine to its present value of more than £20. The life of a villein then had a price based upon the man's value to the community. And if this all sounds very remote and mediæval we can compare it with a transaction of 1826, when a wife was sold for 30s., with a toll of 1s. being collected by way of official recognition. That was in Brighton.

In order to secure a conviction on a charge of poaching it was necessary for the offender to be taken in the manner, and this might be in any of four stages, all of which had colourful names. They consisted of "stable stand", or lying in wait for the deer; "dog draw", or chase by dogs; "bloody band", which was the cutting up of the carcase; and "back bear", or carrying the carcase.

In the time of Henry II the death penalty was done away with, it being decreed that "henceforth no man shall lose life or member for taking the King's deer". This was certainly a step forward. We may also assume that many offenders against the Forest Laws were, in fact, never sentenced. The more serious cases had to be referred by the Verderers Court to the Court of Eyre, which normally met in Gloucester, but the meetings of this court were infrequent, with intervals of as much as ten years, so that many of those arraigned by the Verderers are unlikely to have appeared before the higher court.

Manwood, a sixteenth-century authority on forest laws and procedure, gives a list of five beasts of the chase, which sounds quite impressive until it is found that the list is made up of hart, hind, hare, wild boar and wolf. Hart and hind both being red deer, and the wolf apparently never having been preserved for hunting, we are reduced to three, of which the hare was not really a beast of the forest. So we must be content with the red deer and the boar, the latter surviving until the time of Henry VII. Wolves were plentiful here all through Norman times, but it is not certain when they ceased to live in the Denes, for records only speak of their existence, and extermination is to be inferred by the absence of any reference.

By way of consolation we have fallow deer as a relic of the old Highmeadow estate. These pretty creatures are generally light brown with white spots, though individuals may vary to dark brown or white. The bucks have antlers which grow to a wide or palmate shape—unlike the other two deer. Their antlers are shed in late spring, and the fawns are born in early summer. While the fawns are young the herd will be scattered, coming together again in the autumn. They live mainly in the remotest part of the Highmeadow woods, though some are not infrequently seen in the neighbourhood of the Buck Stone and the Yat Rock.

There is persistent rumour of a solitary hart or hind now living on the east side of the Forest, particularly on the slopes of May Hill. It is said to be a night-raider of the gardens in that neighbourhood, but I have never seen any proof of this, and an agitated sheep can leave a "slot" very like that made by a deer. If any such creature does exist it is probably an escapee from Lydney, or other parkland.

So we claim no wild creature larger than the badger, and these, while by no means scarce, are not so numerous as on parts of the Cotswolds.

The change of policy under the Commissioners, as compared with that of William the Conqueror, had led to a change of outlook towards wild life. Economic timber production is now the important item, bringing the rabbit under a cloud, because of the damage he does to trees, at the same time placing the stoat and weasel on something of a pedestal. Foxes, too, are looked upon with official favour for the part they play in keeping down rabbits, but the Commissioners meet the inhabitants with a reward of 5s. a head for those destroyed. It is necessary to use great lengths of small-mesh wire fences to protect young plantations, but this is an expensive item in first cost and upkeep, for there are always some who will kick a hole in the wire to make a handy catching place.

Unless the fences are watched constantly they will soon be completely ineffective.

The depression of the 1930's did more than anything else to reduce the rabbit population, for lack of work gave the opportunity and the incentive to a form of poaching that does not incur heavy disapproval. It is, in fact, a very ill-advised rabbit that raises its head within the present limits of the Forest.

There is now no hunt centred on this district, and neighbouring packs, while they share the country on the east side, pay very little attention to the woodland area. Attempts have been made to pursue foxes amongst the trees, but scent is always very uncertain, particularly in the early part of the season. This may seem a little perplexing to those who have picked up the heavy odour of fox in the autumn woods, but the trail which is at the level of the human nose is of no use at all to a pack of hounds.

The hunting for which this region was famous was, of course, quite unlike the performance with which we are familiar today. Old drawings of the chase, while they convey no impression of life or movement, do show quite graphically what happened. They generally portray the unfortunate quarry closely pursued by a lean and hungry dog, while a man (or sometimes a woman) armed with a bow manages to shoot an arrow into its neck with the most commendable symmetry. The important point is that the deer were driven, being brought to a suitable spot where they could be shot or chased by dogs, according to the whim of the hunter.

It is easy to imagine the scene in some clearing, such as that where the Speech House now stands, with a large company of Foresters driving the animals so that they must pass close to the "tryst" where the royal party is waiting. Fences may have been put up to help the drive, and shelters of green boughs will protect the hunters from sun and rain. An old rhyme makes this clear, and also shows that hunting was no male monopoly, when a king promises his daughter:

> "Ye shall be set at such a tryst,
> As hert and hynde shall come to your fyst."

In such circumstances steep banks and old diggings need not present any great difficulties, whereas they could play havoc with a "field" such as disports itself across the pages of our Society press.

Today the only hunting carried on in much of this country is by local enterprise, and with far more democracy than tradition. But then it aims only at destroying foxes, without any idea of enriching the landscape with pink coats or well-groomed horses. First indication of this hunt comes in the form of a vague stirring in the air which grows imperceptibly into the combined din of human voices, rattles, yelping dogs, whistles, the occasional bray of a trumpet and the report of a gun. The party is led by a nucleus of local talent, well versed in the movements of all that flies or runs; next comes the main body of beaters and noise-makers, whose equipment comprises a vast amount of enthusiasm and energy. Then, well in the rear, trails the oldest inhabitant supported on two sticks. But if the membership is a little less exclusive than in some packs, there is no slackness in technique. The procedure consists of surrounding a likely copse or briar-patch, then turning in the dogs and turning on the full blast of vocal and instrumental persuasion. If the fox is at home he is left with the option of going to ground or making a bolt for it. Either way the odds are about level; a jolly Sunday morning is had by all; and the score card shows that a fox has considerably brighter prospects when chased by an organised pack.

Squirrels are of particular importance in a region devoted so largely to tree-growing. The red variety were numerous in the early part of this century, and no doubt caused a lot of damage. There is now a marked tendency to place the red squirrel nostalgically amongst the good things of yesterday, but such a view can only arise by comparison with the grey invaders. A writer before the "Grey Conquest" refers to the pretty red creatures as ". . . considered to do much damage . . . mischievous in young larch and fir plantations". He was right. Many a "stag-headed" conifer owes its deformity to the bite of a red squirrel, but with the establishment of the more villainous greys we are inclined to forget these bad marks. We often hear that the grey has driven away the red, though such is not the case here. In fact, the red squirrels very nearly disappeared just after the Great War. Disease is believed to be the cause, though the clear-felling of so much woodland probably played a part. This meant that the greys, after a slight delay in crossing the Severn, came into a land of endless opportunities and no competition. They spread amazingly, until the authorities became really alarmed, but there is no indication that they are likely to reach the numbers which, we are told, infested the land from which they came to us. In the State of Pennsylvania bounties were paid for the destruction of 640,000 and squirrel hunts in New York State dealt with as many as 2,000 a day.

My own impression is that the newcomers reached their peak in 1944-5, and have decreased since then, though whether by reason of the campaign waged against them, the severe winter of 1947 or by natural ebb and flow of animal life, I would not venture to suggest. The present high price of cartridges has had a depressing effect on the fight against this menace. Many people who are in a position to take up arms are quite unable to afford to shoot at a very elusive target on the present terms. One method of attack is with small-bore rifle and shot-gun. The rifle disturbs them from the drey, while the shot-gun comes into use when they bolt. In younger plantations a telescopic metal pole replaces the rifle. But it is a slow and expensive job either way.

During the last war the drive to reduce animal pests came to this area just as it came elsewhere, but conditions here were, in many ways, unlike those elsewhere. Throughout the Denes, where the absence of some amenities should have encouraged the spread of rats, these pests were less in evidence than would be expected. This was largely due to the fact that rat hunting, as a recreation, has a strong following. This has a very direct bearing on the balance of nature, and the changed interest of present-day youth to machine worship has contributed quite largely to the increase of certain birds and animals. But that is a big subject.

East of May Hill conditions may be described as "normal"; by which is meant that some game is still being preserved, the hunt cherishes a fair number of foxes, and rabbits meet only enough hazards to keep them fit and flourishing. In places they flourish magnificently, as in the case of a very deeply established bury on the top of a gently sloping marly bank at Highleadon. When the order went out for this to be ploughed local opinion said that the rabbits could not be exterminated, and someone suggested the only method would be to drive them out with tortoises, carrying lighted candles on their backs. This was a new idea to me, and was not tried. Two hundred traps were set, which gave a catch of 109, 84 and 76 on the first three nights. Trapping went on for a fortnight. In the following season twenty of these holes were open. A trap was laid in each one, and on the first night a 100 per cent catch was taken, but on the following night the luck changed with the arrival of gypsies. Next morning there were no rabbits, no traps and no gypsies.

The balance sheet of the badger had always presented difficulties. There is a wide range of debits and credits, and there was only very meagre information about these most interesting animals until an excellent book appeared last year. The number of badgers in this area is much greater than is generally reckoned, though they are not as plentiful here as on the Cotswolds. But their habits cause them to be overlooked, for only those with a good deal of enthusiasm will have the patience to watch for them. No direct evidence as to the killing of lambs or poultry has come to my notice here, which is a little surprising in view of the number of cases that have been proved beyond reasonable doubt on the other side of the Severn. But such cases should not be allowed to bring the whole family into disgrace, for they are exceptions, generally being the work of old badgers with bad habits, that may be due to loss of speed, or teeth.

On balance the badger is definitely beneficial. Their chief service to those who grow timber is in the destruction of young rabbits and chafer beetles, while fruitgrowers benefit by the destruction of wasp-nests. My opinion is that much of the annoyance caused by badgers rolling in corn crops is due to their taste for this delicacy. I have watched a badger dig a nest out of a hedge bank, eat the grubs with obvious relish (and tightly closed eyes), then roll in the standing straw to remove the infuriated wasps. One habit of the badger is, however, rather troublesome; that is a great determination in the matter of tracks. If one of these creatures is in the habit of going by a certain route no ordinary fence will stop him. He will make holes in stout wire netting rather than turn aside.

There are otters in the Forest, but who would care to estimate their numbers? Perhaps no creature is more difficult to observe, and few travel more widely. Their footprints can be found anywhere from the Severn mud to small streams up in the hills. A balcony view is sometimes offered from the Wye Valley road; they are very interested in the fish preserved at the Soudley Pools. For all that it is easy to spend a lot of time searching for them, and to be rewarded with no more than a whistle or a splash as they disappear. It is some months since I have seen one, but like all the other fishermen, they are probably telling each other what a rotten season it has been, with no water in the river—and that badly polluted.

Hares are found, just as might be expected, in the bigger fields from Westbury, right round the eastern side of our area, though never in great numbers. The Denes are no place for them, the country being too rough and the enclosures too small for any feeling of security. And there are too many interested onlookers.

In the animal kingdom size is no indication of importance, and those who grow trees are more concerned about voles and long-tailed field-mice than with some of the bigger creatures. These two small animals are vegetarians, and in favourable conditions they can increase at an astonishing rate. Unfortunately these conditions are often found in young plantations, with the result that small trees may be bitten right through, and even those which have reached the height of a man are not safe from "girdling". It is here that the natural enemies, buzzards, hawks, owls and weasels, play such an important part.

Any reference to snakes might well be omitted on the grounds that there is nothing unusual to report, for we have what may be regarded as a normal supply of adders and grass snakes. Instructions for distinguishing them are about as numerous and varied as advice on mushrooms—and as useful. In my travels around the Forest I have not heard of any recent case of snake-bite, and it was only recently that I met an adder—in the road. When examined closely these creatures are not a bit alike, but if in doubt, try a little caution first.

Birds are often more limited in their territory than are animals. In view of their greater mobility this may sound surprising, but it is true. The otter is a veritable gypsy by comparison with the stay-at-home robin, while swallows and martins, when their migration flight is over, settle down to an area in which a hare would feel cramped.

The explanation is primarily food supply, with nesting accommodation playing an important part. Our birds are, in the main, more restricted in menu than our animals. The otter and the fox are carnivorous, but within that limit their taste is not exacting and they will travel far to satisfy hunger. The badger and the grey squirrel will eat almost anything, and they are not difficult in choice of a housing site. The water vole, so unfortunately mis-named the water rat, is the only one coming to mind whose choice of food normally keeps him close to the rivers and ditches where flags and horsetails may be found. In the same way a number of our birds are restricted to a small feeding area during any particular season. But here we are lucky in having a geo-graphic range from mudbank to semi-moorland which lends itself to the accommodation of many species, and in being situated between east and west, where many casual visitors show them-selves at times.

A few birds are ubiquitous, and of these the most familiar are the chaffinch, blue-tit, crow and magpie. There are others, of course, but these four may be seen at any time from Severn shore to the pine trees on May Hill. There must be a strong case for naming the chaffinch as our commonest bird, for they are unobtrusively everywhere. The house sparrow likes a bit of life; the starling leaves no doubt of his presence as he travels in a chattering, bustling flock; the robin covers the whole area with a thin and carefully regulated system of territories; but the chaffinch will visit the town garden in twos or threes as happily as he will search for seeds after the threshing machine in great flocks. By the riverside they will hop in the shallow water, and on the highest and bleakest of our hills they will forage in small groups. But all these birds belong to the whole country and so, though they are no less interesting or important on that account, they must here give way to those species which have some special local significance; the ones that find in this area some conditions not to be found in all counties. So let us first examine those conditions.

Our most striking feature is undoubtedly the river with its ribbon of mud and salting. A narrow ribbon by comparison with some marshy estuaries, but enough to bring a very useful collection, mostly of winter visitors.

The next special area consists of the thick conifer plantations where the trees press so close together that bright midday brings only a lightening of the gloom to the bare ground with its carpet of needles. Nothing could be more marked than the contrast in bird life between these two environments. The birds of the shore are bright, noisy, impetuous, whereas in the thickness of the wood it is easy at first to imagine that nothing moves. Only as you watch and listen will you become aware of a host of soberly clad points of life, mostly fitting well to their background, often working singly or in pairs and announcing themselves in a subdued chorus of tiny chirps. There are bright and noisy birds, such as the jay and the woodpeckers, belonging to the woodlands, but they are associated more with open, broad-leaved or mixed woods than with conifer plantations.

The last region is the wind-swept hilltop, where a keen struggle is waged in silent watchfulness; silent except for the coarse voice of the crow, the petulant mewing of young buzzards and the scream of the evening swift. Here it is that the windhover lives true to his name and, if you are lucky, you may see the superb airmanship of the buzzard.

Having named the habitats from sea level upwards I should, perhaps, follow that order in mentioning the more noteworthy birds, but if you have enjoyed the sight of five buzzards floating majestically within a space of two hundred yards you will understand why I insist upon starting at the top. In all this area the only place where I have repeatedly—almost regularly—seen the buzzard is around the upper slopes of May Hill. This may be due in some degree to the fact that I have most opportunity there, but that can only apply to a very limited extent, because these great birds can be seen from a considerable distance, and I have rarely noticed them anywhere else in our Forest area, though there is good reason to think that a pair nested this season in the High-meadow Woods, near to the steep banks of the Wye. There appear to be two main reasons for their choice of May Hill as a nesting site: the extensive tract of high ground that is clear of trees, and the near-circular shape of the hill. The importance of this latter condition becomes obvious to anyone watching these birds as they fly.

The kestrel, which is plentiful here, will hover with quick wing-beat that is little more than a quiver, then stoop with all the speed of his streamlined body, or fly to a fresh hover with charac-teristically rapid wing movements. The buzzard, by contrast, is an aviator of studied leisure, using every air current to carry him on those enormous outspread wings. The wing shape tells the story: kestrel crescent-shaped and carried to single-feather points; the buzzard rounded and wide, with the ability to regulate the pitch of the primary flight feathers in a way that must cause aircraft designers to think furiously. It is this special feature that allows the buzzard to soar, without wing action, on the lightest air currents. No movement of bird, beast or reptile could be more efficient or leisurely, but it can only be used to the full where there is an upward movement of air, and for this no site could be better than a circular hill. Given these conditions there is no need for a weather vane. The buzzards will always choose the side facing directly into the wind.

In the spring of 1949 a pair of buzzards (and I absolutely refuse to call them "common" to distinguish them from the rough-legged variety) built their nest and reared three young ones in this neighbourhood, so that it was quite possible to see the family of five all within camera range. Unfortunately the opportunity and the camera never came into my hands at the same moment, but it is to be hoped that they will become more numerous—as they have done in the south-west during the past few years. In any area where much tree-planting is done there is probably no more useful ally. The diet consists mainly of young rabbits, rats, mice and voles, which is entirely satisfactory; small birds are not usually held in much esteem, which is another good feature; a liking for earthworms is rather surprising, but not of much importance either way, while a weakness for cockchafer beetles is most gratifying.

Field mice and voles are very troublesome to all who grow trees from seed. In the nineteenth century they went a long way towards ruining a scheme for replanting a large area of the Forest. This was trifling when compared with the plagues of these creatures that have from time to time infested the Continent, but in every case the natural enemies (especially buzzards, hawks and owls) have shown themselves to be much more effective than any system of trapping or poisoning. So let us hope that these birds will be protected as they deserve. The chief enemies at present are a pair of carrion crows, and the first indication of the buzzards being in the neighbourhood generally comes in the form of harsh cursing from these ill-tempered birds as they try to drive their opponents away. Attacks are pressed home most persistently, with the buzzards only swerving and looping to keep out of the way, for the buzzard's reluctance to hit back has given him the reputation of being a coward. But some observers say that he will, under enough provocation, even turn the tables on the raven. So I am hoping to see my particular friends tear into those crows.

At the opposite end of the scale is the tiny wren, with body so small that it seems nothing short of a miracle that he can live through frost and snow. Yet the dead bracken of winter carries a large population of wrens, even above the 900-foot line. But here, as elsewhere on downs and uplands, the main breeders are the larks and pipits, with a fair sprinkling of whitethroats, warblers and whinchats. By all accounts wheatears used to visit the Forest in considerable numbers, but they have been noticeably absent from the woodland areas in recent years. This may be in some degree due to a decrease in the extent of open waste-lands, for they are still found in suitable situations outside the National Forest Park. And where thistles seed there is always a fair chance of meeting the goldfinch and the linnet.

That useful bird with the unfortunate name, the hedge sparrow, appears to do something in the nature of a short seasonal migration up and down hill. During the winter they are not common on the high ground, but as the breeding season comes round they become plentiful. And on summer evenings swallows, martins and swifts will travel up from the valleys to hawk for insects on any high grassland. In this way they snatch a few extra minutes of feeding time, for they are still busy on the hill when the valley is in deep shadow, and the last journey home to the nest is often made in very dim light.

Before leaving the hilltops and the bracken I must sound one note of disappointment. The nightjar, bird of many names, and even more queer stories, has not come to my notice during the last two seasons. I hardly expect to see this fern-owl, for few birds are more difficult to find, but there is no mistaking the weird cry. In the summer nights of 1946-7 their sewing-machine-like call came almost continuously from the bracken round my house, though I never caught a glimpse of one. But if they should return the event will not go unheralded, even if it has to be forced on to the last page, for we can ill afford to lose a bird that is so interesting and so harmless. There appears to be absolutely no justification for the name "goat-sucker", while one alternative, fern-owl, is easily understood, as the bird spends much time in bracken and is not unlike an owl in shape or in his liking for the darkness.

Odd as it may sound, the hills are interesting on account of the birds that do not live there. In other words, there is a very definite limit to the territory of such common birds as the thrush, blackbird and house sparrow. But this limit is fixed by the use to which the land is put rather than by the height above the sea. For example, none of these birds were in the habit of visiting my garden, which stands on the edge of bracken and gorse at about 800 feet and had been completely neglected until four years ago. But on the other side of the hill, where houses and gardens stand side by side at the same height, they are plentiful. During the past year the field adjoining my garden has been ploughed and some clearing has been done in my garden. This season a pair of blackbirds have moved in, and thrushes are to be seen occasionally.

Obviously their food is more easily found amongst humans than in the great open spaces.

Rather more difficult to explain is the comparative absence of seagulls from the higher ground. This is not due to the height, for they can be seen in great flocks following the plough on Cotswold fields even at a thousand feet. Certainly we are not able to offer the big fields such as are plentiful across the Severn. Can it be that they do not like the disturbed air currents of this steep country, for the eye of memory pictures them wheeling and swooping over level ground rather than in steep valleys? If this is so we might expect a surfeit of those grubs and creeping things for which the seagulls hunt, but the balance is probably preserved by birds from the adjoining woodlands.

Those who are responsible for timber production in State Forests are well aware of the good work done by many birds, including the nuthatch, tree-creeper, the flycatchers and the tits. It is sufficiently appreciated that active steps are being taken to encourage them in Dean Forest. In a young plantation there is likely to be food for a considerable population of insect-eating birds, and it is here that they will serve the most useful purpose. There are, however, certain limiting factors, apart from food supply, which may keep the bird population below the number which would be most helpful to the trees. Water is of the greatest importance, but here we are well placed, for the whole area is so well watered by pond and stream that no part of our woodland can be considered out of reach of a natural supply.

Housing is another problem, for though there are ample branches from which the birds can sing, the nesting sites are limited, and we cannot expect summer visitors to settle, or residents to stay, if there is no suitable place in which they can build a nest. Collectively the birds of the woodland use a very wide range of sites, but taken individually they have quite definite likes and dislikes. The wood-warbler will not leave ground level; blue-tits like holes in trees or walls; long-tailed tits make their beautiful ball-like nests in bushes; tree-creepers prefer crevices in broken bark, but will sometimes be satisfied with an ivy-covered tree or wall; pied flycatchers look for holes in decayed trees;

woodpeckers make their own homes when given the right sort of tree; goldcrests hang their nests under the branches of conifers or yews. And so the list might go on, but these few are sufficient to illustrate the needs of a mixed population.

All the birds just mentioned, and many others with equally varied tastes in nesting sites, are beneficial in woods on account of the insects they eat, so it is important that they should find accommodation. Those with ideas like the wood warbler will have little difficulty in placing their nests amongst the undergrowth of young plantations or in rough banks; goldcrests need never be short of a branch from which to hang their tiny homes; wood-peckers will provide their own diggings where their food is to be found; but the others may not find the right spot in well-managed plantations. The sort of trees that appeal to the blue-tits, tree-creepers, nuthatches and pied flycatchers are usually just the ones that the timber merchant does not want, and although they provide nesting sites they also form a breeding ground for many of the insects that damage timber.

The felling of trees in the last war and the routine removal of those which are dead or diseased has greatly reduced the sites available to these birds, which is one reason for the provision of nesting boxes. Another reason is that these boxes make it possible to watch and record the movement of certain species with much more accuracy. And because they are being watched by experts in this area I will not mention the exact locality. It has been said that the return of pied flycatchers as a nesting species is due to the pro-vision of these boxes. This may be correct, but it is well to bear in mind that the arrival of the boxes coincided very closely with the clearing away of a number of likely sites, and with a stepping-up of observation, so it would be rash to say that there were no pied flycatchers here before the boxes were introduced.

There is competition for the tenancy of these nesting boxes, and the records will show a number of domestic tragedies. In several cases great-tits have built their nests and laid some eggs, but later inspection has shown a pied flycatcher to be established. Closer investigation has discovered the first nest and eggs to be under that of the flycatcher. To me this suggests the presence of a third party as villain, for the great-tit is not the sort to yield to any bird of his own size.

With the exception of those noisy natives of the more open stretches of forest such as jays and magpies, the woodland birds are not conspicuous. This is not due to nervousness, for they appear to be very largely indifferent to the presence of humans. It is probably because they are not subject to much persecution, and it is noticeable that many of them, particularly the wren, have a well-developed curiosity. Many times, when pausing under a tree to eat sandwiches, a wren has made a deliberate journey to get a good look at me—scolding most of the time, though it was not the nesting season. It is only by standing quite still, preferably against the trunk of a tree, that it is possible to watch these smaller birds. The tits and goldcrests are with us all the year (though the goldcrests have a complex system of migration, many of them are resident), and to me there are few sights or sounds more charming than those provided by a flock of these restless creatures making their way through the trees in a thick conifer wood. The tits frequently hunt in mixed flocks, though long tails are not generally included in the mixture, but goldcrests are less sociable. In either case the first news of a flock comes in the form of a distant confusion of twitterings, which gradually becomes clearer—like the rendering of the Song of the Volga Boatmen—until they reach a climax and fade away again into the distance.

The redstart would qualify for the title "Robin of the Woods" were it not that the robin is just as much in evidence in the more open woodland as in the garden. These two birds are very much alike in movement and general behaviour. Their feeding habits also have a good deal in common, and it is probably on this account that they appear to avoid much overlapping of territories —or such is my impression. I am of opinion that the black redstart nests here, though this has been declared unlikely. But it is these unlikelies that give added interest, and I shall watch the "suspected area" very carefully next season.

There are many other birds of this mixed woodland and open country that will be met with by those who look for them but which there is no space to discuss in detail. Crossbills may drop fragments of larch cones on your head if you stand quietly under these trees; siskins are not uncommon, living mainly amongst conifers during the nesting season, but moving to beeches and alders when mast and cones are ripe; tree-pipits are summer visitors, preferring the outskirts and seldom venturing deep into the plantations. And last among this group of birds is the nightingale, patron of bush and coppice rather than high wood. There used to be an idea that nightingales do not cross the Severn, but there is no truth in this. They visit us each summer, though not in large numbers, and the likeliest places in which to hear them at most times of the day and night during their short season are around Beauchamp Pitch, between Highnam and Churcham, and in the Wye Valley below St Briavels.

Many people express surprise on hearing that the nightingale sings during the greater part of the day. This is due, in part, to the very sombre colouring, and to the perch from which he sings being situated, more often than not, near the centre of a bush. But anyone who really knows the song will have no difficulty in identifying it amongst the daily chorus.

The birds of the riverside differ very widely in most respects from those of the other regions—if we overlook the jays and magpies for the moment. The ducks, sea-birds and waders are either brightly dressed, noisy or spectacular; sometimes all three. Another distinction is that many of them nest on remote, rocky cliffs in other parts of the country, or abroad, so that they are present in greatest numbers during the winter. This is fortunate to the extent that it provides interest at a season when other wild life is at a low ebb, but those who have waited and watched on any of our river estuaries in winter will readily understand that there are distinct drawbacks. No coldness is quite as penetrating as the damp mists of the river in January.

We can lay very little claim to the various geese visiting the New Grounds across the Severn, for they seldom set foot on this shore, though we hear them fly over at the times of migration. There are not enough open meadows for them, and those we have are rather too carefully watched. The only place where I have seen white-fronts and brents is between Westbury Hall and the railway line, but they do sometimes make a foraging expedition further down. Their season, like that of most winter visitors, is from about mid-October to mid-March.

None of the gulls breed here, though all of them may be seen as winter visitors or in passage. The black-headed and lesser black-backed usually leave a few young birds here through the summer. Those who do not know the gulls should be very wary of their names, for they can be misleading. The common gull is much less plentiful in these parts than the black-headed or the lesser black-backed, and the black-headed gulls are only seen wearing the dark head feathers for a very short time before the spring departure for the nesting grounds. And when they return in late summer the distinguishing feature is gone again. The kittiwake, razorbill, great skua and guillemot are occasional visitors, and the cormorant, as mentioned elsewhere, is a familiar sight on the Severn. The gannet, Manx shearwater and storm petrel have all been recorded, but I am not aware of having seen any of them here. Amongst other winter visitors there is a reasonable chance of seeing the whimbrel, jack-snipe, knot, dunlin, sanderling, curlew-sandpiper and green sandpiper.

The curlew and lapwing stay with us all through the year, and their choice of nesting site is very wide, ranging from wet Severn-side meadows to open fields and rough heaths. Woodcock and snipe also nest here, but while they have many features in common their feeding habits differ, for the snipe will come down to the river, but the woodcock will seldom leave the margin of the wood.

Ducks, again, are more numerous in winter, when we can fairly hope to see the teal, wigeon, shoveler and tufted duck. Pintails and pochards sometimes look in as they pass, but only the mallard and the sheld-duck stay with us all the year. Even this is, apparently, not quite accurate, for the latest news tells of the migration of many sheld-ducks just after midsummer. It seems that they go on an extended picnic to the Heligoland Bight, leaving the youngsters in large batches, watched over by a few adults. It has often been noted that broods of this species do join forces, for groups of mixed ages numbering fifty or more have been seen.

The linking of this with the short migration of the parents is recent, and still the purpose of the summer trip is not understood. These beautiful and interesting ducks nest in fair numbers along the lower Severn, though it must be admitted that they generally choose the far bank.

Mallards live in flocks on both our rivers during the autumn and winter, and from the fact that they seem to be equally happy on the Severn tideway or in the shade of the Yat Rock it is clear that they take a wide range of food. A quiet spot out of reach of stalking guns is their chief requirement, which is not surprising, yet as soon as they divide up for the nesting season much of this shyness disappears. The caution remains, but they will find sites on ponds quite near to dwellings and even main roads.

Amongst the more attractive birds so far overlooked are the woodpeckers (all three), pied wagtails, dippers, kingfishers and ravens. And at the moment of writing I can see from my window a perfect illustration of Dignity and Impudence. Two small birds are mobbing a buzzard high up over the valley. They are too far away for certain identification, but they fly like martins.

The listing of items, whether of the plant or animal kingdom, to be found in any locality shows a good deal of recklessness on the part of the writer, and may prove a very mixed blessing to the reader. It may encourage those who search, but it can cause disappointment to those with limited opportunities, such as a summer holiday. Nature's procession goes on throughout the year, and though spring and early summer bring the biggest display, the visitor who comes to see us only in May and June will miss a lot. I can tell you that lilies of the valley may be found in flower at The Slaughter in May, and that June is the time to look for Solomon's seal near Aylburton, but no such easy directions can be given for birds, animals and other moving creatures. Also, it is important to keep in mind that the situation is never static. The species declared absent today may put in an appearance at any time. This has happened quite recently in the case of the Death's Head moth.

I know a bank where the wild thyme blows—and because a ridge of limestone runs along its crest, that bank is strewn with rock roses, with early purple orchis in plenty and an occasional bee orchis, if you care to search. Wild roses and travellers' joy grow thickly, with privet making the air sickly-sweet at mid-summer. These things are certain, but when I say that the marbled white butterfly, the chalk-hill blue, ringlets and hedge browns all come here when the sun is shining you may have to accept my word, for any of them may not be there when you call.

There are many rules by which to ensure a view of this creature or that. Rabbits come out to feed before or after rain; foxes come home at dawn; hawks raid the pheasant-rearing grounds around 12 and 5 o'clock; if a badger does not come out, in summer, before the last bird-song he will stay in for the night; the move-ments of fish are an open book, to judge by some writings on the subject. And with all this knowledge we shall still have to rely largely on luck. In a five-mile car ride at dusk in the first week in September I noted the following: 1 pair curlew, 1 tawny owl, 1 little owl, black-headed and lesser black-backed gulls, 2 sand-pipers, 1 heron, 1 badger crossing the road, several pipistrelles and 1 large noctule bat, rabbits *ad lib*. Another time a carefully planned walk will discover only the rabbits.

The same conditions that control the bird population apply in an even greater degree to plant life. Plants, being fixed (except in the dispersal of seed) and feeding directly from the soil, are more severely controlled by situation and soil. But fortunately this peninsula is able to supply accommodation to suit a remarkably wide range of plants, from the seaweed growing so luxuriantly around St Tecla's Chapel to the shy little sundew, catching flies in one or two "quabb holes" at the 900-foot level. The woodlands provide shelter for some of the plants that will not venture too boldly into the open; the cliffs, particularly those of limestone, give natural rockery settings which would make absolutely no appeal to the more luxuriant growth of the vale. Patches of bog are still to be found, though the draining and ploughing of recent years have reduced them considerably.

According to the *Gloucestershire Flora*—that great work pub-lished in 1948—the county has 1,039 native plants, out of a total of 2,369 for the whole of Great Britain. This figure, which does not include subspecies and varieties, compares very favourably with Monmouth (791) and Hereford (821). A number of these species have, unfortunately, become extinct in the county since the record was compiled, so we may take a round figure of 1,000 species, of which 900 have been found in the Severn–Wye peninsula. Somewhere about 50 species choose the west side of the Severn only, but 35 of these are brambles which will make a stronger appeal to the specialist than to the general observer.

The comparatively equal distribution on each side of the Severn is due in no small degree to the recurrence of the Coal Measure formation to the north of Bristol, for a considerable number of plants on the county list are found only in these coal-field areas. The limestone formation is also repeated in the Avon Gorge, but here west loses to east, for there are several plants peculiar to the cliffs of Bristol, while the Wye rocks have nothing all their own.

Backhanded though it may appear, I think it may be useful to mention a few well-known plants that are not found wild in this district. These include fritillary, purple milk vetch, pellitory of the wall, berberis and the red, broad-leaved, green-flowered and violet helleborines. Woad, once so much used by our ancestors, used to be found near the High Beeches, but it has now retreated to the Tewkesbury area.

On the credit side of the account we may claim a walk-over on sundews, as all three have been recorded here. It must be admitted that the oblong-leaved and the great sundew have not been seen recently and may have disappeared, but the round-leaved species still grows here, though it is in danger, as will be mentioned later. Others favouring this area are the intermediate enchanter's night-shade, three or four species of hawk's-beard, woody chickweed and the purple ramping fumitory (unless it has died out very recently). Streaked crane's-bill will have none of east Gloucestershire and is rare on this side, being reported only in three instances.

The list of plants gets quite a lot of help from the tide-washed lower reaches of Wye and Severn. Here many plants such as sea purslane and sea trefoil find conditions to their liking. The rock sea-sand spurrey is even more choosey, growing only on the Wye estuary.

Rivers, as our earliest channels of trade, are the most likely landing places for plants coming in from abroad. However welcome these may be, and though they may have "come with the Conqueror", they remain aliens to the botanist. This often causes difficulty, as the wanderer by the Wye will find if he wishes to identify the handsome pink-flowered plant with the tall angular stem which may be found growing profusely beside the Wye above Brockweir. This plant is probably a stray from cultivation rather than from commerce, for it is also found on the Chelt, where no ships pass. It is the Indian balsam (*Impatiens glandulifera*), which, as an immigrant, does not appear in many text-books. The same applies to monkey-flower (*Mimulus langsdorfii*) and a tiny veronica (*V. filiformis*). The surprising tree mallow, with stem as thick as a blacksmith's arm, has a liking for the alluvial soil near the Severn. But in this case size is probably a big handicap, for it seldom manages to grow the whole ten feet or more of its height outside the protection of a garden.

In the area now forming the Royal Forest four main features affect plant life to the extent of producing local associations that may be regarded as typical. They are soil poverty, generally found in the Coal Measure formation; height, which gives semi-moorland conditions; woodland shade, which encourages a preponderance of those plants which can tolerate shade; and peat bogs. While each set of conditions, or the combination of more than one, favours certain species we must face the fact that many of these highly specialised plants are fighting a losing battle for survival. To those who are interested in plant life it is disappointing to find rare plants dying out in any locality, but it is only a small part of the price we have to pay for the movement we call Progress.

The coalfield area has a soil with an acid tendency and low fertility, on which the natural growth of plants is anything but luxuriant. Added to this a large part has, at some time, either been dug out or covered by the spoil from mining operations. This exposed subsoil and rock is in the slow process of clothing itself with soil, a process that is almost entirely dependent on an indefinite group of pioneer plants. Any big waste-tip will provide an illustration of the patient struggle that starts immediately the unsightly heap is made. At first the material is too shifting and unattractive to carry even the humblest growth, and heavy rain will spread the material over surrounding land, but within two or three years mosses will make a start.

Then will come fescue grasses, with narrow, wiry leaves and strong, adventurous roots. Shepherd's purse and chickweed will struggle to hold a place, and though they make a poor show at first it is all part of the scheme of reclamation that may produce an inch of soil in a thousand years. At least, that is one estimate of the speed at which this work is done. But the pioneer plants are not all dull drudges. Gorse and silver birch will not be long in finding a place and I have more than once been surprised to meet a thriving plant of mignonette right on the summit of a tip where no other growth had managed to climb. In this case the seed had probably been carried on the coat of a wayward sheep, by a bird, in the casual hand of hiker, or however you like to imagine. Mignonette seed would not be lifted so far by the wind. Small colonies of plants growing from wind-borne seeds—such as the hawkbits and groundsel—will often be found well above the mixed army advancing from the base, showing how widely these seeds are distributed, and bracken spores will sometimes find a home on the flattened top. But the most surprising instance of this method coming to my notice was on the New Fancy tip, where three small mushrooms grew on a slight ledge half-way to the summit.

The planting up of waste-land, especially steep slopes, is of particular importance in this part of the country, as may be gathered by watching any of these tips during heavy rain. Where there is no plant growth the water runs down the slope, forming channels as it goes and carrying all the finer particles with it. This results in miniature floods followed by drought. But when plants are established, their roots act like a sponge, holding the rain and releasing it gradually. In this way tree-covered hills act as vast natural reservoirs which keep the springs running in dry weather. This process was illustrated very clearly when the rounded top of May Hill was ploughed. While the surface stood bare any heavy rains washed out deep gullies and carried away much valuable soil. In the following years the springs on the upper part of the hill dried up more readily than had previously been the case. Now, with a thick turf grown again, the water no longer rushes off the surface, and the springs are running more steadily.

This question is in no way confined to Dean Forest, but unless it is given more attention in the future the rapidly extending system of water pipes will be in danger of running dry in summer, as they have threatened to do more than once in recent years.

Some old quarries and scowle-holes provide just the cool, moist conditions in which ferns thrive, and they are probably the most characteristic feature of the Denes. They are everywhere, from a bleak perch on some old wall to the near-darkness of disused pit-shafts. And if, when exploring some of these gloomy corners, you come face to face with *Gymnocarpium dryopteris* and *Phyllitis scolopendrium* do not be dismayed. Brought to the light of day they are merely the oak-fern and the hart's-tongue. The botanical names of ferns are rather terrifying, but to make up for that their popular names are altogether delightful: prickly shield, soft shield, lady-fern, broad bucklers and mountain bucklers, they are all here. But unfortunately we can no longer claim the magnificent Royal fern.

Under the high oakwoods, in moderate shade, the prevailing plants will be tufted and wavy hair grass, with wood sorrel and wood violet (which you may prefer to call *Viola reichenbachiana*). Here also may be the common tutsan, of the St John's wort family.

The marsh bedstraw, lesser skull-cap and red rattle choose ditches and damp clearings. In the same position, but far from common, are the bird's-foot fenugreek and the bird's-foot (*Ornithopus perpusillus*).

Still near the trees, but on dry banks, grow yellow pimpernel, perforated St John's wort, stitchwort, ling, whortleberry, foxglove and—rarely—the petty whin.

Bog plants are a most exclusive collection, and all the rarer species seem to be doomed, for they absolutely demand their special habitat. A bog is not just a patch of wet land, for that definition would apply equally well to a marsh, whereas the two are quite different. The essentials of bog formation are acidity and a high water table. Given these conditions dead vegetation will turn to peat, and only a very limited range of plants will manage to grow. The most typical bog plant is the sphagnum moss, and where it is found there is always a chance of meeting sundews, bog St John's wort, bog asphodel and bog pimpernel. The butterwort, though a true bog plant, is not found here. Bog bean, in spite of its name, will live in marsh or stream, but that adaptability does not look like preserving it here, for it has become quite rare.

Arrowhead, flowering rush, bur-reed and mimulus (monkey-flower), though they love to have their feet in water, are plants of the stream and marsh, to be looked for in such places as Walmore Common and the wet meadows near Lydney.

The speed-up of draining during the late war did a lot to reduce the sites on which all such plants will grow. At present there is a scheme afoot for the drainage of Walmore Common by means of pumps. This would cause a great change in the wild plant life, and we should lose a number of species, but it would be quite unreasonable to raise any objection to the scheme on these grounds. The agricultural value of such land would be raised out of all recognition, and the holding up of water at this level serves no useful purpose. It is the draining of high ground that needs very careful thought, and though it is repetition I would stress the point again.

In natural conditions, with a thick growth of plants, rain soaks into the ground and finds its way slowly downhill. But where drainage carries the water away quickly it is liable to cause sudden floods and subsequent droughts, a state of affairs which is becoming all too familiar in many parts of the world. The obvious remedy is to keep the uplands planted with trees as far as possible so that their roots may act as a sponge. And yet, when I look from my window and see trees being planted on one of the few remaining sites where we grow sundews and bog asphodel, I am sorry. But officials of the Forestry Commission have lent a most understanding ear, so we have hopes of keeping our sundew.

The clear-felling of woodland has a most disturbing effect on plant life. Thickly grown conifers allow no undergrowth, so that when they are cleared the land will be occupied by a few strong growers that delight in such opportunities; foxglove, ragwort, willow herb and bracken being the chief species. In more open, broad-leaved woodland there will have developed a carpet of shade-bearing species, but this will die out almost immediately on exposure to full sunlight, and the same invaders will establish themselves within two seasons. This happened with startling suddenness when a plantation of Spanish chestnuts was felled at Highnam. Although a thin covering of trees was left the foxgloves moved in like an invading army, taking possession of the land to the exclusion of everything except the bluebells. Wood sorrel, sanicle, spurge, enchanter's nightshade, all disappeared as if they had never lived there, only the bluebells surviving because they managed to do their flowering each year before the foxgloves overwhelmed them. In some parts, on the limestone, the cleared ground will produce a luxuriant crop of deadly nightshade, the real *Atropa belladonna*, not the common woody nightshade.

In this connection a most interesting step has been taken on the Forestry Commission's Highmeadow estate. This great tract of woodland is already of special interest because of the varied conditions of soil and situation which it affords, and because it has been less disturbed by clear-felling than any area hereabouts. In 1944 some 90 acres were set aside as an "Ecological Reserve", in which plant life will be left free from artificial control, to work out its own pattern by the "survival of the fittest". Here everything that chooses to grow will live or die according to the law of the jungle, with records being made to show the trend. This will, of course, be a very long-term demonstration of which we shall only see the early stages. A detailed description of the site would serve no useful purpose, even if such a task lay within my powers of description and within the physical capacity of this book. It could only mean anything when read in conjunction with a similar description made at the beginning of the experiment, and then it might be misleading, for the early tendency may not continue.

When normal forestry operations were halted on the Reserve, six years ago, the woodland was of mixed types. One portion had been felled, leaving a few oak, ash and beech trees to regenerate the land with their seed; another plot consisted of a mixture of tall trees growing rather close, and left as a wind-break to a plantation of young spruce; the remainder was mostly mixed coppice, except where the land is too steep to permit of planting and the cover consists of just such trees as can cling to the rock. Thus there will be at least three types of woodland "going native", for it is unlikely that there will be any appreciable change on the steep bank. At present the whole Reserve has a look of moderate neglect, with the tall trees of the wind-break becoming even more spindly in their effort to secure a share of light, the coppice becoming overgrown, and an army of silver birch encamped where the oak, ash and beech should be reproducing their kind.

The Reserve has a north-easterly aspect, on Carboniferous Limestone, and reaches from the bank of the Wye to a height of about 400 feet. Of these conditions the soil is likely to play the most noticeable part, for it is too thin—in the main—for good oak, but appears well suited to beech and ash. At the moment quick-growing birch is overshadowing a sprinkling of young oak, with naturally sown beech very little in evidence. But a quick start may not give a winning lead, particularly against the shade-bearing beech, so that our grandchildren may see high woods of beech, with some ash and oak, and little undergrowth. Whatever may happen in the battle of the giants there will be a wealth of interest in the smaller plants forming the carpet.

When travelling through unfenced woodland, such as is found in the vicinity of Speech House, there is a temptation to regard such scenery as "natural". This is far from being correct. In the natural state there is very keen competition for living room, and it is the species best suited to soil and other conditions that survive in any particular locality. This means that we should expect to find beech and ash predominant on the limestone rim of the coal basin and on the cliffs of the Wye Valley. Under these would be yews, for we have already noticed how they follow the lime. In the coal basin the soil is naturally poor and inclined to be acid, so that the range of plants would, in the natural state, be quite limited, with oak as the chief tree, undergrown with the hardier shrubs down to the bilberry. Bluebells and spurge grow in these woods, but it is noticeable that they are meagre by comparison with the specimens growing in other parts, and the primrose is conspicuously absent. The Old Red Sandstone produces a deeper and more fertile soil, growing the majority of plants that do not demand lime. Eastwards, towards the river, all the more luxuriant types flourish.

The main difference between the tree-covered parts of this forest and a naturally grown woodland lies in the absence of undergrowth, which in this case is kept down by sheep. During the time that the area was preserved as deer forest sheep were severely discouraged because they deprived the deer of food and shelter, but we can feel more charitable towards them as we walk on soft turf under a high canopy of leaves. Natural woodlands, where such remain, may send a botanist into raptures, but they just cannot be walked through.

Under the pretence of following some thirteenth-century document our boundary was set as wide as Newent. Now I may as well come into the open and admit that the territory was decided at Easter, when the daffodils were in flower, so there was a golden reason as well as an historic excuse for including this country to the north-east. There is something about this area that suits wild daffodils, but there seems to be no one who can say just what it is. The Old Red Sandstone offers itself as an explanation, and there is a strong temptation to regard this formation as essentially their home. The main part of the crop certainly follows this rock, running from Preston, past Dymock and Newent, round May Hill to Blaisdon. They are found in smaller numbers, though still plentiful, at Awre, Blakeney and Newnham, and again at Redbrook and Brockweir where the same soil formation reappears. Then the link with the Old Red is rather strained by their presence at English Bicknor and St Briavels. *Gloucestershire Flora* speaks of their absence from the Silurian formation. Taking

*Mixed woodland and open country*

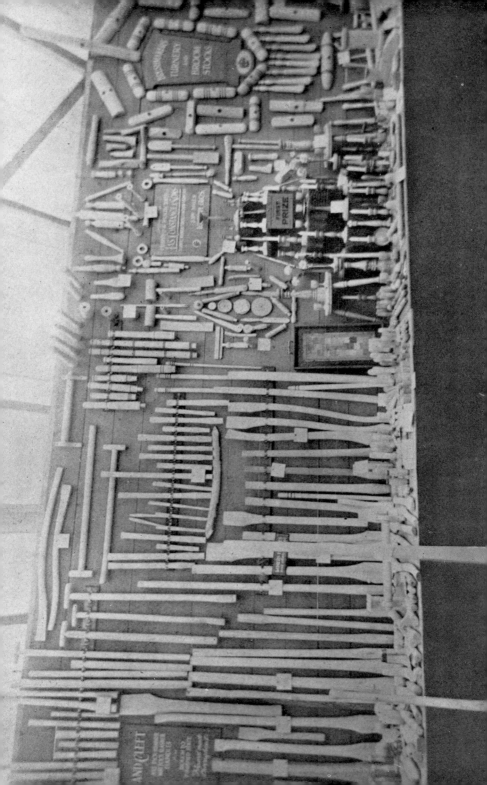

my hat humbly in hand, and without leaving my seat, I can see two very vigorous patches just above the limestone layer in this formation. These have all the appearance of being natives, but if they are aliens they seem to find the country of their adoption quite congenial.

When the top of May Hill was returned to grass after the war-time ordeal by plough a few daffodil bulbs were still unconquered. These are now growing at a height of 950 feet, in Silurian Sandstone. No, the soil is not entirely responsible for the way in which this plant flourishes here, for it grows in sandy meadows and on clay banks, in woodlands and roadside ditches. But they must have some strong local attachment, for they seldom bear removal out of this district, though they can be transplanted without difficulty within the limits of Daffodil Land. It has been suggested that bulbs taken from Dymock fifty years ago played an important part in the development of some of the Dutch strains. However that may be, the process is not reversible. Attempts to found a bulb industry here with imported Dutch varieties have always failed.

But however much we do not know about our daffodils will not in any way dim the splendour of the golden fields where they choose to grow. Wartime ploughing cleared many fields (much to their agricultural advantage), but the bulbs in hedgerow and adjoining woodland very soon return when the plough turns its back. Even the queues of cyclists and motorists who make the pilgrimage, to return in a state that can only be described as "dripping daffodils", do not seem to check the triumphal career in any way.

But while the daffodil has the popular vote, William Cobbett put up a strong case for the autumn crocus. Writing in his *Rural Rides* on 13th September, 1826, he mentions a clump of these flowers in an orchard between Huntley and Bollitree, calling them "the prettiest sight in the way of flowers that I ever saw in my life", as they grew amongst grass that was freshened by rain after a parched summer. I like to think that the colchicums growing near the road just below Dursley Cross are the same ones that Cobbett saw, as they very well may be. These are the little items that bring history to life.

14*               201

*Wood-turning is firmly established*

In giving these two flowers first place I have merely echoed the opinion of others. My own choice is for a plant that gives pleasure through the whole year, through snow and frost just as much as in the crowded months of summer flowering; in fact, the silver birch. Judging for order of merit is full of pitfalls. How, for instance, can it be said that heather is more beautiful or more useful than foxglove? It is like making a comparison between stew and peach sundae, or between Gloucester Cathedral and Severn Bridge. Each has its particular function and is appropriate to certain conditions, which is exactly why I give first place to the silver birch. In wide green parkland oak and elm will look at ease, with plenty of room for head and roots. But when we come to quarries and waste-heaps, where the crumbling rock will not grow grass, and where heavy rains scour away the soil as it is formed, that is where the humble, thrifty birch comes into her own. Everywhere from sour swamp to high rock-crevice these trees are struggling to preserve beauty, but the spot most clearly in my mind is the big quarry beside the road from Longhope to Mitcheldean, for there they have worked little short of a miracle. No sooner has the waste settled down than the seeds manage to take root, growing with amazing rapidity as though anxious to cover up the scar that man is making. And there they will flourish until, as is happening at present, the removal of rough stone undermines them. Not until they fall do they give up the struggle. The silver birch is said to have grown here before any other of our trees, and by sheer adaptability is likely to outlast them all.

Taking the whole year round no tree does so much to brighten the landscape, from the first mauve bloom of the twigs in late winter, through the fairy-lightness of summer shade, to the exquisite lacework of branches outlined by frost or snow. And against blue-black storm clouds the white bark stands out as one of the most startling contrasts in Nature.

But, you may argue, however pretty this tree may be it is of no use, and foresters regard it as a weed. Admittedly it has frequently been left to lie where it has grown, unwanted for firewood or fence. But that is just a sign of times that can, apparently, afford to ignore the material that lies to hand, for until recent years there was no lack of uses. It is, perhaps, symbolic that a tree so closely associated with the enforcement of discipline should be out of favour. From Roman times downwards the birch has been the standby of the schoolmaster; the means of coaxing unwilling pupils over early jumps in the course. But that was not the only use.

> Even afflictive birch
> Curs'd by unlettered idle youth, distils
> A limpid current from her wounded bark,
> Profuse of nursing sap.

So we see that Youth was not slow to take revenge, first by inscribing initials (probably with twined hearts) on the silvery bark, then by making a drink from the sap. Here is a recipe:

Make an incision in the bark in March, keeping the wound open by a small stone, and making a bottle fast to catch the flowing juice. Boil each gallon of juice with a quart of honey, a few cloves, lemon peel, cinnamon and mace. Ferment with yeast and bottle.

Whatever the results may have been, the old folks certainly did have fun in making their drinks. But it is unfortunate that there appears to be no evidence as to the comparative straightness of footpaths since home-made wine went out of fashion.

The uses of the birch tree did not end there by any means. The bark had a reputation for burning so brightly that it was in demand for fire-lighting, while cotton reels, spindles, plates and mugs were made from the wood. One other use was particularly appropriate to this neighbourhood—the flooring of carts used for stone-carrying. Its peculiarly woolly texture saved it from splitting under the falling stones. The Forestry Commission are planting various conifers, including the stone pine, with a view to hiding waste heaps and the production of timber. In many cases, however, growth is so puny that it would seem to be a better proposition to let the natural salvagers do the first rough work of reclamation, especially if we could cultivate a taste for birch brew.

Dean Forest and oaks are as inseparable as sausage and mash, or Bath and Wells. It is a partnership of long standing that has found its way into song and poem. But, sad to relate, the Denes do not grow good oak trees according to popular standards, and for two perfectly good reasons. The soil is poor, making for a slow growth which brings with it toughness of fibre rather than imposing size. The strength of timber (which was of the utmost importance before the days of steel girders and reinforced concrete) depends to a great extent upon the closeness of the annual rings, a condition more likely to be met with here than in more genially situated parkland. Also, the builders of wooden ships knew better than to cut curved ribs out of straight timber.

The result of this was that the pedunculate oaks with their short trunks and spreading heads, grown on these poor soils, produced just such timber as the shipyards demanded. Now, with no demand for bent timber, sessile oak is being more generally planted. Apart from the difference in length of main stem, which may be greatly influenced by conditions of growth, the distinction between these two lies mainly in the presence or absence of a stalk to the acorn cup. The leaf runs rather contrary, the sessile oak (*Quercus petræa*) having a shorter stalk to the acorn cup and a longer leaf stalk than the pedunculate oak (*Q. robur*). There is also a variation in leaf shape, the sessile oak having the lobes less developed. But to confuse the issue there are endless hybrids in which these characters are blended in varying degrees.

According to one authority the oak tree plays the host to 500 insects, 36 fungi, 16 hanging mosses, 7 leaf mosses and 3 liverworts. And I am not prepared to argue. This is unfortunate for the tree and for those who decide to picnic beneath its shade. Kipling, in *Puck of Pooks Hill*, warns us against the elm and advises:

> But whether a lad be sober or sad,
>     Or mellow with ale from the horn,
> He will take no harm when he lieth along
>     'Neath oak and ash and thorn.

Well, 500 species of insects may do no harm to him who lies beneath, but they can be mighty unpleasant. And to the tree they can be very harmful, sometimes eating away the leaves so completely and so early in the season that a second crop grows. In this case a second narrow ring may be formed in the trunk, thereby upsetting the calculation of age from the annual rings.

A Forest of Dean oak is mentioned in *The English Forest* (1853) as being an even more accommodating host:

"On the topmost branches a pair of sparrow hawks had made them a nest which, at the time I examined it, contained four eggs. In a hollow near the top was a jackdaw's nest with five young ones. A little lower a woodpecker had another with five eggs in it. Still lower was a nuthatch's nest with seven young ones. And near the foot of the tree, in one of the crevices of the bark, which was overgrown with ivy, a pair of wrens had made another nest in which were several eggs."

For a forest area specialising in tree-growing we are unfortunately short of really outstanding specimens. This has been laid at the door of Sir John Winter and his 500 axemen, but though he certainly did almost strip the region of timber we must remember that timber was a commercial proposition and would have been cut by others, if not by Sir John. It requires 200 years or more to decide whether an oak stands any chance of developing into an outstanding specimen, and by that time the tree is well past its prime for timber. Future generations may condemn our own time for the absence of forest giants, but real giants are very widely spaced, whether it be in trees or in humans. Kent of Tidenham and Bright of Longhope cannot be repeated *ad lib*.

The age of trees is a topic that is always inclined to arouse interest, so it may be in order to give a very rough guide to the age of the oak, which applies in some degree to other broad-leaved trees. During the first 300 to 400 years the annual rings will run about ten to the inch. After that age they tend to become closer. Take as an example a tree with a girth of 22 feet. This gives a radius of $3\frac{1}{2}$ feet which, at ten rings to the inch, represents about 350 years. When this is applied to the biggest trees in the Forest (apart from the Newland Oak) it gives an age of 300 to 350 years.

Another point—a forest is not the ideal kindergarten for record-breaking trees. The competition in early life is inclined to draw the trunk up to a shape which produces useful timber but which is very badly suited to withstanding gales, especially when the surrounding cover has been removed.

It is in the parkland that the finest trees grow, and though the area of such land here is limited there is enough to carry some very fine specimens. In Lydney Park are elm, oak, beech, pine and chestnut (horse and Spanish) growing as if the site is entirely to their liking, and if the elm prefers the lower edge of the park that is perfectly natural. Sedbury Park has changed hands, a change which deprived it of many beautiful trees. The main item of interest remaining is a yew-tree walk in which the figures of a fox hunt have been most realistically clipped. Let us hope that the portrayal of a fugitive fox, hard pressed by hounds, will have a salutary effect on the inmates of the remand home which is now in possession.

In the private woodland of the Highnam Court Estate there is, amongst a great variety of trees, a Spanish chestnut that may be unrivalled throughout the whole country. I can give no girth measurements, for the tree divides in four stems almost from ground level. Each stem, however, is equal to a tree of fair size.

Winter did not get his hands on all our woodlands, for there are very many acres of trees here that did not belong to the Crown in the seventeenth century. From all sources, however, we can only produce one real patriarch among oaks, and that one is now carrying his age very heavily, though he has managed to greet another season with a thin covering of leaves. The Newland Oak has some claim to be considered as runner-up for the title of Britain's oldest tree, being thought by some to stand second only to the yew on Merrow Down, near Guildford, described as old at the time of the Domesday Book. Estimates of the age of any great oak vary so widely as to invite a charge of guessing, but it is safe to say that the parent tree could have been in full vigour when Offa built his dyke. This tree is now so deformed with age that a fair measurement of girth cannot be taken. A hundred years ago, however, it was recorded as measuring 41 feet at 5 feet above the ground. The branching head is now gone and only a few small shoots give any sign that there is still life in the Newland Oak.

Jack of the Yat stood beside the Monmouth road not far from

Sallow Vallets Lodge. A promising youngster this, with a girth of about 22 feet, and a place in map and guide-book until the early part of this century. Now only the rotting stump remains, but the name serves as a reminder that Yat meant "road" just as much as "gate".

Beside the same road, about a mile nearer to Coleford, stand those of the High Beeches now remaining. The years are weighing heavily upon them, so heavily that several have collapsed and lie in ruins, though reckoning in years they are mere infants when compared with our older oaks. One hundred and fifty years is a long life for the beech, while Dryden tells us what to expect from the oak:

> Three centuries he grows; and three he stays
> Supreme in state; and in three more decays.

On this basis it might be thought that, growing in competition, the oak would master the beech by sheer longevity; yet such is the vitality and smothering habit of beech that, in the opinion of John Evelyn, ground growing both trees strongly will probably revert to pure beechwood if left untouched. Evidence on this point may come from the Ecological Reserve, already mentioned, but not in our time.

There would be no difficulty in writing of trees and woodlands just as long as there is any opportunity to move amongst them. Every hour of every day brings subtle changes of colour and outline; every passing cloud heightens the magic of light and shade. To those who love the country there is no dead season, but nowhere is the scene more enchantingly varied and alive than in undulating woodland. Look down over a birch coppice in winter, or up through the first transparent green of the beeches; marvel at the bluebell carpet of spring, or watch lazy white clouds drifting across gaps in the oak-leaf canopy; walk in the sighing peace of thick spruce plantations when the wind outside is blowing a gale: the woods are always lovely for those who can tune their minds to such quiet, satisfying joys.

# CHAPTER IX

## LOOKING TO THE FUTURE

"The slender and negligent execution of the forest law hath been the decay and destruction (in almost all places within this realm) of great wood and timber, the want whereof, as well in this present time as in time to come, shall appear in the navy of this realm."

MANWOOD, *Lawes of the Forest* (1592)

WITH the entry of the present century came a trembling of the balance of industry. At first it came so gently as to pass unnoticed, for there was no certain date and no particular event that can be pointed out as marking the turn of the tide. The tide of prosperity had, in fact, never exceeded a ripple in this part of the country, which would make it even more difficult to decide just when the ebb set in. There had been plenty of bad patches before, and they had not yet reached the dignified status of "trade recessions", so belts were pulled in again. It was not until the first quarter of this century had passed that the outside world began to realise that acute distress had reached this land; that our Mesopotamia held much lovely scenery, and very many people with hopes as empty as their bellies.

The figures of coal production are a very fair guide. The peak had been reached in 1898, when production passed the one million tons mark by a comfortable margin, though the task must have been anything but comfortable for the lads who often hauled the trucks along the galleries by means of a chain and strap round the neck. This figure was a big step forward from the 350,000 tons dug in 1856, but it marked the top of the tide and was soon followed by a steady decline. Many of our better small pits were becoming worked out just at a time when improved methods in other coalfields were bringing increased competition. The iron industry, which offered a handy market for the right type of coal,

208

had reached its top level rather earlier. In 1856 there were eight blast furnaces producing 100,000 tons of iron a year, but by 1910 this trade had ceased to be of any account. Many iron-miners found work in the coal pits, while others managed somehow with a plot of land and their common rights.

If any date must be mentioned as marking the start of the decline I should suggest 18th May, 1900. This was the day on which the *Dean Forest Guardian* published a prospectus of the newly formed Forest of Dean Stone Firms Ltd, an amalgamation that linked established businesses at Parkend and Mitcheldean with a Bridgend enterprise. Quarrying never employed large numbers of men when compared with the coalfield, but it was a useful subsidiary industry. The formation of this company was no bad thing, and was probably necessary for efficient working at a time when the amalgamation of small units was the order of the day. It did, however, mark the start of a series of such fusions which appear to have worked against the best interest of the Forest. Quarrying and the iron industry of this area both linked themselves with partners in South Wales, and in each case local employment seems to have suffered in subsequent consolidation. Natural conditions played a big part in this decline, for our small iron deposits do not lend themselves to mechanised methods, and many of our quarries were somewhat inaccessible before the days of efficient road transport. Brewing, which was carried on in a small but highly successful way at Mitcheldean, withstood the outside offers of partnership until 1936; then an alliance was formed which left another gap in our industrial front. Ship-building had dropped right out of the picture, and a change of fashion had put an end to the making of grandfather clocks.

These tall clocks came chiefly from the workshops of the Voyce family at Mitcheldean and the Shortmans of Newnham. A number of specimens of both are still to be seen, and though it is likely that the mechanism was made by bigger firms, the cases and dials are distinctive. Two Voyce clocks are still owned by members of the family, while Shortman models may be seen in the Angel Hotel, Monmouth, and the New Inn, Gloucester. But this is straying from the track, for grandfather clocks belong to the past, however interesting they may be.

During the first decade of this century forestry supplies the only relief in an otherwise depressing picture. The dates, together with initials of officials of the Forestry Commission, on cottages at Cannop and Miry Stock tell the story of progress in woodland management. The road from Parkend to Miry Stock was made by the Crown at this time to meet the needs of forestry, and it was this road which brought a trial of strength between the Commissioners and the Common Right Holders a few years later. Having made the road through enclosed woodland the Commissioners saw no reason why they should fence it on either side, maintaining that grazing animals had no right to use the new road, which was the only means of entry into the enclosures. But the animals and their owners held other views, and subsequently won the day.

But woodlands never did provide a great amount of employment, even in the days when oak trees were barked and the smaller wood converted into charcoal on the site where it had grown, and both these sidelines were dying out. Writing in 1912, A. O. Cooke gives details of the open-pit method of charcoal making as practised here, but he was doing us less than justice in saying that the craft was no longer carried on by local men. At Flaxley we have a man who has been at the trade all his life, which goes back before the days when Cooke was writing. True, he generally uses the portable kiln, but his hand has lost none of its skill in building the open pits. But it seems unlikely that there will be anyone to follow him in the trade.

Rail facilities were considerably more extensive at this time, for it was possible to travel from Lydney through Speech House Road to Coleford, and from Cinderford through Lydbrook to Ross. But this brought almost no broadening horizon to people who had little inclination to leave home and desperately little money for rail fares. Gloucester was a long way off; Ross and Monmouth could be visited on special occasions; but mostly they lived very much to themselves.

It was in these circumstances that the Forest came to be

regarded over a wide area as a dump of humanity from which it was sometimes convenient to draw cheap labour. "You know, my dear, I've had such trouble with servants. Now I'm getting a girl from the Forest of Dean. If you're lucky you can get quite a good girl without having to pay these ridiculous wages, and they're much easier to feed." Remarks such as this were being made in drawing-rooms anywhere between Gloucester and London, and the reply was always ready. "I hope she'll be satisfactory; but of course you won't leave anything of value about." Under these conditions it is gratifying to hear that there were any good girls. But this had very little effect on the invisible barrier, for the girls seldom really took root in the basements of Cheltenham or Chelsea, Bath or Bournemouth. By a strong homing instinct they generally returned to find a mate in the Forest, probably within sight of home.

The cumulative result of these factors was to make the unemployment and distress of the 1930's felt more severely here than in most places. The situation became so acute as to give rise to a report that steps might be taken to transfer a big section of the population to other parts of the country. How this was to be done —without recalling Oliver Cromwell—has never been made clear, nor have I been able to trace the rumour to any source. But the very existence of such a story shows how serious the position was, though anyone who knew the Forest in those days will need no reminder. At any time of day men could be seen standing at cottage doors and street corners, or squatting on the pavements when the sun shone. They stood singly, or in silent groups, so bored with enforced idleness that they seldom talked amongst themselves. But their eagerness to talk with outsiders was pathetic, amongst people who are normally so self-sufficient. When the public houses opened there was no hurry, for those who had the price of a drink probably had to make a pint last all the evening, and those who had not would just go on standing.

All these remarks apply, of course, only to the industrial area, to the coalfield and immediate surroundings, and the past has been brought up once more in order to show how important it is that we should prepare for the future. The rest of the region was subjected to the ordinary ups and downs of farming, which at that time consisted very largely of downs. But there is nothing peculiar in that to claim attention.

The only good that has come out of so much adversity is a resolve that the same thing shall not happen again. The forces marshalled to resist industrial depression, headed by the Forest of Dean Development Association, have not yet fought a major engagement, though they have done a lot of reconnaissance work. No small part of this has been to obtain agreement between all the parties concerned as to the steps that should be taken, and it is pleasing to note that at present there is a very fair measure of such agreement. Let us hope that understanding and the spirit of co-operation are established firmly enough to withstand whatever may lie ahead.

Those who have only heard casual mention of the Development Association may have the impression that its purpose is to bring industry to this district *ad lib*. Such an idea would be wrong. New industries are wanted, but only so far as they are reasonably suited to the district and likely to prevent unemployment. At the same time the countryside must be protected from unsightly development, for the Association are fully alive to the natural beauty of the district and to the possibilities of the tourist trade. This presents some very big problems, the biggest of which concerns the future of the coal mines.

The outlook for the pits was difficult enough to forecast under the old system, though quite a few well-informed opinions have been given. Now, however, new conditions have developed so rapidly that I cannot find anyone whose view is worth having who cares to make a prediction. When I say that nationalisation of the mines has not yet done anything to clarify the situation please do not think that I am doing any cheap political tilting. Before the advent of nationalisation the view most generally held was that coal-mining would decline steadily until, in twenty years or so, it would play a trifling part in our economy. (This was gone into more fully in the chapter on coal.) The National Coal Board may alter this figure in either direction, as a variety of conditions demand. The need to reduce production costs might lead to concentration on other coalfields that can be worked more efficiently, with rapid closing down in this area; on the other hand, a demand for coal regardless of cost might keep these pits open long after they have ceased to be a sound economic proposition. While the first of these courses probably has more support it would be difficult to find anyone willing to stake his future on the outcome, yet very many futures depend upon it.

Two other factors, both well above the horizon, may play an important part in the future, though they cannot now be assessed. Much research is being carried out to discover other sources of power that can be harnessed for our use, and it may be that atomic energy, or some other device, will prove such a blessing that there will be no need for men to spend their working lives in a coal seam. And even if the sceptics amongst us have serious misgivings, we cannot rule out the possibility. The other factor is a development of the process by which the coal can be utilised without the labour of bringing it to the surface, by the production of gas direct from the seam. At one time a good deal was heard about this, chiefly from Russia, and although the layman has not heard about it recently there is quite a chance of this process being used on seams which, for one reason or another, are not economically available to pick and shovel.

Recently there has been dissatisfaction about the policy of dismissal on the grounds of redundancy in some pits. Protests have been made at the putting off of older men while young ones are retained. If the life of these pits is as limited as some declare, it does seem reasonable to let the older men finish out their time in the present jobs, for a change of work is a serious matter to a man who can only look forward to some ten years of working life. It also appears to be bad policy to keep young men in positions that are considered to be only temporary. On the other hand, we do not want to find ourselves in the position of facing an extension of the life of the pits with a labour force composed largely of septuagenarians. But in this connection I should add that the chief complaint that I have heard against the old brigade is that it is quite impossible to stop them working.

With these and many other points in mind the Development

Association are striving to bring in other industries at a rate that will safeguard the area against serious unemployment as the labour requirements of the older industries shrink. At the same time it is important, in the national interest, that such alternative industries should not attract labour away from the mines, for the figures appearing regularly in the press leave no doubt that coal-mining has drawbacks which weigh very heavily in the campaign to recruit workers. The isolationism of this industry in the past has already been condemned, and there is no doubt that the invisible barrier did very much to keep down the standard of living, but these two factors did tend to keep up manpower in this vital trade. Now we can no longer look for the automatic replacement of one generation by the next. There are "better 'oles", and everyone is entitled to choose the best he can find. Common rights are having some influence here, for men are often reluctant to leave their few sheep even for offers of other employment that sound quite attractive. The history of the past centuries still keeps a hand on them.

Recent reports of the Association's activities make encouraging reading, even when we have in mind that they are words spoken while the enemy of unemployment is not yet at our gates. Factories established during the last five or six years have enormously widened the prospects for all sorts of workers, and will provide opportunities to climb the industrial ladder, a feature that has always been seriously lacking in coal-mining. Amongst these new ventures are bus and coach body-building, light engineering of various types, the manufacture of cinema projectors, plywood and plastics, the bottling of fruit juices, a clothing factory, and large premises now in course of erection for biscuit-making. These new establishments are situated at Lydney, Cinderford, Coleford and Mitcheldean, so that they are quite well situated for the existing centres of population. In my opinion the attempt to develop Coleford looks distressingly like artificial respiration, and I cannot agree with the planning view that this town should form the industrial centre of the Forest. I believe that Lydney must take that position, however frantically we plan otherwise. Apart from any other considerations this would help to preserve the Wye

Valley from industrial invasion, for Coleford is very near to some
of our loveliest scenery, and the siting of two factories on a hilltop
where they cannot be hid gives sufficient cause for uneasiness.

The older industries are chiefly outside the coalfield, which
makes them less suited as alternative employment, though buses
can get over most of this difficulty in such a limited area. These
industries include tinplate-making at Lydney and Redbrook, the
wire and cable works at Lydbrook, woodwork and turnery
around Longhope, pin-making at Lydney and Whitecroft and
quarrying scattered everywhere except on the east side.

Two industries from amongst all these are of special interest for
several reasons. Pin-making and wood-turning both have a strong
link with the past, and both have shown great vitality in adjusting
themselves to changing conditions. Our pin factory (for the two
premises are complementary) is one of very few such enterprises
in the whole world, and the saw mills and woodwork shops are
the only trade relying on local material—apart from mining and
quarrying.

Pin-making is a very old trade in the Forest, and though the
present factory does not represent a continuous growth from the
old root it is following the tradition, in a very modernised form.
A pin, whether we think of the point or the head, is so well
established as a symbol of littleness that it is something of a shock
to find that their manufacture is one of our biggest industries, with
an employment not far short of 500 men and women. The
explanation can be read from the stencils on the wall of the
despatch department. Durban, Liége, Adelaide, Toronto, Jamaica,
Stavanger, Gröningen, Winnipeg and a dozen more names from
all over the world are hanging there for directing packages containing articles of nearly every shape into which wire can be
forced. The pin-maker has his eggs in so many baskets that ill
winds must find him as hard to penetrate as the proverbial duck's
back. And if that is not good metaphor it is hard fact. Changes in
hairdressing fashion only mean a switch from this line to that, for
ladies can lose just as many grips from short hair as they could lose
hairpins from the other sort, and it is unlikely that fashion will
move the same way at the same moment in Bombay, Brussels

and Barking. Babies in every country can be hitched up with safety-pins from the Forest of Dean in white, blue or pink. Those who have no need of either of these productions can hold themselves together with six small plated safeties, made, polished and bunched by machinery, all for a penny. And the sight of paper clips in their shining thousands would bring joy to the heart of an official. There is certainly more in pins than meets the flesh.

Wood-turning and the small timber trade is firmly established around Longhope, so firmly that one family has been in the business since 1788. This industry uses great quantities of coppice wood, which explains why it grew up outside the area where large timber is grown. The passer-by will notice huge stacks of rough poles lying outside these factories, and may well wonder what can be made from such unlikely material. The answer can be found in every home and garden, and on every farm in the land, for this is the raw material of brushes and handles of all kinds. But that is the end of a story whose beginning is lost in antiquity, for this is one of the oldest crafts, showing an unbroken sequence from the first man to shape a club handle, down to the machine which now converts a square stick into a banister brush (except for the bristles) in one operation.

In the days when the handles were turned and the holes bored by hand, willow, lime and alder were in demand on account of their easy-working softness, but the change to machinery has made silver birch the most popular wood. The old favourites will not stand the ordeal of having the holes bored in one operation, so they are only wanted in very small quantities by the few remaining hand workers. The coppice wood is cut when the thick ends of the sticks measure about five inches across, and when the sap is down. The bark is then sliced off in rough strips to help drying, while the sticks are kept in the stacks for at least a year. The wood can be dried in kilns, but that method is not used here. The next process is to cut the wood into shapes that can be handled by the finishing machines, and it is here that skill is needed to avoid waste. A good sawyer will waste very little but bark and sawdust. From the square-sawn stick to the finished article is now a triumph of mechanisation rather than a display of craftsmanship.

*A splendid sandstone*

Once the machine has been set it will do everything, except think, and thought is not needed on a repetitive job after the first article has been turned out. It is the creative thought of the craftsman that gives a touch of his own character to each one of his productions, so that every one is an exciting adventure.

It is a symptom of the present age that men are ready enough to tend these machines, while there is no one in this neighbourhood making wattle hurdles. These are being imported from Sussex, when we have plenty of hazel from which they could be made. I am quite at a loss to explain why Sussex should now have practically a monopoly in the making of such things as hurdles and trug baskets. Manual skill has not always been lacking in our district, or the business that started over 160 years ago would not hold three Gold Medals of the Royal Agricultural Society, in addition to a heap of other awards. But this business, though sending hundreds of gross of machine-turned articles to all parts of the country, has difficulty in finding a man who will make a scythe handle. This leaning towards the machine is, however, quite necessary if the trade is to survive, for a thousand gross of brushes will probably be ordered for each enquiry for a scythe sneath.

To me, the biggest surprise hidden amongst the oak trees of Dean Forest is the stone-working industry. I have said elsewhere that local masonry seldom reached a high level, and that quarrying is relatively unimportant. Both these statements need qualification, for neither is true without some reservation. Though stone has been quarried here for more than two thousand years, it was not until the dawn of the present century that the industry reached its zenith. By that time the quarries were busy to such good effect that a large proportion of public building works within a wide radius are constructed, in part at least, of this excellent material. A splendid sandstone, in blue or grey, comes from a number of workings in the centre of the coalfield, while a first-class red building stone is taken from the steeply pitched beds of Old Red Sandstone beside the Longhope–Mitcheldean road.

There is no need to search for words with which to describe these three types of stone, for mention of a few of the works in which they have been used will be far more convincing. Eastnor

*Fishermen near Lydney*

Castle, near Ledbury, was built rather more than a century ago with stone carried from here by mules, it is said. This was quite a big contract, and another useful one was to follow from Severn Bridge, where the abutments and piers are of grey Forest stone. Here the quality has been tested more severely, for apart from the normal weathering the piers are washed by salt water at every tide. These examples are close at hand, but the fame and the stone were spread far and wide. Littleton Bridge, near Shepperton, is built mainly of grey stone, dressed in the Cannop Valley, while the red facings came from the red rocks of Mitcheldean. And the altar of the Roman Catholic Church of St Gregory, Earlsfield, was fashioned from Forest stone by Forest labour. All these are only odd instances chosen from hundreds.

A process of amalgamation joined the various stone companies in this area with others, including the famous Portland quarries. Of this venture let us merely say that it was spectacular while it lasted. United Stone Firms, as they called themselves, supplied the dressed stone for Thames House and Adelaide House, in London, and still they looked for fresh worlds to conquer. It is widely known that the blocks with which Broadcasting House was built came from the quarries at Portland, but it is not so widely realised that the stone was dressed here in Dean Forest. For many months the little yards at Parkend and Bixslade echoed the sound of saw and chisel all through the night in order to supply the builders in Portland Place. While the job lasted it gave work to a considerable number of men, just at a time when other industries were feeling the pinch of depression. But the stonework appears to have been of a higher quality than the business organisation, for the company came to grief on financial rocks, and the quarries and yards were strangely quiet for a long time.

Now the Forest of Dean Stone Firms are reviving the business in local stone, and though the number of men is not a tenth of those employed fifty years ago this does not mean a corresponding decrease of business. The industry has been mechanised almost out of recognition. Standing in the yard at Bixslade, hemmed in by oak trees, and with the cry of moorhens added to the chorus of machinery, I watched an interesting comparison. On the one hand rabbets were being cut in blocks of stone with a revolving carborundum cutter, cooled by a jet of water; on the other, a man did the same work with hammer and chisel. While the machine finished three blocks the man was still busy on his first, and I am bound to admit that the machine was turning out a better job.

There is not the same international flavour that we met in the packing room of the pin factory, but stone is being sent to build an extension to barracks at Tidworth, and for a new wing to the College at Aberystwyth. Yet you can walk in these woods or watch the water-fowl on Cannop Ponds without being aware of all this activity. More readily noticed, but harder to trace, is the peculiar smell pervading the ponds. This comes from a factory at the crossroads higher up the valley. Let's look.

The general switchover to coal for iron-smelting led to a steep decline in the demand for charcoal, but the demand did not die out. Charcoal is still needed in a number of manufacturing processes, including the case-hardening of steel, so considerable quantities continue to be made, though not in the open pits of the past. This method certainly saved transport, for the burning was done on the site where the wood had grown, and the charcoal is much lighter to carry than the wood from which it is made, but it lost very heavily on the score of efficiency. Each ton of wood yields about 2 cwt. of charcoal, and nothing else, when burned in open pits, a figure which can be improved by about 50 per cent with the use of portable kilns. But these kilns, though they were used considerably in the emergency conditions of the last war, are very wasteful when compared with the more modern process.

It was in 1911 that the Forestry Commission started a factory near Speech House Road Station for the production of charcoal and the extraction of other substances from the cordwood of their forests on each side of the Wye. There are only two other plants of this type in the country, and not many areas could find enough raw material to supply such an undertaking. Here, as with the other two factories, only hardwoods are used, for distillation of the wood from the conifers is an entirely separate affair (carried on quite considerably in France).

The process of wood distillation differs from charcoal-burning in that the wood is burned in sealed retorts, so that carbonisation is controlled and the by-products collected. At this factory all kinds of hardwoods go into the retorts at the rate of 20 tons a day. Oak is available in greatest quantity, though beech is more highly esteemed, while sawmill waste gives too much ash owing to the high proportion of bark. During carbonisation the wood yields up moisture, wood-alcohol and tar, being completely carbonised without losing its shape, though every stick shrinks by about one-third. The charcoal is crushed and graded into various sizes; the tar and any impurities are removed from the distillate, leaving a product that is chiefly used as a base for lacquer.

The extent to which this process has improved upon the pit-burning method is shown by the comparative production figures. While the old method aimed only at the making of carbon, and then achieved no more than 2 cwt. for each ton of wood, the distillation factory obtains 5 cwt. of charcoal and 3 gallons of distillate. The small amount of tar produced is not in great demand at present, so it is being mixed with sawdust and used—with coal —to heat the retorts. And, as if to give the hallmark of authenticity to this factory near the Speech House, Forest sheep make their way amongst the machinery, or take their ease in the shadow of the sacks of carbon.

The wood used in this industry is quite unfit for the sawyer, and much of it would only make very second-rate firewood. Transport is a serious item, as a large area of woodland is needed to supply 20 tons of cordwood every day, especially after the heavy calls made during the war. This supply problem has, of course, increased with the growth of conifers, and so far no plant has been established in this country for the distillation of turpentine from the softwoods. Climate plays an important part here, as it is in the sunnier South of France and in Spain that the biggest supplies of turpentine are obtained by distillation and tapping. Also, there seems more likelihood of our softwood waste being pulped for the manufacture of that ever-increasing range of goods now being made from "reconstituted" wood.

The renewed demand for the silver birch illustrates very clearly the main difficulty that presents itself to those who plant trees.

Birch coppices were grown in the past largely for the tops, from which brooms and vinegar were made. Then birch brooms went out of fashion, and vinegar was made by other methods, so that the birch coppices did little more than add beauty to the winter scene. Now there is a demand for birch for turnery and for veneers, so we turn to the coppices, to find trees that would yield plenty of vinegar and brooms but of poor shape for turnery, and quite useless for veneers. The difficulty is not so serious here, however, as with the bigger trees, for the birch is a quick grower, and it should be possible to produce all the timber we need of this kind on land which is of little or no value for any other purpose. In the meantime the other coppice trees are sadly out of favour, with the exception of sweet chestnut for cleft fencing, and hazel for pea and bean sticks. Even the making of cleft gates and hurdles is dying out. Many times in recent years I have tried to buy a cleft chestnut gate, which is lighter and tougher than any other, but with no success. Progress and a higher standard of living insist that I must be satisfied with a clumsy affair made from sawn oak timber, with plenty of knots and grain so short that the rails can be snapped across the knee.

The outlook for the small timber industries appears to run just contrary to our national fortunes. A feeling of wealth, skilfully played upon by business interests, tempts us to look elsewhere for the things that can very well be grown and made on our own doorsteps. Cheap, machine-made articles of all kinds, and from all parts of the world, are paraded in front of us, while the craftsmen shut up their workshops, and the newspapers scream about financial crises. So shall we look for the other side of the picture?

The lane leading from St Briavels to Brockweir is very narrow and winding; so narrow that bracken, honeysuckle and meadow-sweet will brush both sides of the car travelling that way in early summer; so winding that it was obviously made by people who had no need of anything more than a donkey track from the old-time port on the Wye to the ancient settlement on the hill. Those who use this lane will do well to adjust their speed to that of the pack-trains of old, otherwise they will miss many lovely glimpses of the Wye Valley and a small but very interesting centre where handicraft has taken root. I say this because the weaving and pottery now carried on here are a revival rather than a survival of old industries.

Handicraft is a word that has been cruelly tortured to cover the activities of industrialists and salesmen, but here it can be used with a clear conscience, for the visitor will find no sign of imitation antiques or poker-work verses. There was nothing arty-and-crafty about the cushion cover on the handloom, or in the jugs and dishes waiting their turn to be fired in the kiln when last I visited the place; nor do I feel any concern that the two undertakings will be commercialised while the present artists are in control. These represent, to me, the complete opposite of the machine-watching inclination. Truly, the weaver works to a pre-arranged pattern, and knows what the woven cloth will look like, but that does not detract from the satisfaction derived from seeing the work grow, especially when the wool has been dyed and spun by the weaver. It is in the pottery that the thrill of excitement comes with the opening of the kiln. But for those who know nothing of the routine of a small pottery this is starting at the end, and a brief account from the beginning will be more useful.

The red clay used here comes from a quarry at Lambsquay, outside Coleford, and is just so much waste material until it comes into the potters' hands. Then follows a lot of patient kneading until it is thoroughly mixed and of the right consistency.

The next stage is the most fascinating part for the onlooker, for a lump of most unpromising material is placed on a table which is turned by the foot of the worker, and as the lump turns it is drawn up by hand into whatever shape is required. Plates, egg-cups, teapots or what else you will, they all start in the same way, with nothing but the skilful fingers of the worker to decide what shape they shall take. This is the oldest and most primitive manufacturing process still in use, and there is a strong suggestion of magic in the way that the inert clay responds to the will of the potter. This is particularly noticeable in the deeper vessels, where the fingers seem merely to hold the clay while it shapes itself. But this illusion would be shortlived with a novice at the wheel.

After the clay has been shaped it must dry for some time before the first ordeal by fire, which hardens it in the rough state such as is seen in flowerpots. Then the liquid glaze, with any colouring that may be used, is applied by dipping, pouring or brushing, and the articles go into the kiln a second time. It is at this stage that the climax is reached, for with natural clay and firing that depends on personal skill the results can never be foretold exactly. Undetected draughts in the kiln may produce a crack, and always there is sufficient uncertainty about colours to make the opening of the kiln an exciting event even to an experienced hand, especially when matching sets of bowls are wanted. Broadly speaking, high temperatures produce darker shades, while from the other end of the scale come the sunnier effects, but within these limits there is an endless variety of shades, so that no two pieces are just alike. Large, flat dishes of the traditional pattern, such as were used as oven ware in other days, need a different technique. They are made flat, and the glaze poured over them while the clay is still moist and pliable. They are then left to dry before being shaped over a mould and fired.

As I have watched the potter at work I have tried to decide, in my own mind, where the boundary line lies between industry and the crafts. Manual skill is not the deciding factor, for none of our industries can operate without manual skill at some stage, however much its place may be taken by the machine at others. The profit motive plays an important part, but still draws no clear line, for the genuine craftsman must generally make his living however meagre it may be. No, none of these fix the dividing line, nor can it be said that the machine has really killed craftsmanship, though it has certainly taken the centre of the stage. The only distinction that seems to satisfy all the conditions is much simpler than these. The industries are noisy; the crafts are not. And in saying this I am not overlooking the blacksmith as a craftsman, for the ring of his hammer is as musical as the chirp of a carpenter's plane. At present we are expected to have an infinite capacity for enduring noise in everyday life, so that it is all the more pleasure to watch things being made in surroundings where cattle and wild birds provide the chorus. But there are troubles even here. When I last visited the pottery the tomtits had been drinking the milk, after removing the cap.

In this Forest country our industries and our crafts are widely scattered, so it is no surprise to find a foundry working in the shadow of oak trees, closely grown around with bracken and fox-gloves. Earlier in this chapter I said that the iron industry was of little account here; this is true so far as it concerns employment. We are proud of the part played by Forest iron, though it is mainly in the past. Now there are only three or four small foundries at work, and while the effect they have on employment is small they serve a useful purpose in doing work that would not appeal to the large-scale shops of South Wales and the Midlands. One such enterprise, situated between Coleford and Speech House Road, generally attracts attention because of its position amongst typical forest scenery and close beside the road. Remarks are sometimes made about the heaps of scrap metal that are rather noticeable in such surroundings, but closer enquiry will show that a wide assortment of castings are being made from material that looks quite unpromising to the casual observer. And can it be that the peace of the forest has seeped into industry at this point? Any-way, this foundry is doing its best to remove one unnecessary noise by making manhole covers that cannot be rocked or rattled by traffic.

There is good reason to be proud of the part played by the forges and furnaces of the Forest in years past. It was at Milkwall, just outside Coleford, that the making of steel by the Bessemer process was developed, to be kept a closely guarded secret for some time until Sheffield got the details. Here also Richard Thomas laid the foundations of the enormous business that carried his name far and wide.

One problem which has no simple solution occurs at a point where industry comes into unfortunate contact with agriculture. The shallow workings of the Free Miner cause very considerable damage to farmland, and although the matter concerns only about four organisations and departments there seems little likelihood of the farmer getting any satisfaction, in the near future, against the time-honoured rights of the Free Miners. The subsidences, or wracks, caused by the falling in of disused workings are disturbing enough when they occur in open Crown land, the area put out of use by the wrack and the waste-heap being lost to tree production for quite a long time. But when the damage is done on farmland the loss is much more serious. Quite apart from the question of compensation, which is a matter resting between the parties immediately concerned, there is the loss of food production, which is a national concern. It requires no knowledge of farming to see that a strip of one acre taken at random across a field of ten acres will reduce the productivity of that field by far more than a tenth. Those who cause the damage will say that it is surprising how soon the land returns to use, but they admit that such use will extend no further than grazing. In fact, the edges of the wrack will become smoothed until it forms a hollow more suggestive of a shallow surface working than a subsidence, but still this will be no place for a tractor, much less for combine-harvesters and pick-up balers.

The area of land involved is small by comparison with the areas affected in other parts of the country by opencast workings, but land is our scarcest commodity, though we are slow in adjusting ourselves to the idea.

The farming of this district divides itself into two types. Broadly speaking, this division is into east and west, but the real distinction is between the land on which modern machinery can be used, and that where steepness or surface rock rule out mechanisation. As scientific farming methods become more widely adopted the distinction will become more clearly marked, with the red soils of the Newent, Tibberton, Minsterworth and Newnham region following more closely the pattern which is dictated by machinery, while the Denes will still provide a retreat for the "family" farmers who cannot or will not accept modern standards.

The only problem, except mining damage, which is likely to arise on the farming front and which can claim to belong specially to the Forest is the question of common grazing rights. Naturally this will only affect a limited number, and of those affected a fair percentage have no attachment to the soil except by the exercise of their rights. At present this grazing is quite an item to a certain number of small farmers, but it can be only a matter of time before the grazing rights shrink to a point at which they will be nothing more than an interesting relic, and no one will be able to point to a time at which they suffered acute distress in the process. The main factor in this trend will be the demand for land for building and the effect of coniferous trees on the woodland vegetation. By degrees we shall reach a stage at which only road margins, such as those around the Speech House, will provide any keep, and even under present traffic restrictions the losses by road accidents make this of uncertain value.

It is at this late stage in the history of common grazing that a most interesting development has taken place. This was the legislation for the control of rams on open grazing with the purpose of improving the quality of our sheep, and it came into force in 1949. The best that can be said of these sheep is that they are hardy enough to survive where many would not find a living, but it is only in recent years that the question of improvement was taken up seriously. When the present step was taken there were plenty of remarks—from outsiders—to the effect that it would take more than an Order to reform the sheep keepers of Dean Forest, but that is a typical outside comment. Mr Evan Jones, who, as secretary to the Grazing Right Holders Association, had his fingers on the pulse, has been a most ardent supporter of the attempt to eradicate the worthless rams that have been much too generally accepted as part of the system. He has never wavered in his belief that the Order would bring about a great all-round improvement. From the owners of the sheep I heard no comment.

The first crop of lambs bred under the new regulations are now growing up, so while it is too early for any well-considered verdict, I think there are signs that something has been achieved even in this first season. Lambs very frequently appear to be of better type than their mothers (a state of affairs not peculiar to their kind), but the improvement looks to me more marked this year. There is, however, another feature to which I attach more importance. The lambs roaming under the trees and amongst the waste-heaps seem to be shaping better than others bred of the same type of ewe on enclosed fields in the neighbourhood. This, if it is correct, indicates that the common graziers have been obliged to improve their stock while some of those to whom the Order does not apply have still not grasped the benefits to be achieved in this way. But this is a case in which it is quite possible to have too much of a good thing, for one of the essential qualities of Forest sheep is thriftiness, which is not a feature of many breeds. If some of the best flocks in the country—Hampshire, Leicester or what you will—were to be turned out on the open grazing here most of them would die several deaths in the first few weeks. They would starve, meet disaster on the roads and fall victims to disease. So any improvement must be on lines that will give more meat and a heavier fleece without losing the hardiness needed for these peculiar conditions.

The greatest enemy of improved sheep production will be the tendency to overcrowd. The right to graze the open land of the Forest does not carry with it any restriction on numbers, and as is always the way in such circumstances, each one means to have his share. The result is that there are estimated to be 10,000 sheep being kept mainly on the common land at present, which is greatly in excess of the number that the land can maintain in satisfactory condition. So until some arrangement for restricting the numbers can be worked out and observed the increased production will be negligible. And here I will make a prediction that will not be at all popular amongst the owners of these sheep—at present. The day will come when the present rights will be modified so that the grazing will be confined to certain specified and enclosed areas, which will be a reversal of the present plan since it will mean enclosing the livestock instead of the trees. The advantages of this scheme are clear, and most of the objections would disappear after the first sharp shock. The younger generation are inclined to take a broader view, and they will not be content for long to be tied by a few sheep to the conditions tolerated by past generations.

Our grandchildren will mourn for these picturesque customs, just as we grieve today for those which have already gone, but if we insist on preserving our yesterdays there will be no room for tomorrow.

Oddly enough it is in forestry, with its rotations of anything

from 25 to 150 years, that there seems to be least uncertainty as to
the future. This may be due in some degree to an outlook that
must develop amongst those who plan and plant large areas of
woodland. Who could spend his days planting oak trees and his
nights worrying about the use to which they are likely to be put
by his descendants of the fourth or fifth generation? Forestry
needs faith, for even the quick-growing conifers will not produce
real timber in the lifetime of a middle-aged planter. But there are
good grounds for confidence in future timber demands when we
think of the present shortage, in spite of all the alternative materials
that have been produced in our own time.

There seems to be very little cause for anxiety about a market
for all the timber that we can grow. The natural forests of the
world have been cut into very heavily, so that future supplies must
come mainly from commercial plantations, with a diminishing
quantity from increasingly remote natural sources. According to
figures in front of me the United Kingdom imported more than
£60 million worth of raw timber in 1937, which is the last year of
normal buying, and in the same year home production was about
£2½ million. The apparent threat to the timber trade coming from
steel girders, tubular furniture and many other sources was probably overestimated in the first glow of enthusiasm. Now the
Chromium-Plate-and-Glass Age appears to have been shortlived
in its more acute form, new furniture again shows a predominance
of wood over other materials, and there are no signs of circumstances which will cause a glut of good trees.

Very much has been written about the planting of large areas of
"drab foreigners", mainly spruce, and although we have no plantation of this type to compare with those of Wales and Scotland
there have been patches of fair size planted in Dean Forest. In some
cases these have been edged with beech with the combined object
of amenity and fire protection, but while this helps to hide the
drabness it does not appreciably meet the charge aimed against the
system of mono-culture. Before siding with either party it is well
worth trying to see the position without prejudice, and to listen to
the claims of both sides. On the one hand are the "mixed cul-
turalists", alleging that the growth of one species to the exclusion

of all else means death to the soil, disease to the plants and dreary scenery. Opposite to them we have those who are responsible for producing timber from land which is often unsuited to other crops, the men who have to wrestle with the problems and the figures.

Probably no one admires densely packed rows of evergreens, and they frequently wring howls of despair from the æsthete and the rural preservationist, but in the past they had very much to recommend them on economic grounds. (I say "in the past" because certain serious drawbacks are coming to light.) The most obvious advantage lies in the length of rotation, or the time that the crop will take to mature. Conifers that will yield a very useful crop of softwood, suitable for building, pit props, and a hundred other purposes, in no more than forty years, do make a strong appeal by comparison with oak requiring three times that life. Here two important factors come into play. Steel joists have replaced oak beams for all except a very few uses, and anyway, oak suitable for weight-carrying beams is not grown under any planned system of forestry. The oak that has been so much extolled in verse and ballad was cut from the outer layers of old trees, where slow growth produces close rings and great toughness. As these self-grown giants are felled the supply of such timber will fade out, for its production is quite uneconomic. Thus it will be seen that oak is not what it was—for a good reason—and it will not be in the same demand.

Another point on which the spruces and their kind score heavily is that of weeding and cleaning the plantations in the early stages. The hardwoods (oak, ash, beech, etc.) cannot compete with the growth of weeds for about ten years, and during that time the cost of trimming between the rows is heavy. Conifers, on the other hand, will be grown sufficiently after three or four years to smother the opposition. This is a great relief to the forester, for the work of cleaning puts a big strain on the labour resources at a busy time.

It was with these facts firmly in mind that our forest planners went ahead with a great programme of mono-culture, until experience began to point out some serious drawbacks. First among these is the effect on the soil. All the conifers, if planted close together, kill off any vegetation that tries to grow in their shade. This of itself is useful, but the conditions set up in the soil by the fall of no plant material but the tough needles is so damaging that it will render the land unfit for any other use for quite a long time after the trees have been removed. This can be seen clearly where a plantation of thirty to forty years' growth has been felled. The land, no matter what its natural quality, will look like a barren heath for a number of years, and will not readily support another crop even of the same type. This is no phenomenon of forestry, for the same thing happens in a less spectacular way where any crop is grown in a pure state for a number of seasons. Of recent years this has been noticeable where wheat has been grown year after year.

Another big failing of the all-conifer wood is the risk of fire. The precautions taken in the form of warning notices, beating brooms and look-out posts show what a serious danger this presents, and it is certainly the foresters' main source of headache, especially during the summer holiday season. In spite of all precautions a fire that once reaches the top of a conifer wood will spread until there are no more trees at hand to spread to. When such a fire has started the only hope of arresting it is to clear a path across which the flames will not be carried—if there is time and labour for such a course.

A third consideration, and one which is likely to become increasingly important, is disease and damage by insects. Though the process is slower in forest trees than in farm crops because of the greater length of a generation, there is no doubt that commercial production is bringing with it greater risk of trouble from these sources. Up to the present the larch has shown itself to be the most susceptible to a variety of ills, until the planting of the European variety has been almost abandoned by the Forestry Commission. This is partly due to the fact that it was one of the first trees to be grown in pure plantations, and also to planting in situations very unlike those in which it flourishes naturally. For the larch is a native of the mountainous parts of Europe where it thrives in the short growing seasons and the hard winters found at altitudes between 3,000 and 7,000 feet. We cannot offer such conditions in this country. But the enemies of trees work in cycles, so we may expect to find the larch taking on comparative immunity in due course, while the Sitka spruce (which now flourishes exceedingly) will, no doubt, fall upon less happy days. But as these "prosperity cycles" cannot be accurately forecast they cannot yet be made use of in planning.

On balance, mixed planting is definitely winning the day, which is particularly satisfactory when we know that beech is an important part of the mixture for the benefit which the leaves bring to the soil. Oaks are the traditional trees of Dean Forest, the poets say so, but without the beech we should lose a great measure of spring beauty. So the pattern for planting must, in many cases, read something like the directions for knitting a Fair Isle pullover, with the design and each species in it having a purpose. There may be spruce with a border of beech; this border will serve to hide the drabness of the main block of trees, and to reduce the risk of fire spreading from the dry grass of the rides to the heads of the conifers. Beeches may be introduced in clumps amongst pine and spruce, to leaven the whole with their leaves; a method which is not entirely satisfactory. Oak and larch have frequently been planted alternately, so that the larch may draw up the oak into straight trunks before the larch is felled to make more room for the longer-lived oak. Or the larches may be planted in strips of three rows to every eight rows of oak, in which case the larch will be cleared at about thirty years and replaced by a strip of beech, thus adding valuable leaf mould to the soil and yielding a stand of trees that can be felled in one operation when the time comes.

Other quite local features, such as wet patches and frost-hollows, call for special treatment, and so tend to make the pattern even more complex, to the great satisfaction of all who see these woodlands in spring and early summer. The change of policy shows itself in the solid blocks of dark conifers already yielding pit props while the young plantations promise greater beauty with increased efficiency.

The application of science to forestry is still in its childhood in

this country, for it was not until the war of 1914–18 upset our calculations on imports that we faced up to the situation. Even then
the lesson was only learnt in a small degree, but this may be looked
to as the dawn of organised timber production. There was a stirring of Government interest, but the long record of inertia and
half-measures had left a great amount of leeway to be made up.
Then a second war led to heavy felling and a slowing up of planting. When the war ended there were nearly 4,000 acres waiting to
be replanted, but very satisfactory progress has now been made
with this work, as can be seen in the Haywood Plantation, adjoining Cinderford, and at Wigpool Common. The leeway has been
made up, leaving only some 300 acres to be planted in each of the
next four years. And this programme will include oak trees in
suitable proportion wherever they are likely to grow well.

The very long association of oak trees with Dean Forest has not
been entirely beneficial in the past, for it has given rise to a con-
servatism that insisted on the growth of the wrong type of tree.
Even after allowing for the length of time that oaks take to grow
it must be admitted that those in command have frequently not
kept abreast of the times, much less have they shown foresight.
An illustration comes to mind from the crop that was removed
from Haywood in the early 1940's. These were vigorous young
oaks that must have been planted at a time when the local shipbuilding trade had ceased, and when wooden ships were out of
date; yet the trees stood wide apart and carried widespread
branches such as would have delighted Raleigh and Drake. In
addition to being quite unsuited to present-day requirements this
method lowers the fertility of the soil. We must hope that such
mistakes are not being repeated, but many instances of inept planning in other spheres must cause uneasiness.

The private owner of woodland is not happily situated, since
financial conditions now make it very difficult for him to produce
timber on economic lines. Even if the necessary capital is available
the majority of owners will not consider that the prospects
warrant a heavy outlay. To meet this problem the Government
have introduced a scheme whereby private woodlands may be
"dedicated", a somewhat ambiguous term for a scheme that is

still being looked at with considerable suspicion. Dedication is, roughly, an arrangement by which the owner undertakes to manage his woodland according to an approved system and on a business footing, in return for which the State offers certain technical and financial assistance. The main objection to the scheme is that the decision is irrevocable, except in abnormal circumstances. Once the covenant has been entered into it runs with the land, regardless of changed ownership. Quite naturally an owner will do a lot of thinking before taking such a step, and it is too soon for any opinion to be expressed as to the reaction.

Until recently it has not been easy for the private owner to obtain sound advice, but this question has now been tackled on three fronts. The Forestry Commission has a special advisory staff ready to give advice outside the Dedication scheme, and the various professional societies have formed an advisory panel. Then there is the timber trade. The result of our neglected forestry in the past has been to make our big timber buyers look overseas for supplies. Consequently they have not given any attention to the problems of production. And, whether we relish the thought or not, we have to admit that big business enterprise have been the leaders of industrial research in other directions. Quite recently the timber trade has set up an organisation to undertake contract planting, which sounds to me like a step in the right direction, especially if it can be followed up by a scheme for maintenance.

A lot has been written about the care of timber trees during the earlier years of growth, and of this mass of advice the greater part is devoted to thinning. It is on thinning (we are told most emphatically) that the whole success of timber-growing depends, and there is often a rider added to the effect that private owners are the worst offenders in this direction. Having read all this, take a walk through the plantations of the Commission and you will not have much difficulty in finding areas that are ten years or more overdue for treatment. And that second decade is the most important if the trees are not to be spoilt. I do not blame the local employees of the Forestry Commission for these faults, and the labour problem is very real in this industry, but the trouble arises at a higher level where plans are made beyond the limit to which

16

the money will stretch. In too many cases emphasis is laid on the area planted rather than on the quantity of good timber that is likely to be produced. In fact, sufficient unto the day is an answer with which to lull the public.

One more factory should be mentioned, though it cannot claim any special association with the Forest, for there are many of the same type throughout the country. This is the Remploy depot at Parkend, and it is here that men and women are trained and employed when, through illness or accident, they can no longer follow their normal trades. The rapid growth of this organisation shows how great was the need for such a service of what may be called "human reclamation". This is no short-term training centre, nor is it a convalescent colony; its purpose is to provide permanent employment for those who might otherwise feel that they could serve no other useful purpose. Unfortunately the industries of the Forest, particularly coal-mining, produce a number of such cases, and it is good to know that we have such an establishment—though the capacity is far below the need. It is impossible to classify a Remploy depot by the goods turned out, for the work must fit the employees, but brush-making and light engineering are the main items.

From what has been said it will be clear that the position has changed very materially since the Hungry Thirties, and the variety of trades now offer a bigger choice of employment than this district has previously known. None of the new industries essentially rely on local material, which will safeguard them from one of the big dangers of the past. At the same time the older trades have made good progress. So we may reasonably hope to share in any helpings of prosperity that come to the country.

No small part of the Development Association's work has been the task of reaching agreement between the public bodies concerned. Any plan for prosperity in the Forest must have the support and goodwill of three local councils, the County Council and the Forestry Commission, in addition to the Ministries of Health, Agriculture, Fuel and Power, Labour, Transport, Works, Town and Country Planning and the Board of Trade. Due respect must also be paid to a number of unions, and to the various mining and common rights. With all these working in harmony it is still impossible to move quickly in response to any sudden change in conditions; without harmony it is unlikely that anything could ever be achieved. But we have put all these pieces on the board (except the ones involving ancient rights) and it is up to us to make them work.

# CHAPTER X

# LOOKING FOR TROUBLE

"The country, companions, and the length of your journey will
afford a hundred compensations for your toil."

OVID

AND now the bounds must be beaten. No perambulation could
be complete without the Beating of Bounds, and as we are dealing
with ancient boundaries it is only fitting that we should observe
the ancient custom.

Admittedly the present form of threshing the outer limits with
wands is a colourless substitute for the old habit of fixing the line
by human sacrifice, but even this modern compromise presents
some difficulties in the present case. The short overland trip is no
more than a comfortable walk, but the rest of the journey consists
entirely of water, and somewhat temperamental water at that.
But the idea had taken root, and I was determined to carry it
through regardless of cost—almost.

So it happened that on a perfect morning in early October
(1949) I slid a canoe into the water at Goodrich with the intention
of travelling to Gloucester by Severn and Wye. A number of
boats come down the Wye in spite of, or because of, the obvious
hazards; a few venture up or down the lower Severn; but the
double journey is a severe test of enthusiasm.

For those who are interested, the canoe was a racing kyak, with
a length of sixteen feet and a width that appears quite suicidal at
first sight. This vehicle was chosen for several reasons. It is built
stoutly enough to withstand the rough treatment that it must
expect at the hands of a semi-novice on such water; it is reasonably
light and almost unsinkable; this one came into my hands at a price
that I could very nearly reach.

Well, the canoe was in the river and with a jump and a wriggle
I was in the canoe. Two hundred yards downstream a swan

cruised majestically, and in my ignorance I was pleased to see that swan. He (or she) seemed to complete the picture, a picture of rural England at her fairest and freshest: a meadow dotted with the white-faced cattle so familiar to this Hereford country; willow trees trailing their branches in the clear, placid water; the swan and me. It needed no wandering on a foreign strand to emphasise the calm loveliness of it all, and it was far enough out of the breeding season for the swan to have given up that intensely protective instinct that can be quite upsetting to a boat of great length and negligible width.

I liked that swan for about two and a half minutes. Now I know that swans are Nature's danger signals on the Wye, and by the end of the day I had come to dislike them quite a lot, for I had learnt that every time a white patch appeared ahead it indicated a weir, which might be more appropriately called a rapid.

If you are familiar only with boating as carried out on the Thames at Teddington or Pangbourne you will find the Wye quite diverting. If you have travelled according to the formula given in most of the older school of boys' books on Canada or the Zambesi you can repeat the sensation here in little overcrowded England. For the Wye is not harnessed and domesticated like the Thames, with level stretches of water kept under control by a series of locks that will, on receipt of the appropriate fee, lift your craft gently up or down between the levels. The Wye will charge you no fee, and in return for this freedom will give all the excitement for which the ordinary individual could ask. But we will take our fences as we come to them.

Lost in admiration of the whole scene (including the swan) I had taken no account of the faint sound of rippling, chattering water until the canoe began to respond to some force considerably greater than the two-bladed paddle. We were moving at something like eight miles an hour, unfortunately not quite on the right course. The error was not more than about nine inches, a small matter when compared with the width of the stream, but quite sufficient to bring the nose into rather sharp contact with a barely submerged rock. The result was startling. With incredible speed the tail end swung round and we shot the rapid in reverse gear.

This has the tremendous advantage of giving a splendid view of all that is past, but it does rather interfere with any attempts at planning for the future. However, Providence is proverbially kind to certain classes of humanity, and we reached the placid lower level unscathed, and with a firm resolve to do better next time.

Whenever in this chapter I refer to "we" I mean the partnership comprising the canoe and myself, for this vessel will just hold one. There were times when my pride was only saved by this limitation, though at several places where manhandling seemed the only solution I paid rather dearly in toil and sweat for this exclusiveness.

At the risk of repetition I must stress the complete loveliness of this lower Wye scenery. Nature has laid a grand foundation and man has, with few exceptions, added those final touches in the form of trimly grazed fields and picturesque cottages scattered at wild random amongst the woods and farmlands. And throughout this stretch of river, until the muddy tideway is reached, the banks on either side are thickly grown with balsam amongst the willows, with here and there a patch of Michaelmas daisy. Several times I guided my way across the stream in the opinion that I had discovered some strange plant giving a profusion of small white flowers at this late stage of the year, only to find a clump of these escapees from some garden higher upstream. A good deal of distribution must be carried on in this way, for it appears to be the general rule for dwellings adjoining the river to throw their rubbish over the bank. No one will object to the spread of flowers in this way, but unfortunately there are very clear signs of rats being spread more generously than flowers. Their runs are to be seen wherever this rubbish dumping goes on, and these are not the tracks of the water rat (more properly the vole), but of the pestilential brown rat, untidy humanity's scavenger.

One delight of this way of travelling is the reflection on all the smooth stretches of water. This upside-down scenery is fascinating, whether it shows the Seven Sisters Rocks, or just a hurried glimpse of the kingfisher's rufous undercarriage as he skims along beside the willows. It is not often that we are able to get double value like this, and certainly not in motoring, where a prolonged glance in the mirror is liable to lead to embarrassment.

It was at Lydbrook, opposite the inn, that we met trouble. The inevitable swans had given warning where none was needed, for this weir is in full view of the road and I had stopped many times to look and ponder as to the best channel. Now, seen from so near to water level, it looked quite threatening and there was obviously no best channel. A man walking on the road above pointed out the course I should take. I thanked him, but in face of such a turmoil of rocks and tumbling water my courage failed. Compromise resulted in a broken paddle and considerable loss of face, for there were four rather critical onlookers. But with the experience gained on all the lower weirs and rapids I should still not be prepared to navigate that particular hazard at the start of a journey and with a certain amount of equipment that would be damaged by water.

So the trip continued with a poor single-bladed paddle that had been carried for just such an emergency. This would have allowed very slow progress upstream and it made me feel more than ever thankful that my whole journey was being made the easy way.

It was about a mile below this obstacle that all thoughts of scenery, swans and broken paddles were rudely blasted sky-high by a factory hooter marking the hour of noon—B.S.T., of course, in this age of self-deception. However well one may be aware of the existence of the Cable Works, the hooter comes as a distinct shock. It seems so completely out of place, this grimy outpost of all-invading industrialism. And the strident blast breaks down any illusion that life in the tiny cottage on the wooded slope might still be regulated by the rising and setting of the sun.

The bridge which here carries the railway from Welsh Bicknor to the Gloucestershire side of the river is the scene of much law-breaking. Being somewhere near the middle of the seven-mile reach from Kerne Bridge to Huntsham, and standing close to a Youth Hostel, it is a very convenient route for hikers. A. G. Bradley openly recommends this way in his book on the Wye, but the railway frowns heavily. When I passed a girl was holding her infant child so that he (or she) could look over the parapet.

Thus, apparently, another generation is being reared to carry on the Battle of the Bridge.

For the next two miles the scenery was tuned to the remarkable late-summer weather. On the right bank the sun shone brilliantly and the summer heat was reflected in a shimmering haze that made Coppet Hill ripple and dance, while the steep cliff running up to Rosemary Topping and the Coldwell Rocks lay in deep shadow. Few leaves had yet changed to autumn colour, but the network of traveller's joy festooning the trees and bushes from hilltop almost to the water gave the impression of hoar-frost. The Coldwells are late risers, but they will have a fine view of the sun setting behind the Black Mountains at the end of long summer days, while in winter they can hope for no more than that the midday rays will caress their grey heads. On the map these lime-stone pinnacles carry such ordinary names as Quarry Rock, Ship Rock and Needle Rock, which sound dull when compared with the Bearcroft, Vansittart and Sargeant Adam mentioned in an old verse. I can find none who remember these old names, though they are given as being familiar to boatmen 150 years ago. But my contemplative mood was interrupted by the outrider of a salmon fisher.

A sculling boat, carrying the devoted wife and the attendant ghillie (for I know of no local name), quietly held its place near the sunny right bank and appeared to encourage the angler some fifty yards below by reporting to him the movements of certain alleged salmon. He, poor man, diligently flogged the water within his reach, always, so it seemed, at that point furthest removed from the spot where Local Knowledge and Womanly Instinct had located the fish.

I approached with great diffidence, not wishing to be even the excuse for an empty creel. It appeared that I could, by following a course that was most carefully explained, avoid all those spots in which salmon lurk. This I gathered from the outriders, but the chief performer, so far as he retained any interest in the pro-ceedings, favoured a course some five yards further over to star-board. Compromise again failed, as it did not give satisfaction to either party, especially when a promising five-pounder chose that moment to leap out of the water close beside me. The ghillie broke into a vigorous "View Hullo!" and I had premonitions of a barbed hook fixing itself in my ear, until it became apparent that the wielder of the rod was a bird-watcher in disguise, for he was at that moment much more interested in the movements of a dipper searching amongst the rocks. Perhaps he only used his rod to entertain the party in the boat, in the same way that a cat will keep her tail in motion during sleep to amuse the kittens.

Now the railway, which has kept close beside the river since Lydbrook, dives into the cliff just below Symonds Yat Rock to reach the Yat station in half a mile, while the river must take a journey of four miles to arrive at the same place. But every bit of these four miles was worth the effort on such a day. The long, trailing, grass-like river reed shone in the sunlit water as we expect a mermaid's hair to shine, and grows so thickly in places that it held the smooth-sided canoe as would a gently restraining hand. And amongst these flowing tresses vast shoals of fish swam briskly to hold their position in the swift water.

It was while watching this other world below the surface that I found my thought straying almost unconsciously to another river, some hundred and fifty miles plus fifty years away. Stone steps lead from the water's edge to the tiny church at Whitchurch, and in the eye of memory I could see a boat moored alongside with the Imp and his sister Dorothy, still cuddling her fluffy kitten Louise, leading Lizbeth and Dick to their early morning wedding beside a Kentish stream. But just as Jeffery Farnol always managed to keep some surprise in store for his characters, so there was one waiting for me amongst the willow branches. The engine of a motorboat roared into life so unexpectedly and so near that our balance was quite disturbed for the moment, and our surviving paddle missed a beat.

For eight or nine miles there had been no traffic except one sleepy fishing boat, but now we had reached the point of greatest activity on the whole river—Symonds Yat—and though the season was over, a fine October day had brought a few visitors. The motorboat hurried away to pick up her passengers, leaving our partnership to make tracks for the landing place, where a drink, eagerly awaited if not hardly earned, might be found. And the clock said five minutes to two, which was due to luck rather than judgment.

In the matter of scenery no distinction can be made between the two banks of the lower Wye, but when it comes to more material concerns like eating and drinking we must admit, with as good grace as possible, that the right bank wins rather easily.

Between Ross and the river mouth the left-hand bank makes only two offers to travellers: at Lydbrook, where the hotel tackles the eating side of the catering business with some reluctance, and at Symonds Yat, where the inhabitants on both sides expect visitors —and get them.

Symonds Yat is honest. It caters for the trippers in coaches, the bed-and-breakfast travellers and the visitors who wish to stay for a holiday. It will serve half a pint of draught alongside a double whisky. It makes no attempt at mock-refinement, and seems only once to stoop to the familiar "Ye Olde" tactics at "Ye Olde Ferry", which may or may not be older than the one which merely calls itself "Ferry to Saracen's Head". The fact that the landlord of the Saracen's Head operates this ferry may, of course, explain the simplicity of the name.

To avoid any invidious distinctions I quenched a ten-miles-of-paddling thirst on the Hereford side and then crossed over for a leisurely tea while Old George repaired my paddle. But there was more than chance or a craving for fairness in this arrangement. The first opportunity happened on the right, and there I was told about Old George as the acknowledged doctor of all those ills that befall boats. As a recreation from repairing oars and gunwales he throws a pretty dart at the Saracen's Head, so I had to wait while business gave way to pleasure. But that was time well spent, for Old George is an artist.

Together we examined the broken end and decided that it weren't a mucher. Then we examined the other end and came to the verdict that it never had been a mucher. That was discouraging until I realised that it was only a sign of the artistic temperament; he was assuring himself that the job was worthy of his skill.

"Just ornery deal," came the contemptuous verdict.

I nodded, more in sorrow than repentance, for I was the victim and not the creator of the wretched paddle.

"Have to take nigh a foot off."

I bowed to the inevitable, but some misgiving must have found its way into the bow, for he assured me that it would be none the worse for losing a foot of its length. The circumstances did not seem to favour an argument as to why the makers should have given the handle a superfluous foot, so I retreated to cold pie and salad on the terrace of the inn across the water and watched Old George at work. The ease with which his few simple tools did the job was a pleasure to see, and he worked with a slow deliberation that was deceptively quick, in spite of a succession of interruptions while he explained that the ferry was none of his business, or meekly carried out an order to draw water from the well.

So by half past four I paid a very modest charge and set off again. And at every stroke (until the next rapid took my attention) I blessed Old George, for the paddle was undoubtedly better than ever. As I started off the young daughter of Mine Host called out: "There's lots of lovely weirs before you get to Monmouth." But even though she put a wonderful depth of meaning into the word "lovely" I went on undaunted; such is the restoring influence of high tea, when taken in October sunshine on the banks of the Wye.

For the traveller by water there is no stretch of the Wye that can equal these three miles between Symonds Yat and the point where the river turns at right angles southwards on the straight run-in to Monmouth. There are rapids in plenty, and all with their guardian swans, but these were all taken with paddle flying—except at one point where a most inviting channel held one snag. We found it. But fortunately there is no time for second thoughts on the way down these watery staircases, and the wooden walls of the junior partner held together.

It was here that Robert Bloomfield (author of *The Farmer's Boy*) saw fishermen using coracles when he travelled this route at

the beginning of the nineteenth century. He left a delightful
account:

> each bore,
> Devoid of keel, or sail, or oar,
> An upright fisherman, whose eye,
> With Bramin-like solemnity,
> Survey'd the surface either way,
> And cleaved it like a fly at play;
> And crossways bore a balanced pole,
> To drive the salmon from his hole;
> Then heedful leapt, without parade,
> On shore, as luck or fancy bade;
> And o'er his back in gallant trim,
> Swung the light shell that carried him;
> Then down again his burden threw,
> And launched his whirling bowl anew;
> Displaying, in his bow'ry station,
> The Infancy of navigation.

This poet has often been spoken of disparagingly, but his writings
do not lack vigour and clarity.

On the left bank is The Slaughter, so named as the site of an
early battle. It may have been that the warm afternoon acted as
a benign antidote, or the tea may have been even more satisfactory
than I had imagined, but it seemed impossible that anything in the
nature of a misunderstanding, much less a slaughter, could ever
have disturbed the sunbathed serenity of the wooded slope. This
was not the season when the bare stems of the dogwood show the
truth of their name, *Cornus sanguinea*, nor could I see any festoons
of scarlet-berried bryony on which to hang a gripping simile.
Rather than any thoughts of battle there came to my mind the
words of Fiona Macleod—"Sweet peace of the running stream to
you."

Whatever geology may say, the Seven Sisters must have taken
up their positions before their brothers, the Coldwells. Or perhaps
in that age of chivalry the ladies were given the place where they
could bathe in morning sunshine while looking down on to the

river-mirror below. Perfect ladies these, who, like the Lorelei or
Rhine legend, stand discreetly amongst the partly concealing
leaves as though shyly aware of their charm. One even hides her
face behind an ivy fan. Can it be that she is taking a stealthy peep
at King Arthur's Cave, a few hundred yards away to her right?
There was a time when the rafts of early Man would have sailed
close by their weather-wrinkled faces, and past the entrance to the
cave whose doorstep now drops two hundred feet or more to the
river.

These are just the fancies of a dreamy afternoon, disturbed at
this point by the clatter of a quarry, so close that the alders and
willows are covered with the dust. But by an absurd incon-
sistency this seems to be in quite a different class from the Cable
Works, though they both deal with local mineral products.
Ancient usage is the probable explanation. Stone-working is
established in a place close to Nature, while cables are still one of
the inventions that Man has foisted upon us.

The map will show how entirely remote this region is from any
road. In no direction can a first- or second-class highway be
reached in less than a mile and a half in a straight line—and
straight lines just are not to be found in this part of the country.
This is all to the good as a protection against the scorched-earth
tactics that have ruined so many beauty spots. At the same time,
all who wish can see this lovely reach of the Wye without going
to all the trouble of buying or borrowing a canoe. Footpaths run
on either side, and if this is too strenuous, the railway between
Ross and Monmouth could do no better if it had been planned
entirely for the benefit of sightseers. This is done so tactfully that
only the passing of a train gives any hint that a railway exists, and
the single line does not allow many such reminders in the course
of a day.

Here let me give a word of advice to train users who may be
more familiar with the Flying Scotsman or the Golden Arrow.
Our train normally consists of one coach with the engine hitched
to the front or back end, and therein lies the problem. By travelling in front of the engine all nuisance from smoke and something-
in-the-eye is avoided, but after watching events at the termini

with great care I am completely in the dark as to the rules of procedure. Odd things happen at Monmouth (Troy) when three of
these little trains get together, and there is the strongest temptation to suspect that the whole thing is a conspiracy. If you watch
too closely one of them is liable to become coy and run back into
the tunnel, while another will rush out of the station with a lot of
self-conscious puffing and then steal quietly back down the slope
and catch you on the wrong platform. On one occasion I was very
near to solving the problem when a man hurried towards the
refreshment room calling for two quart jugs. On a hot day this
was quite sufficient to cause a diversion, and by the time the news
got around that he only wanted to milk a cow that was in transit
(and *in extremis*) the three trains had settled into their places with
expressions of the most unutterable smugness. So I can only
repeat, travel in front of the engine if possible, and leave you to
find out how this is done.

The wild ducks appreciate these isolated spots, and they were
here in plenty, generally allowing me to come within about
seventy yards, as though they were perfectly aware of the range of
a smooth-bore gun. Very noticeably they were almost entirely in
the ratio of two ducks to one drake, which is somewhat
irregular, according to some authorities. One sord (or should it be
badelynge) of eighteen swam in front of me for some distance
before taking to the air and dividing into six parties, each consisting of a drake and two ducks. One evening this week a local
paper carried a headline calling attention to the thousands of
surplus women in its area. Yet we humans continue to talk of
Planning just as if we understood the subject.

Once again let us be thankful to the Perambulation of 1282, for
we are now right out of Gloucestershire, with Hereford on our
right and Monmouth to the left. As a Gloucestrian I feel that some
mistake must have been made in the fixing of this boundary
which runs from the southernmost point of the loop of river
through which we have just passed, close by the village of
Staunton, and on to the river again at Redbrook. But Gloucester's
loss must give great satisfaction to the people of Monmouth as
they look across the Wye to the tree-covered slopes of Reddings

Inclosure and the Kymin. The town of C.S. Rolls and Henry V would be as lost without its Kymin as London would be without Hampstead Heath, or Bristol shorn of Durdham Downs.

After the sharp turn at Wyaston Leys the Hereford boundary runs away to the right, leaving the river entirely in Monmouth, and it is here that it undergoes one more of those amazing changes which are such a striking feature throughout its whole length. For about two miles we travelled on a sober domesticated waterway, charming still, but without the careless, rippling laughter of youth. And the hills on either side draw back to make room for placid meadows. The sun was low now, shining into my eyes as I paddled over the last two miles of the day on water which had, with the change of light, lost all movement and depth, reflecting the evening light as would a mirror, reflecting without adding anything of itself.

The eighteenth century saw the creation of a very comprehensive system of hotels to minister to the needs of coach travellers. The twentieth century has adapted many of these to the needs of the motorist. Stabling of yesterday will now accommodate the machines of the moderns, but what happens to those who arrive, travel-stained and weary, by canoe? This was in my mind as I came in sight of Wye Bridge, and weight was given to the problem by the comments of boys on the bank: "Look, here's a smashing boat!" "Gosh, I bet she can shift!" These and other such remarks gave me the satisfactory feeling that the partner looked as well as she had behaved, but they made me hope that a parking place could be found out of reach of over-enthusiastic admirers. Those who go on such trips should, no doubt, be prepared to curl up under a hedge, but setting aside any personal reactions, I was most unwilling to see my kyak curled up anywhere.

Monmouth rose magnificently to the occasion. The boathouse was open and Mr Jones gave the impression of being there specially to receive me. It really is a pity that such a welcome can be so little used, for there cannot be many odd callers to keep it exercised. One complaint only could possibly be raised, and that cannot be laid at the door of Mr Jones, even if I could find his door.

Therein lies the difficulty. Letting you into a secret, it seems that one figure only is used in numbering the group of cottages by the river, and that is the figure one. This appears intolerably restrictive until we remember that it allows II, III, and even IIII, if required. Mr Jones lives at No. II, and when I called to collect the key next morning it should have been perfectly simple to find it. A brief reconnaissance revealed four claimants to No. II. Admittedly they were not in a row, but they all stood within a circle of fifty yards. A trifle disconcerted, I enquired for Mr Jones, only to find that names in this neighbourhood are available on the same terms as numbers. In the moment of despair I caught sight of Mrs Jones waiting by the boathouse.

On the evening of my arrival I must confess to a feeling of aching superiority over my fellow guests at the hotel. What if I had no tie, and if the good red marl decorated my flannels quite liberally. Their costumes would have looked silly enough in my canoe, even as luggage, and my appetite was more than a match for those who had arrived by car. Between nine and ten o'clock, as I sat making notes for this chapter and watching them yawn, I felt that the day had been entirely satisfactory.

In Monmouth the bookshops carried in their windows copies of Mr W. H. Potts' *Roaming Down the Wye*, which, amongst much of interest, showed at this time a danger to which we poor scribes are exposed. Speaking of the restoration of the Monnow Mill to usefulness Mr Potts remarks, "No factory deriving its power from a water-wheel need worry about the possibility of a power cut in this climate". And by the time this book had reached the place of honour in the shop-windows Monnow had temporarily ceased to flow. A mere trickle of pollution was oozing amongst the stones under the old bridge-house. Do not think for one moment that I am criticising the writer. Much more am I thinking of all those charges to which fate and human frailty will expose me in due time.

To be really candid, Monmouth does not quite play the game with this side of the river as far as man's handiwork is concerned. Wye Bridge is certainly impressive, for which we are thankful, but from all her store of treasures the only items dealt out to the

Forest side are one railway station, one timber yard, one hotel and one combined gas-and-water works.

Second thoughts, second glasses of beer (or cups of tea) and second laps of a journey such as this start under a cloud. The first enthusiasm is gone, and habit has not yet taken its place. The atmospheric cloud was hanging over the hills as I carried the canoe from her stable, but it was no more than a mist that had risen from the water thickly enough to hide the rising sun. At least I consoled myself with the idea that sunrise is the time at which the shining disc climbs above all solid obstacles; in this case more than an hour after the official time, for the hills of Dean Forest hold back the dawn from Monmouth at this time of year.

A less material but no less real cloud showed itself in the clumsy stiffness left from the previous day, soon to be shaken off by the succession of rapids under the two railway bridges. A method of classification similar to that used for hotels and brandy seems to operate on the Wye, with swans in place of stars. These rapids were marked by five swans; I recommend ten. My first impulse was to shirk the worst part of them by wading down through the shallows, but one or two remarks from a gang of painters working on the iron bridge goaded me on. Even Mrs Jones had told me that I should be all right if I followed the stream, which is the same as aiming for the V of clear water, but local knowledge had failed to take sufficient account of the shortage of water in this unusually dry summer. The partnership only asked for about five inches of water, which seems quite modest for a river that has been described as navigable up to Welshpool, but even those five inches were not always to be found here, and we scraped the stones hard in several places.

Towards Redbrook the wooded hills again close in on either side, so that the scenery returns to the pattern that is expected of the lower Wye Valley. As far as Tintern the left bank is mainly steeper, while the Monmouth side reaches higher levels, especially at Beacon Hill (1,003 feet) above Llandogo. In reply to this the Hudnalls, by St Briavels, offer only 861 feet. Again there is no purpose in comparing the scenery on these opposite banks, for it

*Newnham in daffodil time*

is all part of one great limestone plateau through which the river has cut a winding path. They are matching pieces.

If The Slaughter has preserved no sign of its name the same cannot be said of Redbrook, for here a turgid, rusty stream carries its discolour well out into the clear waters of the Wye, in sharp contrast to the Whitebrook two miles below. But this Whitebrook enters from the right, so we will not follow it up to New Mills to discover how long it is since they whitened the water, presumably in the manufacture of woollen goods.

At Redbrook there are a number of large stones, cut and dressed to shapes resembling the bricks with which children play, lying so that they are only uncovered when the river is low. I could gather no information as to their origin, but it seems likely that they helped to form the quay for the old copper trade. At the end of the seventeenth century a thousand tons of ore were being imported from Cornwall by sea and river every year. This amount sounds trifling by the standards of today, but the task of carrying even that quantity would have presented many difficulties, with a lot of waiting for tides and rain to help the trows over shallows and rapids. The Wye, being a swift-flowing river with a considerable catchment area on impervious rock, responds very quickly to rainfall in the upper reaches, unlike the Severn, which may not show any signs of "fresh" for a week or more. It is said that in 1795 the Wye rose fifteen feet in twenty-four hours at Hereford.

Again near Redbrook salmon were not being caught. This sounds rather negative, but it is the only expression coming to mind for the non-expectant approach made by the average man who casts a line for salmon. The female of the species undoubtedly takes a more hopeful view, but then, the average fisherwoman is definitely younger than her male counterpart, and may not have met the same disappointments. Perhaps the ladies lay aside the rod and gaff when hope fades, leaving their fellow-men to whip their way through the evening hours.

There were some professionals on the job in the stretch between the Red and White Brooks, and with the sun reflecting on the water ahead I did not see them until only about fifty yards separated us: three cormorants, two squatting on rocks jutting out from the water, the third apparently holding himself out to dry in the sun. This was the one to catch my eye, for against all the brightness he stood out like some oddly shaped black cross, the upright of body and head being about three feet high, with the crossbar formed of the spreading wings much the same length, for the wing tips were not extended. On first sighting me they all turned their heads to stare, then, apparently satisfied with the fact that I had shifted course towards the bank, they lost interest and the sun-worshipper returned to an absurdly feeble flapping of the wings. It would be difficult to imagine any creature looking more damply dejected.

I moved closer and out of the line of the sun to try for a photo, but the two squatters were suspicious and flew away, while their companion moved to a branch of dead wood standing up in mid-stream. Here he stayed while I approached to within twenty-five yards, then dropped to the water and took off in much the same way as a swan.

This encounter pleased me, for while I know that cormorants are found in more inland places, and that they frequent the lower Severn, I have never seen one in this neighbourhood before. The nearest, speaking from memory, was one that I watched from the top of the cliff at Winter's Leap as he dived for fish two hundred feet below.

It is interesting to note these as the only fishers who did not complain of the lack of water or the awkward ways of fish, for I did not hear them utter a sound. On the other hand, in their black suits they looked quite the most dismal, so there may be something in favour of airing a grievance.

While I was still turned to see these birds flying upstream a salmon leapt so near that he showered me liberally and rocked the canoe by falling against the bow. In my ignorance I should put him at about six pounds, though on the scales he would probably weigh as much below that as he would exceed it in a story of "the one that wouldn't".

At Bigsweir you will be well advised to stop and have a look round—for several reasons. Bigsweir House is one of the best and most pleasantly situated houses on our bank of the river; the weir is one of the worst on the journey; it will be your last chance to step out on to clean shingle. Below this point there is a fringe of sticky tidal mud right down to the junction with the Severn. And as we reach the tideway we must say farewell to the balsam that has followed us so far.

At Llandogo there was food for the body and the mind, and if I took them in that order it was because they were offered that way. Besides, after four hours' travelling, even with the stream, there is something very attractive about poached eggs on toast and steamed pudding eaten on a lawn with a view of the Forest's western scarp.

From a white-haired man who stood watching some sort of hydraulic machine by the gate of his cottage I made enquiries about the weir just below, but honesty should have made me ask outright about the machine, for the way over the rapids was quite obvious from this point of vantage. I soon learned that the apparatus used a small stream running out of the bank to make electricity for lighting the cottage; also that the white-haired man was not really absorbed in machinery, he did this for a mechanical son. There was no need to ask what was his life interest; he meant to tell me, and with an enthusiasm that made light of his age. A life that included forty-five years as a lay preacher had done nothing to dim the keenness of this youngster as he shared his treasure with me. In the light of his great discovery how could a few years weigh him down?

It came to me in short sentences, full of burning eagerness, that his chief interest was history—religious history. To this subject he had given much thought and many hours of reading, but it was only recently that he had made the great discovery. Here it was necessary for him to break off and explain that he had, in childhood, lived at Woolaston, where his father kept the forge. A slump in this trade had taken them into the mining area, so that he had played around the caves at Staple Edge and on the old Roman road at Blackpool Bridge.

Now, so many years later, he had discovered the close link between this Forest country and the Roman Empire: the story of

Caractacus (of Caradoc) and his daughter, who achieved the Roman name Claudia; of Pudens and the Epistle to Timothy. Here, on the very ground where he lived, had walked the girl who was to become the wife of St Paul's friend. And the caves had sheltered the Silures—perhaps even Caradoc himself—in the courageous struggle against the invading armies. History had come to life for him, and he only wished that everyone could be told the wonder of it.

Certainly history would have had a new meaning at school if such things had been made clear to us as we pored over the tiresome names and dates of a period that seemed so remote. On the other hand, we should have been less interested in school days, and he would have been robbed of the satisfaction of this later discovery.

So I left my new friend with the joy that had come to him through a millennium and a half, but not until he had lent to me— a complete stranger—the book from which he had gathered the news; surely a grand example of fitting the practice to the sermon.

Being unused to the muddy banks of the tideway the partnership very nearly went into involuntary liquidation at Llandogo. That would have cut short my babblings and, a matter of greater concern, would have deprived me of the opportunity of playing Sir Galahad, or as near to that role as is allowed to us in these days of machinery and enlightened maidens. It happened thus. On the left bank of the river at this stage there runs a footpath backed by the steep wooded slope of the Hudnalls. And by this path there journeyed three comely maidens, very fair of form and feature. Now as I drew level with them I perceived their way to be barred by five monsters standing at a point where they must pass through a closed wicket. Seeing which, I reined in my steed and bowed myself to the ground (an exercise quite worth trying in a racing canoe—in warm weather). To cut a long story short, three smiles drew me over that confounded mud to move five wretched cows from the gate. And when we were alone again I am prepared to swear that one of the cows winked at me!

My reward came quickly and, very appropriately, from a member of the fair sex—though a brunette in this case. At Brockweir Bridge the water runs swiftly amongst rocks and it is difficult to decide where the channel runs. Seeing my uncertainty, a damsel walking briskly over the bridge turned back several paces and indicated with no uncertain hand just which course I should take. Thank you, Miss Brockweir, and I hope you were walking homewards at the time, for then we can claim one more attractive feature for the English side of the Wye.

So on to Tintern and tea, but not until several more rocks had convinced me that more water was absolutely essential. Not being free to order my life entirely by the moon, I was running exactly wrong with the tides. On this particular day there would be no useful depth of water at Tintern until twilight, and then it would move in the wrong direction for half an hour or more, according to the height of the tide. So, with no wish to finish this part of the trip in the dark, I struggled ashore in the shadow of the Abbey. The struggle was mostly due to recent high tides which had flooded the cellars of the hotel and blocked the old quay with nearly a foot of the slippiest mud imaginable.

Yes, there was a swan fifty yards downstream when I stopped, and the bus beat me by about twenty yards.

It was some days later, when the turn of the tide had moved round to about 10 o'clock, that I returned to find everything just as it was left on the bank: canoe, paddles and boots all with their thick layer of estuarine sediment.

Launching a canoe in these conditions is fun—if it works. There is the anxiety of pausing, one foot aboard, the other stuck fast in mud, while some inscrutable law of friction decides the moment to "go". Then there must be no second thoughts or you will (a) land in a mud pack that will have relatively little face value as a beauty treatment, or (b) watch your craft glide aimlessly away. The latter happened once on this trip, but providence, in the shape of an eddying current, brought it back again.

Below Tintern the Wye has a dual personality. The cliffs are steeper and more imposing than anywhere else and the trees grow to the water's edge. It was this which caused great difficulty in the navigation of the river, for it was impracticable to make a towing path through this narrow gorge. It is at the water's edge that we meet the other aspect, the herald of the sea, and it starts as a rigid line set by the highest tide. At this level all greenness ends; the rest is mud, relieved only by sea birds, ducks and waders. The first two miles below Tintern were particularly well supplied with mallards, showing that the road has taken itself out of sight and almost out of hearing as it climbs the bank under Wyndcliffe.

Here is the first sign of barge traffic in the shape of two chutes for loading stone from quarries on both sides of the river. Judging by the scars that are being made in the tree-covered banks a lot of stone is being taken from here, and I was told that it is mostly going for works which are intended for keeping the Severn within bounds. The barges on this trade must travel with the bigger tides, for at the time I passed there was not six inches of water under the chutes, and the tide would run out for another two hours.

And now the Wye, with one of her most convulsive wriggles, gives to the farm at Lancaut the distinction of having nearly two miles of river-boundary to less than half a mile of fence. How the auctioneers, who love to describe a farm as well watered, must yearn to get this one on their books! It was a late occupier of this farm who told me of the difficulty he had in getting animals to leave the farm. With great earnestness he explained how cattle, after living here for a time, would make most determined stands against being driven through the gate to the road. Frequent experience of this behaviour puzzled him a lot, and his efforts to explain it went so far as to consider the possibility of some influence surrounding the ruins of the old church near the river bank.

Immediately after this spectacular loop in the Wye is Winter's Leap, a point on the limestone cliff where the well-known Royalist is said to have escaped from the pursuing Parliamentary troops by jumping his horse from the edge of the cliff to the water. No one believes this to be strictly true, and some have tried to move the scene to the Beachley shore, where there is no cliff on the escape side that would bring the incident up to legend standard. From the river, however, there appears a possible solution. True enough, the limestone is almost vertical for two hundred feet, and this would give dramatic background to the story if

Winter did, in fact, vanish from the top and appear again in the water below. But right amongst these rocky buttresses there is a gap where trees grow all the way down the precipice. To slide down here would need good nerves and good luck, but it would not be impossible for a gallant horse and a desperate man. And we know that Winter had good reason for wishing to avoid a meeting with his opponents. It would then be up to the Roundheads to excuse themselves by reporting that he jumped from the top, a feat which even seventeenth-century religious fervour could not be expected to emulate.

A cormorant, taking quick alarm, flew overhead with sombre dress and outstretched, searching face, for all the world like some disappointed Puritan returned to look for the Royalist who got away. Seaweed now clings to the rocks, showing how much salt is in the water. Flocks of dunlins and sanderlings wade in the shallows at each bend. A few greater black-backed gulls are on the lookout for any opportunity to profit by theft or terrorism. But still the wild, familiar cry of the estuary is missing.

As we hurry down this last stretch the stream is running so swiftly that there is little time to see or appreciate the towering walls of Chepstow Castle before we are shooting under the bridge and looking for a landing place. You may go to Chepstow by train or by bus without misgiving, but if you venture by water watch the tide and then be very careful. Few places can compete with the rapid rise and fall of tide that is met with here. During the spring and autumn peaks there is a variation of as much as 46 feet within two hours. This amazing figure, which is more than the height of the tides in the Severn, is caused by the action of outflowing tides in the Severn which draw the water below normal river level. The great volume of the Severn running past the mouth of the Wye acts in much the same way as the stream of air which draws petrol from the jet of a carburettor. After dead low water the level will make up considerably before the next tide returns.

I left the junior partner just clear of the water, wedged on the stones of an old landing stage. By the time I had reached a settlement with four sandwiches and a tomato she was looking somewhat forlorn in about eight feet of air. I had been warned. Not many years ago the owner of a smart motor launch chose to ignore the advice of the old riversiders just at this spot. His battered launch was brought back down the valley on a timber wagon.

When A. G. Bradley travelled down the Wye he paused at Chepstow and then finished up with the merest handspring on the Beachley peninsula. Mr Potts calls it a day without the handspring. But we are pledged to make our way right out to the point where the sister rivers meet again after parting in infancy high up on the slope of Plinlimmon. And in these last two miles the everchanging Wye produces the biggest surprise of the whole course. Hills and woods are gone as the stream flows sluggishly on between widening mudbanks where now at last the curlew sounds his plaintive cry. The river ends as she began, under a low-ceilinged solitude. Even in the misty sunshine of a glorious October afternoon there is something wild and primitively awe-inspiring in this scene where water, sky and land blend almost imperceptibly, as we imagine they must have done when the earth was born from formless mists and vapours. And out of this meaningless expanse, just as the senses are losing their hold on time and place, there rises up the Chapel on the Rock.

I have already dwelt at some length upon this remarkable light-house, but no apology is offered for mentioning it again. It is to the traveller by water that it must make the strongest appeal; for him it was built.

The change from Wye to Severn is much more than a change of direction. After rounding the rocks of St Tecla's Chapel everything is altered, from the scenery to the rate of progress and the tactics that must be used. To those who do not know the Severn it may seem odd to take the twenty-eight-mile journey to Gloucester in this direction, when the canoe could just as easily be carried on the car for another down-river trip. That would be the right course on most rivers, but here it is easier, and much safer, to travel up with the tide than to attempt going down with the stream.

To say that the Queen of English rivers is temperamental is to put the case very gently. Quite frankly, the whole length of

Severn below Tewkesbury is full of problems and dangers even to those who know it well, and strangers should go very cautiously. A knowledge of the tides and a good map will, together, give warning of most of the pitfalls, but the sands shift so unexpectedly that no map can show the exact channel on any particular day. When travelling downstream with the ebb-tide, therefore, it is easy to follow the wrong channel, or stype, and so become stranded on the mudbanks. And the trouble does not end there by any means, for some of sand and mud is not safe to walk on, even if the boat is light enough to be carried. The alternative is to wait until the next tide, with a fair chance that the rush of water will overwhelm the boat before it can be freed from the mud. On the other hand, by starting upstream about half an hour behind the flood-tide it should be possible to move with the deepening water past all the worst obstacles. It should.

I will make no secret of a feeling of uneasiness as I stood on the landing stage of the ferry, waiting for the tide to turn. I have watched sailing dinghies pass this way in half a gale, when the waves were big enough to hide all but the sail as they slipped into the troughs, but still the two feet of canoe looked very small when compared with the two-mile width of water, sand and mud. But at least there is no doubt about the direction in which the water is flowing. At one moment the stream is running down angrily past the Hen and Chickens rocks; when you look again the threatening ripples have disappeared and the water is starting to move upstream. There is no "head" on the tide here; that will not build up until Severn Bridge is passed, and then only on the bigger tides. But the water moves swiftly, for the time of high water at Sharpness is only about forty-five minutes later than at Newport.

There is a temptation to start immediately the tide has turned in order to get full benefit from the time it is running, but the water will not run steadily until the sands are covered, so it is better to wait half an hour. Two strings of barges are now in sight, on their way up from Avonmouth, so we shall have company as far as Sharpness, though they will not reach the lock gates until near the top of the tide, so we should keep well in front. For the first three miles the main channel runs on the Tidenham side, passing under Sedbury cliffs where Offa and Winter met various turns of fortune. Now only a few cattle look down as we pass, which is fortunate, for in this wide stretch of swift-moving water there would be little enough opportunity for looking round even if big events were still taking place. The ruined arch up in the red rock is not the entrance to a smugglers' cave, just a kiln that has had its approach eaten away by the tides.

The contrast with the Wye is striking, quite apart from the opening up of the whole scene, the difference between stream and tide being more obvious than anything else—at first. With all her weirs and rapids the Wye has several distinct advantages: the banks are never far away on each side and, except over the shallows, there is opportunity for leisure. The tideway has quite another feeling, as if the canoe had some reason for not wishing to go upstream. It is for ever trying to turn this way and that, swinging round on an eddy whenever the paddle is idle. This makes for rapid progress, with paddle always busy and eyes fixed ahead. The gulls that glide and scream round the landing stage follow for a short way, as if summing up the chances of food being thrown from such a small boat. Deciding against, they turn back.

The channel here is called Slime Road, but I have not the slightest wish to find out why, and the slime is now well covered by the incoming water. It is at Pillhouse Rocks, three miles up from Beachley, that a decision has to be made. The main channel swings right across to the far bank, while a shallow stype runs close to the Forest shore. To follow the channel will mean a longer route, but guarantees plenty of water all the way, while the stype alongside Lydney Sands will be dry at low tide. Therefore it is only safe to keep to the near bank when there is a reasonable certainty of reaching Severn Bridge before the tide turns. Once the water starts to fall progress will be slow, if not precarious. But today there should be no difficulty, and with luck I shall be round the bend at Awre, perhaps up to the Nab at Newnham, before the tide turns.

It is pleasant enough here in sunlight, with wind and water as friends, but the picture can be very different when a cold winter mist clings to the surface of the water, or when blustering south-west winds drive the tide up in small, white-capped waves. Those are times for a boat such as the fishermen use, manned by men who know the river in all her moods and tantrums. The banks are low now, and the rising water has lifted me up until I can see the lapwings and curlews on the grass between river-edge and railway, but the railway embankment shuts out the view of all except the high ground of the Forest. Perhaps that is for the best, as the currents are still running cussedly enough over the submerged sandbanks.

Here is a putcheon weir, the framework in which the baskets are placed with their open ends upstream to catch the salmon on the ebb. Quite an old method of fishing, for it was mentioned in a charter of A.D. 956, when the Manor of Tidenham was granted to the Abbot of Bath. The Abbot re-let to the Archbishop of Canterbury, stipulating that the rent should include six porpoises yearly. One of these creatures turned up lately by the entrance to Lydney Harbour, but no one would undertake to find six in a year. Apparently the catching of porpoises and salmon is not quite what it used to be, for this putcheon weir is the first I have seen, standing near the Broad Stone and just outside the boundary of Tidenham parish. In the days of the Charter there were a number of weirs on Severn and Wye.

Another mile and we are opposite Woolaston Grange, near the point where a port is said to have stood in Roman times. No trace is left now, but the shifting channel of the Severn has a habit of moving landmarks if they stand too near the shore. But just here the bank gives the impression of having been built up, so it is quite possible that some remains are still deeply buried. After the isolated railway halt of Woolaston the bank becomes broken and uncertain, a sign that we have reached Aylburton Warth and the Lydney New Grounds. At no very remote date the river came much nearer to the road along this stretch, reaching a point not far from Lydney Church. Then there must have been a sharp bend where the harbour now enters the river, for Nass House stands on land rising above the alluvium of the New Grounds. Aylburton Warth might present some difficulty at high tide and when mist hides the outline, for the bank is quite irregular, with patches of reed. This quiet stretch is the home of reed warblers, curlews, lapwings and many other birds with a taste for solitude and mud.

All is quiet at the entrance to Lydney Harbour, so it looks as if no barges are coming out by this tide. My attention had been so taken up with the course ahead that I had quite forgotten the two strings of barges coming up to Sharpness. They have now drawn nearly level, just passing Berkeley Pill, a mile away on my right. That means that my progress has been rather behind timetable, so I must keep moving. On my left the red cliffs rise again; a pleasant change after seven miles of muddy banks. Even more welcome is the stype running along the shore once more, for though the tide is still running up it is nice to know that the main stretch of sandbank is passed. But a view of Severn Bridge ahead is a reminder that this river is just an obstacle race. ODTAA. I have never tried to get under the bridge against an ebbing tide, and after watching the tremendous rush of water between the piers I have no wish to try.

The barges have swung round, so that they now head downstream as they wait for traffic coming out of the docks. The gates are not opening yet, so there should be comfortable time to clear the bridge, though not to reach The Nab as I had hoped. Mallards and shell-duck are preening themselves on the rocks near to the bridge, no doubt making their toilet in the leisure hour while the mud is covered by the tide. Four spans of the bridge now have water flowing under them, but in two or three hours the river will have shrunk again until the stream will be confined to two spans on the Forest side, while all the rest will be feeding ground for ducks, gulls and waders. A train makes its noisy, echoing way overhead, looking more like a child's toy amongst the framework of girders.

Fortune is on our side, it seems, for by a mixture of luck and judgment the tide is just right for this tricky stage of the journey. If the water is running strongly in either direction there will be swirling eddies around each pier, strong enough to draw the unwary traveller out of his course. And when any boat, large or small, comes into contact with the pillars of Severn Bridge the situation is serious—if not critical. But we are now so near to the top of the tide that the water is flowing gently, with no more than a ripple of protest against the obstructions that man has put in the way. A few strokes of the paddle, and Severn Bridge is left behind; a few more, and we are passing the hamlet of Purton with its historic manor-house. It looks as if Purton has a meaning in some way connected with a ford, for the name occurs just here on both sides of the river, and there is no doubt that the people from either side used to cross with horses. It is now twelve miles back to Beachley, with time for two or three more miles before the ebbing tide is likely to offer much opposition. Purton offers no temptation, for the railway forms the river bank, giving no chance to step ashore. Only a mile further, however, is Gatcombe, which is quite different.

The railway must have altered the scenery along here quite a lot, but it has not managed to rob Gatcombe of its charm. There is an archway where the water comes to meet the few fishermen who live in the cottages huddled in the wooded combe. To the traveller this arch offers a fascinating glimpse of the tiny settlement, but to the people who live here it is of vital importance, for they live in close partnership with the river. At the time of high spring and autumn tides there is no safe mooring on the other side of the railway, so it is through this archway they must haul their boats and carry the cargoes, whether of salmon or firewood.

We have already met the putcheon, but there are three other methods by which salmon may, legally, be caught in the lower Severn. Two of these are carried on from here: lave netting and netting from stop-boats. Lave netting is full of excitement, even for the onlookers, and for the performers it is one of the few surviving methods of hunting which still relies entirely on human skill. Even the weapon, like a huge shrimping net, is no more than the clever fashioning of wood and string to a highly specialised shape. When ready for use it is a formidable affair, but it will fold up to be carried on a bicycle. The fisherman carries the net in shallow water, waiting for the ripple made by fish that can travel at great speed. The aim is to place the net so that the salmon will rush into it; no easy task with a big net, and in a foot of water.

But this is a big subject, and with all the time and space in the world I could not hope to equal the description given by Brian Waters, in his book *Severn Tide*.

Gatcombe and Lydney are the centres for the stopping-boats, the broad-beamed boats that anchor themselves across the stream and fish with a net lowered over the side on wooden spreaders. This net will face downstream for the incoming tide, or upstream for the ebb, and the boats will operate in the deep water of the main channel. One favourite site for these boats is in Well House Bay, a short distance below the bridge. Here two of them will take up their position when tide and season are right, waiting for the pull on the net which tells of a fish. Then the scoop-like apparatus will be raised, the fish removed and the waiting game goes on.

The last method of fishing permitted on the lower Severn is with the long net, but as this needs a narrower, deeper stream it will not be met with until we have passed Framilode. Incidentally, some of the names met with may be puzzling to strangers. The word "lode" has two meanings, both of which apply to Frami-lode. It may denote a place where the river may be crossed, or a stream to which the lower tides will not reach. A pill is a stream or drainage outlet visited by all tides, as distinct from a rhine, which is generally provided with a tide-flap to prevent the back-flow of water from high tides. "Warth" is a name used in these parts to describe riverside meadows, being land that has been built up by the river, over which the higher tides and floods still flow. It is, in fact, in process of building.

In the meantime the tide has turned, and the mud-laden water is rushing back to the sea. This is quite normal, though the rate at which the sandbanks reappear is a trifle bewildering when com-pared with the rate at which the sea leaves a sandy beach. Such conditions call for the broad beam of the local fishing boats, and even these can be rolled over like logs if they become lodged across an out-flowing race. A canoe would survive just so long as it could be kept head on to the current; a very uncertain life when the water divides up into a maze of races and channels. Having nothing of the hero in my make-up, and feeling a strong desire to finish the journey, I drew the junior partner well out of reach of the night tide, but I must confess that she looked entirely out of place amongst fishing boats and salmon nets. And in spite of the way in which our legends are heartlessly torn up and thrown in our faces I looked towards the cottage under the wooded bank, just in the hope that Sir Francis Drake would choose that moment to peer out of the window.

In the normal summer it would be too much to expect yet another fine day in which to finish the trip, but such things really happened in that glorious year, 1949. After the now familiar morning mist there was every promise of autumn gold during every minute until the sun slipped out of sight in the west. This season of summer days and winter evenings has been called the nearest approach to heaven upon earth. I agree.

Tide would be later today; about forty minutes by the normal variation and about another forty for the distance we have travelled upstream from Beachley. It would also be a little lower, as we are past the high levels and in a few days there will hardly be enough water to cover the sands. Even so, it would not pay to start immediately the tide turned, for then I should have to steer a course wide of the Forest shore on drawing level with Awre Church, as the channel takes the outside of the bend. But it is not easy to leave salmon fishermen, once they are talking, and leaves floating on the smooth water had been moving upstream for more than twenty minutes when I wriggled aboard.

Whether it was just weariness, or a feeling of climax at the start of the last lap, I cannot say, but that first mile out from Gatcombe seemed very long. Not until the putcheon frames at Poulton Court were behind me, and I had cleared the mouth of the brook that comes down from Blackpool Bridge, not till then did I settle into the stride. Across on my right were the Slimbridge New Grounds, where the wintering geese should be starting to arrive any day. The water is not yet high enough for me to see across the Warth, in fact it probably would not reach that level today, but there is no sign or sound of geese.

Now we are well into the cider country, with meadows and orchards crowded so thickly along the banks that it is said that the men rowing barges up with the tide, in days before the canal,

*Mitcheldean, or Dene Magna*

reckoned one stroke of the oars to each fence. I should like to be able to say the same, but pulling one of those oars was a man's job, of course. At the bend cattle are drinking on the muddy sands, a clear sign that the salt water has not yet reached so far. These animals in their red, dun and white add a pleasant touch of colour to a scene otherwise soberly green, washed with the silvery gold of this St Luke's summer, but with the water so low here I am almost inclined to grudge the drop they drink. On the shore side there is not depth enough to cover the paddle, so that I am half pawing my way over the mud.

Gloucester is now only nine miles away—in a straight line—but such is the course of the river that after the next eight miles there will still be some ten miles ahead. The great horseshoe around Arlingham is nothing short of eight miles from heel to heel, yet so close are these heels that the whole loop will gain me only a mile and a half in straight distance. No wonder there have been suggestions to cut through the narrow isthmus between Fretherne and Framilode. The purpose of such a cut would be to release flood water from the Gloucester area, for there is certainly no traffic to justify such a scheme. Without doubt this would enable the river water to get away more quickly, for the shallows between Longney and Awre play a big part in holding up flood water, but it would seriously affect our geography to find Arlingham west of Severn, and Newnham nowhere near the river.

Another big drawback to the cutting off of this bow would be the loss of Newnham as a mark-point for the tides, for all local calculations are based on the times at The Nab, a point about a mile below the church. Official figures are given for Sharpness Docks, and from these the up-river times are calculated by a simple formula:

High water at Sharpness means flood at The Nab,
High water at The Nab means flood at Gloucester.

To make this clear I should explain that "flood" is the term used for the first ripple of incoming tide. So the high-water level is reached at Sharpness at the same time that the incoming tide first shows itself at The Nab, and by the time the full height has been

18

*A Forest ride*

reached at The Nab the advance guard will be at Llanthony Weir. And the flood covers the fourteen river-miles between Newnham in about an hour, the exact time varying according to wind and "fresh". When estimating the time at which a high tide may be seen at any particular spot it is as well to allow a margin of at least twenty minutes, for although tides generally keep very closely to schedule they sometimes run early or late for no apparent reason.

Travellers on the Gloucester–Chepstow road sometimes remark that they never see much water in the Severn after passing Minsterworth. Knowing that the tides are timed by the moon, running about forty minutes later each day, this may sound surprising—at first. There is, however, a very simple rule to explain this, a rule which also serves as a rough guide for those who want to see the Bore. In its simplest form this rule says that "the tide passing The Nab atween eight and nine will be a big 'un". This may sound ridiculously simple, but it works. All that need be added is a reminder that tides always work up to a climax in spring and autumn, say March–April, and September–October; also that none of the old rules were shaped for Summer Time.

All this time the kyak and I are making what speed we can while the tide is in our favour, for we cannot expect much more help. Since it is on this stretch of river that the phenomenal wave builds up with the big tides this seemed the right time at which to mention it. But now we must hurry.

Our way lies under the electric cables, but there is no need to lower one's head, for the pylons are 303 feet high; past the old port of Bullo Pill, where William Greening ruled for fifty-four years and six months; past The Nab, and so on to the old ferry at Newnham. The honeycomb pontoons are still littering the banks from the last attempt to make a car ferry, but should you wish to make the trip to Arlingham (whether it is for the fine stained glass, or only to sample the draught of the New Inn) it will be necessary to plan the trip in advance. To tell the truth, the ferry service today is rather below the standard of Tudor days. But there is a magic password, so if you have any river problem in this locality, just ask for Bill Hardy.

Bill did not have to learn (as did Mole, in the *Wind in the*

*Willows*) that "there is nothing—absolutely nothing—half so much worth doing as simply messing about in boats". He knew it right from the start. All his spare time is spent by the river, making boats and mending boats, with all the same easy skill that I had watched at Symonds Yat. And he has the advantage of George by forty years.

Somewhere near here the Romans are said to have forded the Severn, leaving evidence in the form of a great elephant bone which can, I am told, still be seen at Westbury. Further round the bend, where the Arlingham shore faces north, is the treacherous Unla Water, still as dangerous as in the days when it brought disaster to Saxons trying to follow the defeated Silures. The Saxon name, meaning disaster, still clings.

All around this great bend the channel clings to the Forest side, until the reverse bends at the heels throw it to the other side. By Newnham and Broadoak the tide normally follows the same course, swinging round with a wave on its left flank, while the water makes a queer hissing roar as it covers the sands. But with the Severn there is no certainty. Without visible reason or warning the incoming water will attack the Arlingham shore, cutting and tearing at the low alluvial bank. But for this peculiarity the encroachment on the Broadoak side would probably be even more rapid. As it is, the gardens here running to the water's edge have lost several feet of their length within memory.

Any boat, however shallow the draught, should keep to the channel and resist any temptation to shorten this bend. Tides will occasionally open up very promising stypes across Pimlico Sands, but these are no more than a snare for the unwary. Quite recently a man who has spent seventy years beside this river had to wait hours for the returning tide to lift his boat off the mud—because he thought there would be enough water in the stype.

On these wide sands there have been great goings-on these last two months. The river has been uncommonly low, and enervatingly warm for the fish, with the result that they have been stranding in considerable numbers with the ebb tides. Riversiders are always on the lookout for such harvests, and in an atmosphere of the keenest competition some families have made quite rich hauls of salmon and other fish. Whatever the letter of the law may be, it is here popularly interpreted as permitting the collection of fish which have died through stranding. This may appear to open up endless possibilities, so it will be well to say that the loophole is not nearly as big as it looks. The Water Bailiff can distinguish between the salmon that has died in this way and the one that has been taken from the water and killed, for an hour or more after the deed is done.

The tide is just about at the top as I pass Garden Cliff (probably taking its picturesque name from the Garne family) and the slabs of stone broken from the old river bed are covered. The sun's warm reflection from the red cliff is a strong invitation to stop and eat my sandwiches, but I had set myself the task of reaching Framilode before the tide turned. Not only was the course set, but I had, in a sense, given hostages to fortune by making no provision against thirst. There is still more than two miles to go, and in half an hour at the most the stream will make the job much harder, so the flat meadows creep past unnoticed as I bend to the paddle.

Of all the villages of the Vale Framilode alone really belongs to the Severn. Church and inn join with the people in looking out across the water that has figured so largely in their lives. Cider and salmon together form the foundation upon which these places were built, but the orchards can be trusted to keep their place, while the river needs watching. And there could be no pleasanter spot than the bench outside the inn from which to look out on a scene that is not disturbed by the ripple of a wavelet or the cry of a gull. But it has not always been so peaceful, if we may judge by the accounts of some big tides that have been handed down. The most graphic one comes from *The Gentleman's Magazine* for 1762:

"On Tuesday, January 27, about nine in the morning, the sunne being fayrly and bryghtly spred, huge and mighty hills of water were seen in the elements, tumbling one over another in such sort as if the greatest mountains in the world had overwhelmed the low vallies, to the inexpressible astonishment and terror of the spectators, who, at first, mistaking it for a great mist or fog, did not on the sudden prepare to make their escape from it; but on its nearer approach which came on with such swiftness as it was verily thought the fowls of the air could not fly so fast, they perceived that it was the violence of the waters of the raging seas, which seemed to have broken their bounds, and were pouring in to deluge the land, then happy were they that could fly the fastest. But so violent and swift were the huge waves, and they pursued one another with such rapidity, that in less than five hours space most part of the countries on the Severn banks were laid under water, and many hundreds of men, women and children perished in the floods. From the hills might be seen herds of cattle and flocks of sheep, with husbandmen labouring in the fields, all swept away together, and swallowed up in one dreadful inundation. Houses, barns, ricks of corn and hay, were all involved in the common ruin. Many who were rich in the morning were beggars before noon; and several perished in endeavouring to save their effects."

Undoubtedly there was something in the nature of a tidal wave on this occasion, for it struck the whole coastal district of South Wales. At the same time, the account appears to have lost nothing in the telling. There have been other floods caused by waves coming up the Bristol Channel, but in recent times there has been far more trouble further up the river, caused by heavy rain and melting snow.

Not long ago, in this neighbourhood, there was an amusing illustration of the suddenness of the tides. Two telephone linesmen were working close to the river bank at the time of the Bore. A northerly wind muffled the noise of the approaching wave, so that the man on the ground only just kept his feet dry, while his companion was well and truly up the pole.

The first wave of a big tide is not the terrific affair that you may gather from some of the yarns that are spread around. It certainly is a thrilling sight, and one that I am never tired of watching, but the main rise in river level is caused by the steady upward flow which goes on for nearly an hour after the flood. If that first onrush reached anything like the heights sometimes mentioned there would be no room for the subsequent rise without the flooding of the whole valley. Another point—riversiders will face the biggest waves standing in the stern of a fishing boat, and such boats could not face the ten-foot waves of popular fiction.

It seems a pity to leave Framilode, and my reluctance is not entirely due to the prospect of ten miles' hard paddling. The rest of this journey is hemmed in by high banks, backed by orchards and meadows; quiet, sleepy country, with few features of particular interest, and no welcome for the traveller. Only at Minsterworth on the Forest side, and Stonebench on the opposite shore, shall I come in sight of the road, and then it will serve only to show how far the transport of today has turned its back on this river. It is a lonely stretch, where men have mostly deserted their old friend the river.

That's Epney, where the elver trade flourished while it was in German hands; then Longney Sands, with the river widening out for the last time, and the channel going over to the far side. The stream is running briskly against me, though not as it will after a big tide. On my left lie the winding lanes and overgrown orchards of Rodley and Bollow, with apple trees standing on the very edge of the bank. On the opposite side is a stronghold of badgers, in a little mound that sometimes has the greatest difficulty in keeping its head above water. They have been here a long time, too, so that I wonder if they will one day develop webbed feet.

I must have let my thoughts stray too far, for I am very close to the bank, to find myself in the shade. Already the air is becoming cool, out of the sun, a pointed reminder that October may have two grand qualities—summer days and winter evenings. The sound of traffic is clear now, so we shall soon be on the two-mile stretch where road and river keep close together. There are fishing punts pulled up on the banks here, heavy things with deep sides and square ends, used for ferrying, fishing and wooding. They are unwieldy-looking boats when handled laboriously with a pole or one paddle, but with four men all dipping paddles they can move quite smartly.

From Minsterworth to Tewkesbury salmon are caught with long nets. In this method one end of the net is secured to the bank while the other end is taken across the river in a boat and gathered in with a sweeping action. This net, made by the fisherman to fit the river on which it will be used, has a slackness or bulge in the centre, known as the "swill". This serves to guide the fish into the "cod" or pouch, from which they are unlikely to escape. The lines at top and bottom of the net are called bridles, and the bridles at the free end are attached to a line known as the muntle. The skill of these fishermen lies as much in making the net as in its use.

This long net seems to be quite the most formidable obstacle salmon have to face on their journey up-river, being much more difficult to avoid than the putcheons, lave nets or stopping boats. But the authorities have made regulations to give the fish some chance of reaching the spawning grounds. The net must not cover more than three-quarters of the river's width; the meshes must not measure less than two inches square, when shrunk; nor must two nets be operated within one hundred yards. And it is illegal to take from the river any salmon measuring less than twelve inches, from tip of snout to fork of tail. In spite of such regulations, and the close season, the numbers appear to be shrinking. The chief reason for this will be met with very soon.

Near to Minsterworth Church is a ledge of rock running across the river bed. The ordinary landlubber may overlook this, and I must confess that I have never located it, but to the riversiders of this neighbourhood it is all-important. Church Rock puts the roar into the Bore, and at a narrow gap in the ledge salmon queue up to pass. And, according to local legend, this used to be a favourite spot for the forbidden art of salmon spearing; the villain standing astride the gap, fetching out large fish just as quick as that. These tales are always good to listen to.

The church has a fine south porch facing the river, and appropriate carvings of salmon and nets decorate the interior. But this door is now closed, though Minsterworth has not entirely lost interest in the river. At one time the people here took quite a lot of their meagre supplies from passing barges, so that the crews did a fair trade in hardware and household goods. In return, a quantity of first-quality cider and perry was taken aboard. And if the casks and packages were not always so innocent—well, the apple trees still grow right to the water's edge.

The last stage of the journey is around Minsterworth Ham;

rich farmland that was reclaimed and drained from swamp less than a hundred years ago; grassland that was ploughed during the last war, to yield good crops in some cases. But the cropping of such land can be no more than an emergency measure, for the general level is not enough above the river to offer any safeguard from high tides and floods. This alluvial soil is still in process of being built up with river-borne silt, and a succession of arable crops definitely reverses the process.

Madam's Pool—what a name to offer to the imagination! I have carefully refrained from making any enquiry about the origin because the truth—if it can be found—might destroy the pleasant anticipation of Madam peeping shyly from amongst the willows as she dives into her pool. There was probably no lady in the case at all, and yet, when we hear that the men who fish Madam's Pool use no cod to their nets, there is a strong temptation to think that Madam is still here, a Miranda who would have something to say if she found herself in a string bag.

At the southern tip of this Ham, on the other side, is Stonebench, favourite spot from which to view the Bore. By the time the tide reaches this point it has reached its greatest height, and from the road it can be watched as it rounds the bend. The perfect form consists of three large waves, in close formation, their flanks breaking furiously along the banks and their crests breaking forward on occasion. Behind this vanguard the water seethes and tumbles in a way that may well be compared to the troubled movement of clouds when stirred by conflicting air currents. The principle is, of course, the same in these two cases—the meeting of contrary streams. Gradually the turmoil settles down, until the water is running quietly but swiftly upstream. This will continue for some forty-five minutes until after the full height has been reached, for the level will begin to fall while the flow is still upstream. This is puzzling to me, just as is the fact that a ripple from a big tide will continue on its course above Tewkesbury, towards Worcester, while the sands at Newnham are uncovering again. All this could probably be explained quite simply with the help of a funnel—but I have not yet found one big enough.

On the last three miles we reach the low-ebb of the whole

journey, and just as I hurry over them in my canoe, so I will not dwell on them here. The pollution of the river below Gloucester has, in the past, been so revolting as to make tragic nonsense of the attempts to preserve the fish or the amenities of our waterways. As I passed this way the water was not only harmful to fish ; it was vilely unpleasant to all who travelled this way at low water. This has been a pleasant trip, and I dislike ending on a note of complaint, so it is good to be able to report that work has since begun on a million-pound sewage scheme which should improve conditions greatly.

So we come "as far as Gloucester Bridge", as set out in the Perambulation. And as the canoe is pulled out of the water near Telford's fine bridge the sun is resting on the hills of the Forest. It was on this bridge, on such an evening, that inspiration came to F. W. Harvey :

> Faint grow the hills, but yet the night delays
> To blot them utterly. Below the ridge
> Of shadow lies the city in blue haze.
> I watch its lamps awaken, from the bridge
> Whereunder, running strongly to the sea,
> Water goes fleeting softly in a brown
> Wild loveliness. In heaven two or three
> Small stars awaken and gaze shyly down.

But this is no place in which to take farewell, here in sight and sound of Gloucester City, when all our travels have been amongst wooded hills and quiet farmlands. So let us go where we can see the day going softly to sleep beyond the Sugar Loaf and the mountains of Wales. And as the lights from distant cottages twinkle to us across the valley, we will repeat words that were written for such a time—"Dear soft sweet breath of the hills, Good-night."

# INDEX

275

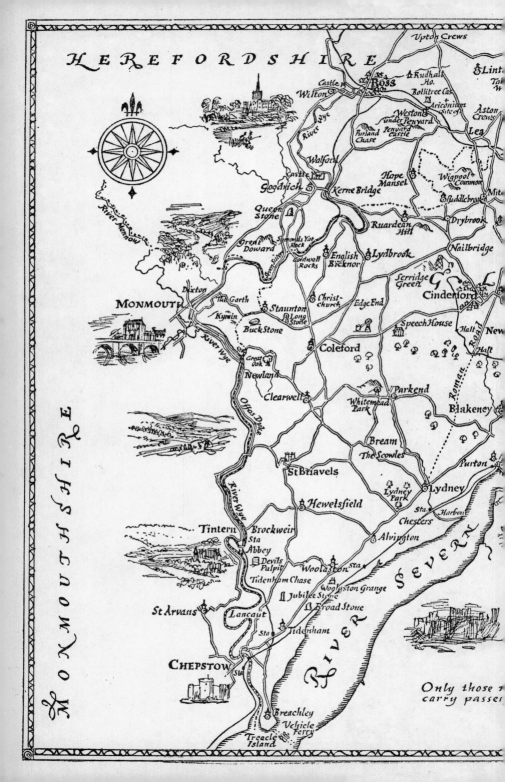